Mary A. Boland

A Handbook of Invalid Cooking

For the Use of Nurses in Training-schools, Nurses in Private Practice...

Mary A. Boland

A Handbook of Invalid Cooking
For the Use of Nurses in Training-schools, Nurses in Private Practice...

ISBN/EAN: 9783744784047

Printed in Europe, USA, Canada, Australia, Japan

Cover: Foto ©Andreas Hilbeck / pixelio.de

More available books at **www.hansebooks.com**

A HANDBOOK OF INVALID COOKING

FOR THE USE OF

NURSES IN TRAINING-SCHOOLS
NURSES IN PRIVATE PRACTICE
AND OTHERS WHO CARE FOR THE SICK

CONTAINING EXPLANATORY LESSONS ON THE PROPERTIES
AND VALUE OF DIFFERENT KINDS OF FOOD, AND RECIPES
FOR THE MAKING OF VARIOUS DISHES

BY

MARY A. BOLAND

INSTRUCTOR IN COOKING IN THE JOHNS HOPKINS
HOSPITAL TRAINING-SCHOOL FOR NURSES; MEMBER
OF THE AMERICAN PUBLIC HEALTH ASSOCIATION

NEW YORK
THE CENTURY CO.
1893

Copyright, 1893, by
MARY A. BOLAND.

THE DE VINNE PRESS.

PREFACE

In preparing the following pages for publication, it has been my object to present a collection of recipes and lessons on food, for the use of nurses. The idea was suggested by the need of such a book in the training-school of the Johns Hopkins Hospital. It is hoped that it will be found useful in other hospitals and schools where the teaching of the subject of food is receiving attention, and also to those who care for their own sick and invalid ones at home.

Part I — the explanatory lessons — includes general remarks on chemistry, lessons on the properties of the different classes of foods, and special articles on Air, Water, Milk, Digestion and Nutrition. Part II consists of recipes, menus of liquid, light, and convalescent's diet, and articles on Serving, Feeding of Children, and District Nursing.

In arranging the explanatory lessons, information has been drawn from many sources, but particularly from the works of Atwater and Parkes. It is the intention that these lessons be studied in connection with the practical work; they contain matter suggestive of that which it is necessary to understand in order that something may be known of the complex changes which take place in food in the various processes of cooking.

The recipes have been carefully chosen and perfected, some having been changed many times before final adoption. In most of them the quantities are small,— such amounts as would be required for one person,— but by multiplying or dividing the formulæ any quantity may be made, with uniform results.

Detailed descriptions have been given in order that those who know nothing of cooking may be able, by intelligently following the instructions, to make acceptable dishes. Repetition and similarity of arrangement will, it is hoped, serve to impress upon the mind certain points and principles.

In some instances the recipes are original, but for the most part the ideas have been gathered from lessons and lectures on cooking, and from standard books, among them Mrs. Lincoln's "Boston Cook Book." Generally the order in which each recipe has been written is the order in which the different ingredients should be put together. The proportions have been placed first, and separately from the description of the process, for greater convenience in using.

Valuable information for the chapter on the feeding of children was found in Uffelmann's "Hygiene of the Child."

I gratefully acknowledge the assistance of Drs. Simon Flexner and William D. Booker of the Johns Hopkins Hospital in reviewing, respectively, the explanatory lessons and the chapter on the feeding of children.

Baltimore, Jan. 18, 1893.   M. A. B.

CONTENTS

INTRODUCTION

PART I

EXPLANATORY LESSONS

	PAGE
PREPARATION OF FOOD	9
CHEMICAL AND PHYSICAL CHANGES	10
ELEMENTS	12
AIR	14, 38
FIRE	14
COMPOSITION OF THE BODY	16
PRINCIPAL CHEMICAL COMPOUNDS IN THE BODY	17
THE FIVE FOOD PRINCIPLES	18
WATER	19
PROTEIN	24
FATS	28
CARBOHYDRATES	31
MINERAL MATTERS	65
MILK	44
DIGESTION	49
NUTRITION	53

PART II

RECIPES

BEEF-JUICE, BEEF-TEA, AND BROTHS	75
GRUELS	83
MUSH AND PORRIDGE	90
DRINKS	95
JELLIES	120
TOAST	128
SOUPS	134

CONTENTS

	PAGE
OYSTERS	145
POTATOES	161
MEATS	168
STEWS	185
SWEETBREADS	188
FISH	191
CUSTARDS, CREAMS, PUDDINGS, AND BLANC-MANGE	195
SALADS	211
ICE-CREAM, SHERBETS, AND ICES	217
COOKED FRUITS	225
BREAD	232
CAKE	246
DIET LISTS OR MENUS FOR THE SICK	254
LIQUID DIET — FIVE MENUS	254
LIGHT DIET — FIVE MENUS FOR BREAKFAST, DINNER, SUPPER, AND LUNCH	256
CONVALESCENT'S DIET — EIGHT MENUS FOR SPRING, SUMMER, AUTUMN, AND WINTER	260

SERVING

IMPORTANCE OF SKILL IN COOKING THE THINGS TO BE SERVED	267
GOOD SERVING A NECESSITY FOR THE SICK	268
PREPARATION OF THE INVALID'S TRAY	268, 270
IMPORTANCE OF HARMONY OF COLORS IN DISHES, LINEN, AND FLOWERS	269
CARE OF DISHES AND TRAY IN CONTAGIOUS DISEASES	271
TRAY DECORATION	272
VARIETY, INTERVALS OF FEEDING, AND QUANTITY OF FOOD TO BE GIVEN	273, 274
A PLAN FOR THE PREPARATION OF AN INVALID'S BREAKFAST	278

THE FEEDING OF CHILDREN

WAYS IN WHICH A CHILD MAY BE SUPPLIED WITH FOOD	280
ARTIFICIAL FEEDING	280
COMPARISON OF THE COMPOSITION OF COW'S AND HUMAN MILK	281
BUYING, CARE, AND STERILIZATION OF COW'S MILK	281, 284
MELLIN'S FOOD AND OTHER ATTENUANTS	283, 290, 291

CONTENTS

	PAGE
PREDIGESTION	283, 284
BACTERIAL POISONS IN MILK	285, 286
APPARATUS FOR STERILIZING MILK	287
CARE OF FEEDING-BOTTLES	287
USE OF CONDENSED MILK	288
PRESERVED MILK	289
FARINACEOUS FOODS, MELLIN'S FOOD, MALTED MILK, ETC.	289, 290
AMOUNT OF FOOD FOR EACH MEAL — DILUTION OF — MANNER OF GIVING	293
TEMPERATURE OF FOOD WHEN GIVEN, AND INTERVALS OF FEEDING	294
GENERAL RULES FOR FEEDING	294
FOR THE FIRST WEEK	295
AFTER THE FIRST WEEK AND UNTIL THE SIXTH WEEK	295
FROM THE SIXTH WEEK TO THE SIXTH MONTH	296
FROM THE SIXTH TO THE TENTH MONTH	297
FROM THE TENTH TO THE TWELFTH MONTH	298
FROM THE TWELFTH TO THE EIGHTEENTH MONTH	299
AFTER EIGHTEEN MONTHS	299
FOODS TO BE CAREFULLY AVOIDED	300

DISTRICT NURSING

DISTRICT NURSING	301
TO MAKE A FIRE	302
TO WASH DISHES	303
SWEEPING AND DUSTING	303
BILLS OF FARE FOR SATURDAY, SUNDAY, MONDAY, AND TUESDAY:	
IN MAY	304–308
IN SEPTEMBER	308–310
IN JANUARY	310–313

LITERATURE

A LIST OF BOOKS ON THE CHEMISTRY OF FOODS, BACTERIOLOGY, NUTRITION, HEALTH, PRACTICAL COOKING, AND ALLIED SUBJECTS, USEFUL FOR REFERENCE	313
CHARTS OF THE COMPOSITION OF VARIOUS FOODS FOR USE IN A COOKING-SCHOOL	314
APPARATUS FOR FURNISHING A COOKING-SCHOOL	315

INTRODUCTION

THE work of the nurse is to care for her patient, to watch, to tend, and to nurture him in such a way that he shall gain and maintain sufficient strength to overcome disease, that he may finally **be** restored to a state of health. Her greatest allies in this work consist in the proper hygienic surroundings of good air, warmth, cleanliness, and proper nourishment.

The most scrupulous cleanliness in the care and preparation of food is an important point in her work, and practically to appreciate this, some knowledge of bacteriology is necessary, for the various fermentative and putrefactive changes (often unnoticed) which take place in both cooked and uncooked foods are caused by the growth of microscopic forms of life. Most of us realize the necessity for removing all visible impurities, but that is not enough; we should also combat those unseen agents which are everywhere **at** work, in order that we may prevent their action upon food material or destroy the products of their growth. Often these products are of a poisonous nature, and cause grave physical disturbances when they occur in our foods. When such knowledge is more general, we shall have arrived at a state of progress in the care and preparation **of** foods not yet universally reached.

The indications at present are that nothing of importance will be **done** to change **for** the better the existing methods of housekeeping, until housekeepers are educated in the science of household affairs. They should comprehend (1) that the atmosphere is an actual thing; that it has characteristics and properties like other actual things; that it is a necessity of life, and may be made a medium for the transmission of disease; and that it is as necessary that it should be kept clean as the floor, the table, or the furniture; (2) that food is a subject which may be studied and mastered like any other subject; that the changes it undergoes in its care and preparation are governed by fixed laws; (3) they should have a knowledge of heat in order to appreciate the effects of temperature on different food materials, to regulate the ventilation of their houses, and to control fires wisely and economically; and (4) they should have some knowledge of bacteriology, that milk and water, flesh, fruit, and vegetables may be kept, or rendered, absolutely free from disease-giving properties, and that perfect cleanliness may be exercised in preparing all materials that enter the body as nutrients.

It is not the intention to imply that all microorganisms produce injurious effects wherever they are found; on the contrary, they are as essential to man's existence as are the higher forms of life; but often they seriously, even fatally, interfere with that existence, and in order to discriminate and to combat the evil a knowledge of their ways and modes of life is essential.

A Harvard professor is credited with saying that no man could be a gentleman without a knowledge of chemistry; and forthwith all the students took to chemistry, for all wanted to be gentlemen. Would that somebody would authoritatively declare that no woman could be a lady without a knowledge of the chemistry of the household—what a glorious prospect would there be opened for the future health of the nation!

We read in history that after a grand medieval repast the bones and refuse of the feast were thrown under the table and left to decay. The scourges which have swept over Europe in past centuries we know, to-day, were not visitations of Providence, but were simply the result of natural causes, due to ignorance of all hygienic laws on the part of the people. Compared with the barbarians of old, in these matters, we are a civilized people; compared with the possibilities of the future, we are still little more than savages.

The ideal life is one in which there shall be no sickness except from accident or natural causes. When we have mastered the laws of hygiene, then will such life be possible. Meanwhile, with sickness always in our midst, we should keep the ideal ever before us, and endeavor by all means to restore suffering human beings to a perfect state of health. A sound body is a material thing, prosaically nourished by material substances, which produce just as exact results in its chemical physiology as if those substances entered into combination in the laboratory of the chemist. The cooking of food should be governed by exact laws which for the most part as yet remain undemonstrated. It is a foregone conclusion that many young women fail in their first attempts at cooking; that they do so is not surprising, for not only are their friends unable to teach them, but the majority of books on the subject furnish no intelligible aid.[1] The science of cookery is still in the empirical stage.

Even among experienced housekeepers there is not enough knowledge of the nature of foods and their proper combinations; the result is a great deal

---

[1] A notable exception is the "Boston Cook Book."

of unwholesome cookery and the consequent injury and waste which must follow. Dislike for the work is usually due to want of success, and failure is attributed to ill luck, poor materials, the fire, or any cause but the true one — which is ignorance of the subject. Of course good dishes cannot be made out of poor materials, but too often poor dishes are made out of good materials.

The systematic teaching of the subject of household affairs cannot fail of good results. Especially is this true in the case of the nurse, who will need at all times to exercise care and wisdom in the choice of food for the sick, to avoid the use of injurious substances, and to select that which is perfectly wholesome and suited to the needs and condition of each individual.

It may be said that most women can prepare a fairly satisfactory meal for those who are well, but very few are able to do the same for the sick.

Count Rumford says: "I constantly found that the richness or quality of a soup depended more upon the proper choice of ingredients than upon the quantity of solid nutrient matter employed; much more upon the art and skill of the cook than upon sums laid out in the market." This is equally true of other dishes than soup. The skill to develop the natural flavors of a food, to render it perfectly and thoroughly digestible, to convert it into a delicate viand, cannot be acquired in a haphazard way. Cooking cannot be done by guesswork. There are right and wrong methods in the kitchen as well as in the laboratory, and there is no doubt that the awakening interest in the subject of domestic science generally is neither an accident nor a whim, but the result of a necessity for better ways of living. We live different lives from those of our grandfathers before the days of the steam-engine, electricity, the telegraph, and the telephone. Now much more energy is needed to meet each day's demand than was required a hundred years ago, and so, much more nutriment is needed to sustain that energy. When the food does not supply the material to meet the demand, the whole being suffers.

A course of study in cooking taken by the nurses of a hospital, while they are still pupils, is valuable for their present and future work. A nurse with the information that such a course should give, will be able to care for the feeding of her patients more wisely,[1] will see the necessity for variety, will learn to avoid suspicious substances, such as fermented meat or fish, canned foods, etc., and will put forth every effort to secure that which is appetizing and wholesome, and suited to the needs of those in her care. She will more easily exercise patience and forbearance with the idiosyncrasies of the sick in regard to articles of diet, knowing that these are usually the symptoms of disease. The proper modes of caring for milk, eggs, oysters, and other perishable foods, the practice of economy in the use of wines, cocoa, and like costly substances, and an appreciation of the value of food materials in general, are some of the points which she will have learned.

She will not forget that cleanliness in the kitchen in the preparation of all food, and in the washing of dishes, towels, waste-pails, sinks, and all receptacles in which easily decomposing substances are kept, means protection against many evils. The little knowledge of bacteriology that it is possible to give in a course in cooking, will enable her to understand that many animal foods, such as oysters, fish, and lob-

[1] Although in some hospitals it is not practicable for a nurse to do much cooking for her patients, she has the control and distribution of the food which is prepared.

sters, are extremely prone to decay, and, although *apparently* good, may have been the camping-ground of millions of organisms which have produced such changes in them as to render them suspicious articles of diet. She will, therefore, always endeavor to have such food alive if possible, or at least fresh, and to keep it in such conditions of temperature as shall preserve it in a wholesome state.

The actual practical knowledge of how a certain number of dishes should be made has, of course, its value; but it is not the only consideration which should enter into the teaching of cookery. Perhaps the most important point in all such work is the recognition in certain cases of the *necessity* for particular dishes, and the reasons for, and the value of, their ingredients. Why one kind of food is better for one person and a different kind for another is, without doubt, an essential point in all such study.

A system depleted by disease, exhausted by long-continued illness, is an exceedingly delicate instrument to handle. It requires the greatest wisdom and good judgment on the part of physician and nurse to restore a patient to health without a lingering convalescence. There is no doubt that the period of convalescence may be much shortened by the wise administration of food, and that the subsequent health of the patient may be either made or marred by the action of the nurse in this respect.

PART I

EXPLANATORY LESSONS

PART I

EXPLANATORY LESSONS

PREPARATION OF FOOD

Digestibility. There are comparatively few kinds of food that can be eaten uncooked. Various fruits, milk, oysters, eggs, and some other things may be eaten raw, but the great mass of food materials must be prepared by some method of cooking. All the common vegetables, such as potatoes, turnips, carrots, beets, and the different grains, such as rice, wheat, corn, oats, etc., neither taste good nor are easily digestible until their starch, cellulose, and other constituents have been changed from their compact indigestible form by the action of heat. Some one has spoken of cooking as a sort of artificial digestion, by which nature is relieved of a certain amount of work which it would be very difficult, if not impossible, for her to perform.

Flavors. The necessity of cooking to develop, or to create, a palatable taste is important. The flesh of fowl is soft enough to masticate, but only a person on the verge of starvation could eat it until heat has changed its taste and made it one of the most savory and acceptable of meats. Coffee also well illustrates this point. When coffee is green — that is, unbrowned — it is acrid in taste, very tough, even horny in consistency, and a decoction made from it is altogether unpleasant. But when it is subjected to a certain degree of heat, for a certain time, it loses its toughness, becomes brittle, changes color, and there is developed in it a most agreeable flavor. This flavoring property is an actual product of the heat, which causes chemical changes in an essential oil contained in the bean. Heat not only develops but creates flavors, changing the odor and taste as well as the digestibility of food.

Effects of Cold. Some foods are better for being cold; for example, butter, honey, salads, and ice-cream. Sweet dishes as a rule are improved by a low temperature. The flavor of butter is very different and very much finer when cold than when warm. It is absolutely necessary to keep it cool in order to preserve the flavor.

CHEMICAL AND PHYSICAL CHANGES

Chemical Changes. Since many of the changes which cooking produces in the different food materials are of a chemical nature, it is well to consider what constitutes a chemical process. This idea may perhaps be best conveyed by a few experiments and illustrations, the materials for which may be easily obtained.

Exp. with Cream of Tartar and Bicarbonate of Soda. Mix two teaspoons of cream of tartar with one of bicarbonate of soda, in a little warm water. A union of the two substances follows and they neutralize each other; that is, the cream of tartar is no longer acid, and the soda is no longer alkaline. Owing to the power of chemical affinities a separation or breaking up of these compounds takes place, and new substances, *carbonic acid* and *rochelle salts*, are formed out of their constituents. The effervescence which is seen is caused by the escape of the carbonic acid.

Exp. with Hydrochloric Acid and Soda. Put a few drops of chemically pure hydrochloric acid into a little water; then add soda. A violent effervescence will follow. Continue putting in soda until this ceases, when the reaction should be neutral. Test it with litmus-paper. If it turns blue litmus-paper red, it is acid; if red litmus-paper blue, it is alkaline. Add acid or soda, whichever is required, until there is no change produced in either kind of litmus-paper. The results of this experiment are similar to those in the first one, namely, carbonic acid and a salt. In this case the salt is *sodium chlorid* or *common salt*, which is in solution in the liquid. Evaporate the water, when salt crystals will be found.[1]

Oxid of Iron. A piece of iron when exposed to the weather becomes covered with a brownish-yellow coating, which does not look at all like the original metal. If left long enough it will wholly disappear, being completely changed into the yellowish substance, which is *oxid of iron*, a compound of oxygen and iron, commonly called *iron rust*.

Burning of Coal. A piece of coal burns in the grate and is apparently destroyed, leaving no residue except a little ashes. The carbon and hydrogen of the coal have united with the oxygen of the air, the result of which is largely the invisible gas, *carbonic acid*, which escapes through the chimney.

Formation of Water. Water is formed by the union of two invisible gases, hydrogen and oxygen. It bears no resemblance whatever to either of them. Its symbol is H_2O.

All these are examples of chemical changes.

Definition of Chemical Change. Chemical changes or processes may be defined as those close and intimate actions amongst the particles of matter by which they are dissociated or decomposed, or by which new compounds are formed, and involving a complete loss of identity of the original substance.

Physical Changes. Mix a teaspoon of sugar with an equal amount of salt; the sugar is still sugar, and the salt remains salt; and they may each be separated from the mixture as such.

Water when frozen is changed from a liquid to a solid; its chemical composition, however, remains unchanged.

Water converted into steam by heat is changed from a liquid

[1] Carbonic acid is composed of one part of carbon and two parts of oxygen. Its symbol is CO_2. One volume of hydrogen united with one volume of chlorin forms hydrochloric acid, HCl. Common salt, or sodium chlorid, is composed of one part sodium and one part chlorin. Symbol, $NaCl$.

to a gas, but chemically there is no difference between the one and the other. *Steam, water,* and *ice* are forms of the same substance, the difference being physical, not chemical, and caused by a difference in temperature.

Lead melted so that it will run, and the solid lead of a bullet, are the same thing.

These illustrate physical changes.

Definition. When substances are brought together in such a way that their characteristic qualities remain the same, the change is called physical. It is less close and intimate than a chemical change. The transition from one state into another is also frequently only a physical change, as is seen in the transformation of water into steam, water into ice, etc.

ELEMENTS

One feature of the work of the chemist is to separate compound bodies into their simple constituents. These constituents he also endeavors to dissociate; and if this cannot be done by any means known to him, then the thing must be regarded as a simple substance. Such simple bodies are called *elements*.

Definition. An element then may be defined as a simple substance, which cannot by any known process be transformed into anything else; that is, no matter how it is treated, it still remains chemically what it was before. Gold, silver, copper, iron, platinum, carbon, phosphorus, calcium, oxygen, hydrogen, nitrogen, and chlorin are examples of elements. Once it was believed that there were but four elements in the world — earth, air, fire, and water. Then it was learned that these were not elements at all, but compounds, and the number of elements increased, until now sixty-eight are admitted to be simple primary substances. Some of these may in the future be proven to be compounds. Sulphur is at present in the doubtful list.

Oxygen. Oxygen is an element. It is an invisible gas, without taste or smell. It is the most abundant substance in the world, and an exceedingly active agent, entering into nearly all chemical changes and forming compounds with all known elements except one — fluorin. It is a necessity of life and of combustion.[1] It constitutes about two thirds of the weight of our bodies and one fifth of the weight of the air.

Hydrogen. Hydrogen is a gas. It is the lightest substance known. It unites with oxygen to form water, and, as will be seen later, enters into the composition of the human body.[2]

Nitrogen. Nitrogen is also a gas, but, unlike oxygen, is an inactive element. It supports neither fire nor life. It is not poisonous, however, for we breathe it constantly in the atmosphere, where its office is to dilute the too active oxygen. A person breathing it in a pure state dies simply from lack of oxygen.

Carbon. Carbon is a solid and an important and abundant element. It is known under three forms: diamond, graphite, and charcoal. The diamond is nearly pure carbon. Graphite (the "black-lead" of lead-pencils), coal, coke, and charcoal are impure forms of it. Carbon is combustible; that is, it burns or combines with oxygen. In this union carbonic acid is formed, and there is an evolution of heat, and usually, if the union be rapid and intense enough, of light. It is the valuable element in fuels, and in the body of man it unites with the oxygen of the air, yielding heat, to keep the body warm, and energy or

---

[1] Oxygen is often called the *supporter* of combustion, but it is no more so than the carbon and hydrogen of fuels, since they are necessary for a fire.

[2] Hydrogen is 14.44 times lighter than air.

muscular strength for work (Prof. Atwater). The carbonic acid formed in the body is given out by the lungs and skin.

Other Elements. There are many other elements about which it would be interesting to note something, such as calcium and phosphorus (found abundantly in the bones), magnesium, sulphur, sodium, iron, etc. Samples of these may be obtained to show to pupils, and descriptions given and experiments made, at the discretion of the teacher. Of the four most abundant elements of the body and of food,— oxygen, carbon, hydrogen, and nitrogen,— it is extremely important that some study be made, and if the apparatus can be procured, that it be of an experimental nature rather than simply descriptive.[1]

AIR

Air is made up principally of two elements, nitrogen and oxygen. It also always contains vapor of water and carbonic acid. Its average composition is as follows:

Nitrogen	78.49%	Aqueous Vapor	.84%
Oxygen	20.63%	Carbonic Acid	.04%

These are mixed together, not *chemically united*. Oxygen and nitrogen do unite chemically, but not in the proportions in which they exist in the air. Nitrous Oxid (N_2O), sometimes called "Laughing Gas," is one of the compounds of nitrogen and oxygen.

FIRE

Exp. with a Candle. Take a tallow candle, and by means of a lighted match raise its temperature sufficiently high to start an action between the carbon in the candle and the oxygen

[1] See Eliot and Storer's "Chemistry," the revised edition, edited by Nichols, and the "Elementary Text-book of Chemistry," by Mixter.

of the air; in other words, light the candle. A match is composed of wood, sulphur, and phosphorus. The latter is a substance which unites with oxygen very easily; that is, at a *low temperature*. By friction against any hard object, sufficient heat is aroused to effect a union between the phosphorus of a match and the oxygen of the surrounding air; the flame is then conveyed to the sulphur, or the heat thus generated causes a union between it (the sulphur) and the oxygen, sulphur burning somewhat less freely than phosphorus; this gives enough heat to ignite the wood, and with its combustion we get sufficient heat to light the candle, or to start a chemical union between the combustible portion, carbon chiefly, of the candle and the oxygen of the air. Allow the candle to burn for a time, then put over it a tall lamp-chimney; notice that the flame grows long and dim. Next place on the top of the chimney a tin cover, leaving a small opening, and make an opening into the chimney from below, with a pin or the blade of a knife placed between it and the table; note that the candle burns dimly. Then exclude the flow of air by completely covering the top; in a moment, as soon as the oxygen inside the chimney is consumed, the candle will go out.

This shows (1) that air — in other words, oxygen — is necessary to cause the candle to burn; (2) that by regulating the draft or flow of air the intensity of the combustion may be increased or diminished; (3) that by completely excluding air the candle is extinguished. This experiment with the candle illustrates the way in which coal is consumed in a stove. By opening the drafts and allowing the inflow of plenty of oxygen, combustion is increased; by partially closing them it is diminished, and by the complete exclusion of air burning is stopped.

The products of the burning of coal are carbonic acid and a small amount of ash. Twelve weights of coal, not counting the ash, will unite with thirty-two weights of oxygen, giving as a result forty-four weights of carbonic acid. Accompanying the union there is an evolution of light and heat. The enormous amount of carbonic acid given out daily from fires is taken up by plants and used by them for food. In the course of ages these plants may become coal, be consumed in combustion, and, passing into the air, thus complete the cycle of change.

Fuel and Kindlings. The common fuels are coal, coke, wood, gas, coal-oil, and peat. For kindling, newspaper is good because, being made of straw and wood-pulp, it burns easily, and also because printers' ink contains turpentine, which is highly inflammable.

COMPOSITION OF THE BODY

Before entering upon the study of foods it is well to consider the composition of the human body, that some idea of its chemical nature may be gained. In the United States National Museum at Washington may be found some interesting information on this subject. From there much that is contained in the following pages is taken.

A complete analysis of the human body has never been made, but different organs have been examined, and chemists have weighed and analyzed portions of them, and from such data of this nature as could be obtained, estimates of the probable composition of the body have been calculated. Thirteen elements united into their compounds, of which there are more than one hundred, form it.

The following table gives the average composition of a man weighing 148 pounds.

Oxygen	92.4	Sulphur	.24
Carbon	31.3	Chlorin	.12
Hydrogen	14.6	Sodium	.12
Nitrogen	4.6	Magnesium	.04
Calcium	2.8	Iron	.02
Phosphorus	1.4	Fluorin	.02
Potassium	.34		

PROF. ATWATER.

It will be seen from this that oxygen, carbon, hydrogen, and nitrogen constitute nearly the whole, the other elements being in very small proportions.

PRINCIPAL CHEMICAL COMPOUNDS IN THE BODY

The following interesting table, obtained at the National Museum, gives the principal compounds of the body. Some of the more rare organic compounds are omitted.

WATER:—A compound of oxygen and hydrogen.

PROTEIN COMPOUNDS, composed mainly of Carbon, Oxygen, Hydrogen, Nitrogen.	*Albuminoids* or *Proteids.*	Myosin and syntonin of muscle (sometimes called "muscle fibrin"). Albumen of blood and milk. Casein of milk.	
	Gelatinoids.	Collagen of bone and tendons. Chondrigen of cartilage, gristle,	which yield gelatin.
	Hemoglobin.	The red coloring matter of blood.	

FATS, composed mainly of Carbon, Oxygen, Hydrogen,	*Neutral Fats.*	Stearin, Palmitin, Olein, etc.	These make up the bulk of the fat of the body. They are likewise the chief constituents of tallow, lard, etc.
	Complex Fats, containing phosphorus and nitrogen.	Protagon, Lecithin, Cerebrin.	Found chiefly in the brain, spinal cord, nerves, etc.

CARBOHY-
DRATES,
composed
of
*Carbon,
Oxygen,
Hydrogen.*
- Glycogen, "animal starch." Occurs in the liver and other organs.
- Inosite, "muscle sugar." Occurs in various organs.
- Lactose, "milk sugar." Occurs in milk.
- Cholesterin. Occurs in brain, nerves, and other organs.

MINERAL SALTS.

- Phosphate of lime, or calcium phosphate.
- Carbonate of lime, or calcium carbonate.
- Fluorid of calcium, or calcium fluorid.
- Phosphate of magnesia, or magnesium phosphate.

Occurs chiefly in bones and teeth, though found in other organs.

- Phosphate of potash, or potassium phosphate.
- Sulphate of potash, or potassium sulphate.
- Chlorid of potassium, or potassium chlorid.
- Phosphate of soda, or sodium phosphate.
- Sulphate of soda, or sodium sulphate.
- Chlorid of sodium, or sodium chlorid.

Distributed through the body in the blood, muscle, brain, and other organs.

Now, since the body is composed of these substances, our food, including air and water, should contain them all in due proportion, that the growth, energy, and repair of the body may be healthfully maintained.

THE FIVE FOOD PRINCIPLES

For convenience of comparison foods may be divided into five classes: Water, Protein, Fats, Carbohydrates, Mineral Matters.

Some scientists include air in the list, but it has been thought best in this work to speak of it separately as the greatest necessity of life, but not in the sense of a direct nutrient.

An average composition of three of the principles is as follows:

PROTEIN	Carbon	53
	Hydrogen	7
	Oxygen	24
	Nitrogen	16
FATS	Carbon	76.5
	Hydrogen	12
	Oxygen	11.5
	Nitrogen	—
CARBOHYDRATES	Carbon	44
	Hydrogen	6
	Oxygen	50
	Nitrogen	—

It will be seen from the above that the protein compounds contain nitrogen; the fats and carbohydrates do not.

WATER

We will now consider the first of the food principles—water. Water is one of the necessities of life. A person could live without air but a few minutes, without water but a few days. It constitutes by weight three fifths of the human body, and enters largely into all organic matter. Water is an aid to the performance of many of the functions of the body, holding in solution the various nutritious principles, and also acting as a carrier of waste. It usually contains foreign matter, but the nearer it is to being pure the more valuable it becomes as an agent in the body. Ordinary hydrant, well, or spring water may be made pure by filtering and then sterilizing it.

Exp. Put a little water into a test-tube, and heat it over the flame of an alcohol-lamp. In a short time tiny bubbles will appear on the sides of the glass. These are not steam, as may be proved by testing the temperature of the water; they are bubbles of atmospheric gases which have been condensed in the water from the air; they have been proved to be nitrogen, oxygen, and carbonic acid, but as they do not exist in the water in the same proportions as in the air, they are not called *air*, but *atmospheric gases*. Continue the heating, and the bubbles will continue to form. After a while, very large bubbles will appear at the bottom of the tube; they increase rapidly and rise toward the top; some break before reaching it, but as the heat becomes more intense others succeed in getting to the surface,—there they break and disappear. If the water now be tested with a thermometer, it will be found to have reached 212° Fahrenheit or 100° Centigrade, provided the experiment be tried at or near the level of the sea.

Steam. The large bubbles are bubbles of steam, or water expanded by heat until its particles are so far apart that it ceases to be a liquid and becomes a gas. True steam is invisible; the moisture which collects on the sides of the tube and is seen coming out at the mouth is partially condensed steam, or watery vapor. Watch a tea-kettle as it boils on a stove; for the space of an inch or two from the end of the spout there seems to be nothing; that is where the *true* steam is; beyond that, clouds of what is commonly called steam appear; they are watery vapor formed from the true steam by partial condensation which is produced by its contact with the cool air.[1]

Boiling-point of Water. Water boils at different temperatures, according to the elevation above the sea-level. In Baltimore it boils practically at 212° Fahr.; at Munich in Germany at 209½°; at the city of Mexico in Mexico at 200°; and in the Himalayas, at an elevation of 18,000 feet above the level of the sea, at 180°. These differences are caused by the varying pressure of the atmosphere at these points. In Baltimore practically the whole weight of the air is to be

[1] Mattieu Williams, in "Chemistry of Cookery."

overcome. In Mexico, 7000 feet above the sea, there are 7000 feet less of atmosphere to be resisted; consequently, less heat is required, and boiling takes place at a lower temperature. By inclosing a vessel of water in a glass bell, and exhausting the air by means of an air-pump, water may be made to boil at a temperature of 70° Fahr., showing that much of the force (heat) that is consumed in causing water to be converted into steam is required to overcome the pressure of the air. The foregoing illustrates the point that *boiling water* is not of invariable temperature; consequently, that foods which in some places are cooked in it may in other places be cooked in water that is not boiling,— in other words, that it is not ebullition which produces the change in boiling substances, but heat.

Changes Produced in Water by Boiling. By boiling water for a moderate time the greater part of the atmospheric gases is driven off. The flavor is much changed. We call it "flat"; but by shaking it in a carafe or other vessel so that the air can mingle with it, it will reacquire oxygen, nitrogen, and carbonic acid, and its usual flavor can thus be restored.

Water which flows through soil containing lime is further changed by boiling.

Exp. with Lime-water. Pour a little lime-water into a test-tube. With a small glass tube blow into it for a few minutes, when it will become milky; continue the blowing for a few minutes more, when it will lose its cloudy appearance and become clear again. The following explains this: in the first place there was forced into the lime-water, from the lungs, air containing an excess of carbonic acid; this united with the lime in solution in the water and formed carbonate of lime. Carbonate of lime is insoluble in water which contains no carbonic acid, or very little,[1] but will dissolve in water which is charged with it, and this is produced by the continued blowing.

[1] The carbonic acid breathed in has united with the lime, thus leaving the water without excess of it.

Now if this water be freed of its excess of carbonic acid by boiling, the carbonate of lime will be freed from its soluble state, and will fall as a precipitate and settle on the sides of the vessel. From this we learn that water may be freed from carbonate of lime in solution in it by boiling.

Organic Matter in Water. There is another class of impurities in water of vastly more importance than either the atmospheric gases or lime. These are the organic substances which it always contains, especially that which has flowed over land covered with vegetation, or that which has received the drainage from sewers. The soluble matter found in such water is excellent food for many kinds of micro-organisms which often form, by their multiplication, poisons very destructive to animal life. Or the organisms themselves may be the direct producers of disease, as for instance the typhoid fever bacillus, the bacillus of cholera, and probably others which occur in drinking-water. These organisms are destroyed by heat, so that the most valuable effect produced in water by boiling it is their destruction. Such water is, therefore, a much safer drink to use than that which has not been boiled. Water should always be boiled if there is the slightest suspicion of dangerous impurities in the supply.

Use of Tea and Coffee. This leads us to the thought that the extensive use of tea and coffee in the world may be an instinctive safeguard against these until recently unknown forms of life. The universal use of cooked water in some form in China is a matter of history. The country is densely populated, the sewage is carried off principally by the rivers, so that the danger of contracting disease through water must be very great, and it is probable that instinct or knowledge has prompted the Chinaman to use but very little water for food except that which has been cooked. Whatever the reason, the custom is a national one. The every-day drink is weak tea made in a large teapot and kept in a wadded basket to retain the heat; the whole family use it. The very poor drink plain hot water or water just tinged with tea.

That tea and coffee furnish us each day with a certain amount of wholesome liquid in which all organic life has been destroyed, remains a fact; they may be, in addition, when *properly made* and of *proper strength*, of great value on account of their warmth, good flavor, and invigorating properties. There is no doubt that it is of the greatest importance that tea and coffee be used of *proper strength;* for if taken too strong, disorders of the system may be produced, necessitating their discontinuance, and thus depriving the individual of a certain amount of warm and wholesome liquid.

To Summarize. The effects produced in water by boiling which have been spoken of are: (1) the expulsion of the atmospheric gases; (2) the precipitation of lime when in solution; and (3) the destruction of micro-organisms. The most important points to remember in connection with water are, that a certain amount each day is an absolute necessity of life, and that unless the supply be above suspicion it should be filtered and then sterilized.

Filtration and Sterilization of Water. Filtration as a general thing is done by public authorities, but sterilization is not, and should be done when necessary by the nurse. For immediate use, simply boiling is said on good authority to be sufficient to destroy all *organisms* then in the water. *Spores* of organisms are, however, not killed by boiling, as they are very resistant to heat. Fortunately they are not common. As they do not develop into bacteria for some hours after the water has been boiled, they may be entirely gotten rid of by allowing them to develop and then destroying by a second boiling; but for all practical purposes, and under ordinary circumstances, water is rendered safe for use by boiling it once.[1] Should the water be very bad, boil it in a jar plugged with cotton for half an hour three days in succession, keeping it meanwhile in a temperature of 70° or 80° Fahr., so that any *spores* of organisms which may be in it will have an opportunity to get into such a state of existence that they will be capable of being killed by the next boiling. The third treatment is for the purpose of making sure of any that may have escaped the first and second.

PROTEIN

The second of the food principles, protein, is a complex and very important constituent of our food. The protein compounds differ from all others as to chemical composition by the presence of nitrogen; they contain *carbon, oxygen, hydrogen,* and *nitrogen,* while the fats and carbohydrates are composed principally of *carbon, oxygen,* and *hydrogen,* but no nitrogen. The so-called extractives or flavoring properties of meats are nitrogenous, and are consequently classed with the protein compounds.[2]

The body of an average person contains about *eighteen* per cent. of protein. The proteins of various kinds furnish nutriment for blood and muscle, hence the term "muscle-formers," which is sometimes given them. They also furnish material for tendons and other nitrogenous tissues. When these are worn out by use, it is protein which repairs the waste.

[1] As a general thing water does not contain organisms that form spores.
[2] Atwater.

Most of the valuable work upon the analysis of food has been done in Germany. From estimates made by chemists of that country it has been decided that the amount of protein in a diet should not fall below *four ounces daily*. This is to represent an allowance for a man of average weight doing an average amount of work, below which he cannot go without loss in health, in work, or in both. Although protein is the most expensive of all food materials, one should endeavor to use at least four ounces each day. Meat, milk, eggs, cheese, fish of all kinds, but especially dried cod, wheat, beans, and oatmeal are all rich in this substance. The protein compounds are divided into three classes:

ALBUMINOIDS, GELATINOIDS, EXTRACTIVES.

Albuminoids. The most perfect type of an albuminoid is the white of egg. It is a viscous, glairy, thick fluid which occurs also in the flesh of meat as one of its juices, in fish, in milk, in wheat as gluten, and in other foods. It is soluble in cold water.

Exp. Mix some white of egg in a tumbler with half a cup of cold water. As soon as the viscousness is broken up it will be found to be completely dissolved. It is insoluble in alcohol.

Exp. Pour upon some white of egg double its bulk of alcohol. It will coagulate into a somewhat hard opaque mass.

Heat also has the power of coagulating albumen.

Coagulation of Albumen by Heat. Put into a test-tube some white of egg, and place the tube in a dish of warm water. Heat the water gradually over a gas-flame or an alcohol-lamp. When the temperature reaches 134° Fahr. it will be seen that little white threads have begun to appear; continue the heating to 160°, when the whole mass becomes white and firm. Now remove a part from the tube and test its consistency; it will be found to be tender, soft, and jelly-like. Replace the tube in the dish of water and raise the heat to 200° Fahr.; then take out a little more and test again; it will now be found hard, close-grained, and somewhat tough. Continue the heating, when it will be seen that the tenacity increases with rise of temperature until at 212° Fahr., the boiling-point of water, it is a firm, compact solid. When heated to about 350°, white of egg becomes so tenacious that it is used as a valuable cement for marble.

These experiments illustrate a very important point in the cooking of albuminous foods. They show that the proper temperature for albumen is that at which it is thoroughly coagulated, but not hardened; that is, about 160° Fahr. Most kinds of meat, milk, eggs, oysters, and fish, when cooked with reference to their albumen alone, we find are also done in the best possible manner with reference to their other constituents. For instance, if you cook an oyster thinking only of its albuminous juice, and endeavor to raise the temperature throughout all of its substance to, or near, 160° Fahr., and not higher, you will find it most satisfactory as to flavor, consistency, and digestibility. The same is true of eggs done in all ways, and of dishes made with eggs, such as custards, creams, and puddings. With the knowledge that albumen coagulates at a temperature of 52° below that of boiling water, one can appreciate the necessity of cooking eggs in water that is not boiling, and a little experiment like the above will impress it upon the mind as no amount of mere explanation can possibly do.

The cooking of eggs, whether poached, cooked in the shell, or in omelets, is of much importance, for albumen when hard, compact, and tenacious is very difficult of digestion; the gastric juice cannot easily penetrate it; sometimes it is not digested at all; while that which is properly done—cooked in such a way that it is tender and falls apart easily—is one of the most valuable forms of food for the sick.

Albumen should always be prepared in such manner as to require the least possible expenditure of force in digestion. Those who are ill cannot afford to waste energy. Whether they are forced to do so in the digestion of their food depends very much upon the person who prepares it.

Advantage is often taken, in cooking, of the fact that albumen hardens on exposure to certain degrees of heat, to form protecting layers over pieces of broiling steak, roast meats, etc. If a piece of meat is placed in cold water to cook, it is evident, since albumen is soluble in cold water, that some of it will be wasted. If the same piece is plunged into boiling water the albumen in its outer layers will be immediately hardened, and form a sheath over the whole which will keep in the juices and the very important flavors. When broth or soup is made, we put the meat (cut into small pieces to expose a large extent of surface) into cold water, because we wish to draw out as much as possible the soluble matter and the flavors. If, on the other hand, the meat is to be served boiled, and broth or soup is not the object, then this order should be reversed, and every effort made to prevent the escape of any of the ingredients of the meat into the liquid.

In broiling steak, we sacrifice a thin layer of the outside to form a protecting covering over the whole by plunging it into the hottest part of the fire, so that the albumen will become suddenly hard and firm, and plug up the pores, thus preventing the savory juices from oozing out. More will be said on this subject in the recipes for cooking these kinds of foods.

Gelatinoids. The second class of protein compounds comprises the gelatinoids, gelatin being their leading constituent. It is found in flesh, tendons, cartilage and bone; in fact, it exists in all the tissues of the body, for the walls of most of the microscopic cells of which the tissues are composed contain gelatin.

Exp. Boil a pound of lean meat freed from tendons, fat, and bone, in a pint of water for three hours; then set the liquid away to cool. Jelly resembling calf's-foot jelly will be the result. The cell-walls of the flesh have been dissolved by the long-continued action of heat and liquid. This is commonly called stock or glaze.

Exp. Put a piece of clean bone into a dilute solution of hydrochloric acid. In two or three days the acid will have acted upon the earthy matters in the bone to remove them, and gelatin will remain. The average amount in bone is about thirty per cent.

Calves' feet were formerly used for jelly because of the excess of gelatin which they contain. They were cooked in water for a long time and the liquid reduced by further boiling; it was then clarified, flavored, and cooled; the result was a transparent, trembling jelly. The prepared gelatin of commerce, or *gelatine*, has now largely displaced this, for it is much more convenient to use, and less expensive.

Extractives. The extractives or flavoring properties of meats and other substances are usually classed with the protein compounds. Their chemical nature is not well understood.

FATS

Fixed and Volatile Oils. There are two classes of fats, called *fixed oils* and *volatile oils*. All kinds of fats good for food belong to the class of fixed oils. A volatile oil is one which evaporates away, like alcohol or water, and leaves no residue. The fixed oils, at least most of them, will not do this; they do not vaporize even at very high temperatures, but they become dissociated or decomposed,—that is, their chemical structure is broken up before their boiling-point is reached. Volatile oils, on the contrary, are capable of being boiled and transformed into gases. Some one illustrates this by the changes which take place in water. When water is heated to 212° Fahr. it is converted into a gas, which on cooling below 212° returns to the liquid state again without loss. The essential oil, turpentine, if heated to 320° Fahr. ceases to be a liquid and becomes a gas, which on cooling becomes a liquid oil again without loss of weight. Other volatile oils are oil of cloves, oil of bitter almonds, orange and lemon oil, oil of cinnamon, bergamot, and patchouli.

The boiling sometimes noticed in a pot of lard is owing to the presence in it of a little water which is very soon converted into steam, when the bubbling ceases, and after that the temperature of the fat rises rapidly, reaching in a short time four or five hundred degrees Fahrenheit, when a separation of its constituents takes place, and carbon is revealed as a black mass.

Composition of Fats. Fats are *hydrocarbons*—that is, they are composed chiefly of carbon united with hydrogen and oxygen. They must not be confounded with the *carbohydrates*, which are always composed of carbon with the elements of water—that is, the proportion of hydrogen to oxygen is as two to one,—whereas in the hydrocarbons this is not the case. These elements enter into the compositions of fats as various fatty acids and glycerin; the acids are not sour, as one would suppose from the name, but are so called because they behave chemically toward bases as sour acids do, that is, they unite with them. The glycerin of commerce is obtained by decomposing fats.

Fat in Milk. The white color of milk is given to it by minute globules of fat suspended in it.

To prove this: Put a little milk into a bottle with a ground-glass stopper; pour upon it three times its bulk of ether and shake gently; let it stand for two or three days, when it will be found that the ether has dissolved the fat and left a semi-transparent yellowish white liquid resembling blood serum. By pipetting or carefully pouring off the ether, and evaporating it by placing the vessel containing it in a dish of warm water, clear oil will be obtained. Care must be taken not to put the ether near a flame or the fire, as it is highly inflammable, and an explosion might occur. Ether boils at 94.82° Fahr.

The proportion of fat in milk is from 2.8 to 8 per cent. It varies in milk from different species of cows, and from the same species at different times, according to age, feeding, and other circumstances.

Cream. When milk is allowed to stand without disturbance for a time the globules of fat, being lighter than water, rise to the surface and form cream. Cream is the most wholesome, palatable, and easily digested form of fat. Butter is obtained by beating milk or cream in a churn until the little globules of fat break and stick together in a mass.

Olive-Oil. Olive-oil is one of the most easily digested and palatable of fats. A genuine oil of the first quality is, in this country unfortunately, expensive, much of that sold under the name being adulterated with cotton-seed oil, poppy-oil, and essence of lard.[1]

---

[1] The decline in the sardine trade during the last few years is accounted for by the fact that cotton-seed oil has so largely replaced olive-oil in the packing of these fish. People who once regarded them as a great delicacy no longer find them satisfying.

Cotton-seed oil has no especially bad flavor, but it is unpleasant and indigestible when used raw as in sardines and salads. The after taste which it leaves reminds one too forcibly of castor-oil.

Olive-oil of the best quality is almost absolutely without flavor. It is prepared in several grades: the first pressing from the fruit is the best, the second is fair, the third inferior, and there is sometimes a fourth known as refuse oil. For deep fat frying nothing is so good as olive-oil, but its costliness in this country excludes it from common use.

The fat of the sheep and ox, after it has been rendered, and deprived of all membrane and fibers, is called *tallow*. The term is also applied to the fat of other animals, and to that of some plants, as bayberry-tallow, piny tallow, and others. The uncooked fat of any animal is called *suet*, but the name has come to be applied to the less easily melted kinds, which surround the kidneys or are in other parts of the loin. The fat which falls in drops from meat in roasting is called *dripping*.

THE CARBOHYDRATES

Starch. Starch is a substance found in wheat, corn, oats, and in fact in all grains, in potatoes, in the roots and stems of many plants, and in some fruits. In a pure state it is a white powder such as is seen in arrowroot and corn-starch. Examined by a microscope this powder is found to be made up of tiny grains of different shapes and sizes, some rounded or oval, others irregular. Those of potato-starch are ovoid, with an outside covering which appears to be folded or ridged, and looks somewhat like the outside of an oyster-shell, although its similarity extends no further than appearance, as the little ridges are true folds, and not overlapping edges.

Size of Starch Grains. Starch grains vary in size according to the source from which the starch is obtained. Those of ground rice are very small, being about $\frac{1}{3000}$ of an inch in diameter; those of wheat are $\frac{1}{1000}$ of an inch, and those of potato $\frac{1}{300}$ of an inch.

Starch is a carbohydrate, being composed of six parts of carbon, ten of hydrogen, and five of oxygen. Its symbol is $C_6H_{10}O_5$. It is insoluble in water, but when the water is heated, the grains seem to absorb it; they increase in size, the ridges or folds disappear, and when the temperature reaches 140° Fahr. or a little over, they burst, and the contents mingle with the liquid forming the well-known paste.

Test for Starch. Mix a teaspoon of starch with a cup of cold water and boil them together for a few minutes until a paste is formed; then set it aside to cool. Meanwhile make a solution of iodine by putting a few flakes into alcohol, or use that which is already prepared, and which may be obtained at any pharmacy. Add a drop of this solution to the paste mixture; it will immediately color the whole a rich dark blue. This is known as the "iodine test," and is a very valuable one to the chemist, for by means of it the slightest trace of starch can be detected.

Exp. with Arrowroot. Make a thin paste by boiling a little arrowroot and water together. When cool test it with a drop of the iodine solution. The characteristic blue color will be very strong, showing that arrowroot is rich in starch.

Similar tests may be made with grated potato, wheat-flour, rice-flour, tapioca, and other starch-containing substances. Also powdered sugar, cream of tartar, and other substances may be tested, when it is suspected that they have been adulterated with starch.

Although starch grains burst and form a paste with water at 140° Fahr., that is not the temperature at which it should be cooked for food, and the thickening which then takes place should not be confounded, as often happens, with the true cooking of starch. In order to understand the difference between the proper cooking of starch and the simple bursting of the grains, let us consider the changes which take place in starch when it is subjected to different degrees of heat, and also those which are produced in it during the process of digestion. All starch in food is changed into dextrine and then into sugar (glucose, $C_6H_{12}O_6$) in the process of digestion. Glucose is a kind of sugar, resembling cane-sugar, but it is not so sweet.

Dextrine. Dextrine is a substance having the same chemical nature as starch, but differing in many of its properties. It may be described as a condition which starch assumes just before its change into glucose.

Exp. to show Dextrine. Carefully dry and then heat a little starch to about 400° Fahr. Keep it at this temperature until it turns brown, or for ten minutes. Then mix it with water, when it will dissolve, forming a gummy solution. Starch will not do this. Test it with iodine; it will not change color. The remarkable thing about the relation of dextrine to starch is that although they differ so much in properties they have the same chemical composition.

The change of starch into dextrine is an important point in cooking, because starch cannot be assimilated until the conversion has taken place, either before or after it is eaten. Now it will be seen that unless this change is either produced or approached in the cooking of starch-containing foods, they are not prepared as well as it is possible to prepare them; also, that it is not possible to cause this change at a low temperature; therefore 140° (the temperature at which the grains burst) should not be regarded as the cooking temperature of starch. It should be such a temperature as shall actually convert it into dextrine, or at least change it to such an extent that it will be more easily converted into dextrine, and ultimately into sugar, by the digestive fluids. This should be as near 401° Fahr. as practicable,— not that a potato, or a loaf of bread, or a pudding will have all the starch in it changed when it is put into an oven of that temperature. It would not be possible, on account of the water contained in each; but that in the outside may be, and the preparation of the remainder will be better than at a lower temperature.

There are other means of changing starch into dextrine than by heat, one of the most remarkable of which is *diastase*, a substance found in sprouting grains, which has the power to transform the starch stored in the grain by nature into soluble dextrine, in which form it can be taken up by the young plant for food. The crude starch could not thus be absorbed. The starch which we use as food is of no more value to us than it is to the young plant until it has been changed into dextrine or sugar. Now, if art outside of the body can accomplish what nature is otherwise forced to do in the alimentary canal, the body will be saved a certain amount of force,— a point of great importance, especially in the case of the sick or invalid, who can ill afford to waste energy.

Starch constitutes half of bread, our "staff of life"; nearly all of rice, the staff of life in the East; and the greater part of corn-starch, sago, arrowroot, tapioca, peas, beans, turnips, carrots, and potatoes.

Arrowroot is the purest form of starch food known. *Rice* is richest in starch of all the grains. *Tapioca* is prepared from the root of a tropical plant; it is first crushed and the grains washed out with water, then the whole is heated and stirred, thus cooking and breaking the starch grains, which on cooling assume the irregular rough shapes seen in the ordinary tapioca of commerce. Probably a part of the starch is converted into dextrine, which accounts for the peculiarly agreeable flavor which tapioca possesses. Mixed with the grains, as they are taken from the plant, is a very dangerous poison which, being soluble in water and volatile, is partially washed away and partially driven out by the heat,— in fact the heating is done for this purpose. *Sago* is principally starch. It is obtained from the pith of the sago-palm. Imitations of both tapioca and sago are sometimes made from common starch.

Starch may be converted into grape-sugar by treating it with acids; that of corn is generally used for the purpose. Much of the glucose of commerce is made in this way. In the United States it is estimated that $10,000,000 worth is manufactured every year. It is used for table syrup, in brewing beer, in the adulteration of cane-sugar, and in confectionery. Honey is also made from it. The nutritive value of vegetables is due largely to the starch and sugar which they contain.

In the economy of the body starch is eminently a heat producer. Pound for pound it does not give as much heat as fat, but owing to its great abundance and extensive use it, in the aggregate, produces more. (Atwater.)

Starch is an abundant and easily digested form of vegetable food, but it is incapable of sustaining life. It contains none of the nitrogenous matter needed for the nutrition of the muscles, nerves, and tissues. Indeed, it is said on good authority that many an invalid has been slowly starved to death from being fed upon this material alone.

Sugar. There are many kinds of sugar, the most familiar of which is *cane-sugar*, or *sucrose* ($C_{12}H_{22}O_{11}$). It is obtained from the juices of various plants, for instance, sugar-cane, beet-root, the sugar-maple, and certain kinds of palms. By far the greatest amount comes from the sugar-cane. It is made by crushing the stalks of the plant (which somewhat resembles Indian corn) and extracting the sweet juice, which is then clarified and evaporated until, on cooling, crystals appear in a thick liquid; this liquid is molasses, and the grains or crystals are brown sugar. White sugar is obtained by melting this brown sugar in water, removing the impurities, and again evaporating in vacuum-pans, which are used for the purpose of boiling the liquid at a lower temperature than it could be boiled in the open air, thus avoiding the danger of burning, and otherwise preserving certain qualities of the sugar. *Loaf-sugar* is made by separating the crystals from the liquid by draining in molds; and *granulated* sugar by forcing out the syrup in a centrifugal machine. The process of making beet-root sugar is similar. Sugar from maple sap is obtained by simply evaporating away the excess of water. In the East a considerable quantity of sugar is made from the juices of certain varieties of palm, especially the date-palm. Maple-sugar and palm-sugar are generally not purified.

Sucrose dissolves readily in water. By allowing such a solution to stand undisturbed for a time until the water has disappeared, transparent crystals are obtained, known as *rock candy*. Again, sucrose melted at a temperature of 320° Fahr. forms, on cooling, a clear mass, called *barley-sugar*. Heated to 420° Fahr. dissociation of the carbon from the water of crystallization takes place, the carbon appearing in its characteristic black color. This dark brown, sweetish-bitter syrup is called *caramel*. On cooling it forms a solid, which may be dissolved in water, and is used to color gravies, soups, beer, and so forth.

Exp. with Sulphuric Acid. A very pretty experiment to show the separation of the water from the carbon may be made by treating a little sugar in sulphuric acid. Put a tablespoon of sugar in any vessel that will bear heat, a thin glass or stout cup. Pour over enough concentrated sulphuric acid to thoroughly moisten it, let it stand for a few minutes, when it will be seen that the mass has changed color from white to a yellowish brown. The color increases in intensity until it is perfectly black, when the whole puffs and swells up, fumes are driven off, and a mass like a cinder remains. This is charcoal, or nearly pure carbon.

The explanation is as follows: So strong is the affinity of the acid for the water that it breaks up the chemical combination between it and the carbon, unites with the water, and leaves the carbon free. So intense is the chemical change that an enormous amount of heat is evolved,— so much, in fact, that a considerable part of the water is vaporized, leaving the more or less solid charcoal. The light color noticed during the first part of the union indicates that the chemical dissociation is just beginning, and that only a small amount of carbon has been set free.

Glucose. Glucose or grape-sugar ($C_6H_{12}O_6$) is one of the kinds of sugar found in grapes, peaches, and other fruits. It is about two and one half times less sweet than cane-sugar. It is manufactured on a large scale from the starch of corn.

Lactose. Lactose or milk-sugar is the sugar found in the milk of the *Mammalia*. That of commerce comes chiefly from Switzerland, where it is made by evaporating the whey of cow's milk. For sweetening drinks for infants and for the sick, milk-sugar is said to be less liable to produce acid fermentation than cane-sugar, and also to be more easily digested.

Sugar is a valuable nutrient, being very easily digested and absorbed. Cane-sugar is converted into glucose in the process of digestion by the pancreatic juice, and after absorption it is completely utilized in the body, furnishing heat and probably energy.

Effects of Heat on Sugar. Sugar undergoes various changes, with different degrees of heat, by loss of some of its water of crystallization. One of the most remarkable of these is seen in caramel sauce, which is a rich crimson-brown syrup generally supposed to contain foreign coloring matter, but which does not. It is made by melting sugar without water, and heating it until the desired hue and thickness are reached. Nothing is added, but something is taken away; that is, some of the water is driven out, with the result of change in both color and taste.

In a recent article in "The Century Magazine" (November, 1891) Prof. Atwater touches upon the subject of the production of artificial foods from the crude materials of the earth, and states, among other things, that a sugar resembling fruit-sugar has been made artificially by synthesis, by Prof. Fischer of Würzburg, Germany.

AIR

Air is a gaseous elastic body which envelops the earth on every side, extending possibly two hundred miles from its surface, but all the while growing more and more rare as the distance increases. When pure it is tasteless and odorless. We really live at the bottom of an atmospheric ocean, and are pressed upon by its weight. At the sea-level the pressure upon every square inch of surface is equal to fifteen pounds.

Atmospheric Pressure Variable. Atmospheric pressure diminishes and is constantly variable, according to the height above the sea-level. If we ascend into the air 5000 feet, it is perfectly evident that there are 5000 feet less of atmosphere pressing upon us than at the point from which we started. This diminution of pressure is often measured by the temperature at which water boils at different heights.

Composition. An average composition of the atmosphere has been previously stated. Besides nitrogen and oxygen, it always contains water in the form of vapor, and carbonic acid. The amount of aqueous vapor in the air changes according to the temperature; the amount of carbonic acid is also constantly variable. Air usually contains, in addition to these, traces of ammonia, organic matter which includes micro-organisms, ozone, salts of sodium, and other mineral matters in minute and variable quantities.

Air in Motion. The atmosphere is almost always in motion. We feel it in the gentle breeze and the more forcible wind. If it moves at a slower rate than two and one half feet a second this motion is not noticeable. Motion in the air is caused by the unequal heating of portions of it. If from any cause the atmosphere over a certain region becomes warm, it will expand (all bodies expand with heat), become lighter, and its tendency will be to move in the direction of least resistance,— that is, upward; so we say heated air rises. Currents of cooler air will immediately flow in to take its place, and thus we have a breeze, a wind, or a gale, according to the velocity and force with which the currents move. It is upon a knowledge of these movements that the theory of ventilation is based. It is because of the constant motion of air-currents that out of doors, except in densely populated cities, air remains constantly pure. When poisonous gases and other impurities accumulate, winds scatter them far and wide until they are so diluted as to be harmless; or under some conditions they unite with other things and form new and simple substances of a harmless nature, while under others, if they are compounds, they may be decomposed or washed down to the surface of the earth again.

Impurities. The chief chemical product of fires and of that slower combustion breathing is carbonic acid. Plants during the day, and under the influence of sunlight, take it up from the air for food, use the carbon for their growth, freeing the oxygen which man and the lower animals need. Thus is the balance most beautifully maintained.

Air is purest over the sea and over wind-swept heights of land. It, however, always contains some foreign substances, and always micro-organisms except over mid-ocean. Even the upper strata of atmosphere are not free from microscopic forms of life, as has been shown in experiments made with hail at the Johns Hopkins Hospital in 1890 by Dr. Abbott. Large hailstones were washed in distilled and sterilized water, and then melted, and cultures made from different layers; in all of these organisms were found, showing that they extend into the air a long distance from the earth.[1]

Impurities of various kinds are constantly passing into the air, but so vast is the expanse of the atmosphere as compared with the impurities daily thrown into it from the lungs of man and the lower animals, from fires, manufactories, and decomposing matter, that they quickly disappear.

Air is the greatest or, as one writer says, the most immediate necessity of life. We could live without

---

[1] This is not the first instance of the discovery of organisms in hail; but Dr. Abbott, if not the first, is one of the first bacteriologists to demonstrate the fact in this country.

it only a few seconds. We constantly use it, whether sleeping or waking, and perhaps this accounts in part for the utter carelessness and indifference which most people have for the quality of that which they breathe. Even those persons who know something of the nature of air, make but little effort to provide themselves with a constantly pure supply.

Effects of Breathing Bad Air. If the effects of breathing bad air were immediate, there would then be an immediate remedy for the present total lack of any systematic means of ventilation in most houses. But the effects of breathing bad air are, like those of some slow and insidious poison, not noticeable at once, and often manifested under the name of some disease which gives no clue to the true cause.

Dr. Van Rensselaer, in the Orton Prize Essay on Impure Air and Ventilation, makes the statement that statistics show that of the causes of mortality the most important and farthest-reaching is impure air.

Amount of Air Required for one Person. Sanitarians have agreed that each individual requires at least 3000 cubic feet of air every hour. A room 10 x 15 x 20 holds 3000 cubic feet of air, which should be changed once every hour in order that one individual shall have the required amount. If three persons are in the room, it must be changed three times.

The effect of bad ventilation is well illustrated by the condition of the horses in the French army some years ago. With small close stables the mortality was 197 in every 1000 annually. The simple enlargement of the stables, and consequent increase of breathing-space, reduced the number in the course of time to 68 in every 1000, and later, from 1862 to 1866, with some attention paid to the air-supply, the number fell to $28\frac{1}{2}$ per 1000.[1]

[1] Parkes's "Practical Hygiene."

Necessity for a Constant Supply of Pure Air. When we consider that the food we eat and digest cannot nourish the body until it has been acted upon by oxygen in the lungs, and that this action must be constant, never ceasing, it will help us to understand the necessity for a constant supply of air such as shall furnish us a due proportion of the life-giving principle, oxygen, and which shall not contain impurities that interfere with its absorption.

We take into the lungs a mixture of nitrogen, oxygen, and carbonic acid. We give out a mixture which has lost some of its oxygen, and gained in carbonic acid. Now, unless the amount of oxygen is what it should be, the blood will not gain from an inspiration the amount it should receive, consequently it will be but imperfectly purified and able but imperfectly to nourish the body. So the whole system suffers, and if a person for a long time continues to breathe such an atmosphere, the condition of the body will become so reduced as to produce disease. Even though in other ways one lives wisely, all the factors of health multiplied together cannot withstand the one of impure air. We eat food three or four times daily. Some of us are very particular about its quality. We breathe air every instant of our lives, but generally we give but little consideration as to whether it is pure or impure.

Ventilation. No attempt will be made here to explain different devices for ventilation, but only to touch upon the principle it involves. Its objects are (1) to remove air which has been breathed once; (2) to remove the products of combustion, whether from fires, lamps, gas, or other sources; (3) to carry away all other substances which may be generated from any cause, in a room or building, as the impurities from manufacturing, those arising from decaying matter, and micro-organisms. In a climate where artificial warmth is necessary a part of the year, it is difficult to warm and ventilate a room at the same time, without causing unpleasant drafts; but with some knowledge of the necessity of ventilation, and of the properties of air, one may in some measure work out a scheme of ventilation adapted to the circumstances in which he finds himself.

There are always the doors and windows, which may be thrown wide open at intervals, and in many houses there are fireplaces. If a window be opened at the bottom at one side of a room, and another be opened at the top on an opposite side, a current of air will be established from the first window, passing through the room and out at the second. This plan will do very well in warm weather when the temperature outside is about the same as that of the room, but it would be impracticable in cold weather. Then we may resort to the very simple plan of placing a board about eight or ten inches wide across the window at the bottom and inside of the sash. Then when the lower half of the window is raised, a space is left between the upper and lower sashes, through which the air passes freely as it enters, and, being sent into the room in an upward direction, causes no draft. The board is for the purpose of closing the window below, and should fit quite close to the sash.

Fireplaces are good, though not perfect, ventilators. Then there are the preventive measures, such as burning the gas or lamp low at night, avoiding oil- and gas-stoves, etc.; the latter are the worst possible means of heating rooms, for not only do they draw oxygen for burning from the air, but they give out the polluting carbonic acid and other products of combustion, which in a coal- or wood-stove go up the chimney.

A well-ventilated room should have an inflow of

warm, pure air, and a means for the removal of the same after it has been used, the current being so controlled that, although the air is kept in motion, there is no perceptible draft.

The plan for the heating and ventilation of the Johns Hopkins Hospital, Baltimore, Maryland, is a most admirable one. Air from out of doors is conveyed by a flue into a chamber in the wall, in which are coils of pipe filled with hot water. The air in passing over these becomes warm, and, rising, passes into the room to be heated through a register. On the opposite side of the room is a chimney-like flue, running to the top of the building and containing two registers, by the opening and closing of which the movements of the air in the room can be controlled. The temperature is maintained by the temperature of the water in the pipes, and the rapidity of the flow.[1]

The ventilation by this method of heating is the most perfect known to the author, who has lived for two years in a building thus supplied with warmth and fresh air. The rooms were invariably comfortable as to temperature, and the air as invariably sweet and pure.

MILK

Milk is one of our most perfect types of food, containing water and solids in such proportions as are known to be needful for the nourishment of the body. A proof of this is seen in the fact that it is the only food of the young of the *Mammalia* during the time of their greatest growth. It contains those food principles in such amounts as to contribute to the rapid

---

[1] For a detailed description of this method of heating and ventilation, see the report of the Johns Hopkins Hospital for the year 1891.

formation of bone and the various tissues of the body, which takes place in infancy and childhood; but after this growth is attained, and the individual requires that which will repair the tissues and furnish warmth and energy, milk ceases to be a complete food.

Composition of Cow's Milk. The composition of cow's milk varies with the breed and age, care and feeding, of the animals. Cows which are kept in foul air in stables all the year, and fed upon bad food such as the refuse from breweries and kitchens, give a quality of milk which is perhaps more to be dreaded than that from any other source; for such animals are especially liable to disease, and are often infected with tuberculosis, pneumonia, and other fatal maladies. Cows are particularly susceptible to tuberculosis, and may convey it to human beings either in their milk or flesh. According to Dr. Miller, cow's milk contains the following ingredients:

Water	87.4%
Fat	4.0%
Sugar and soluble salts	5.0%
Nitrogenous matter and insoluble salts	3.6%

Another analysis is that of Uffelmann:

Water	87.6%
Albuminoids	4.3%
Fat	3.8%
Sugar	3.7%
Salts	.6% [1]

Characteristics. Milk from healthy, well-nourished cows should be of full white color, opaque, and with

[1] Variations in the composition of cow's milk (300 analyses):

	Minimum.	Maximum.
Albuminoids or Protein	2.04%	6.18%
Fat	1.82%	7.09%
Sugar	3.20%	5.67%
Salts	.50%	.87%

—KÖNIG.

a slightly yellowish tinge sometimes described as "cream white." It should vary but slightly in composition from the above analyses. The fat should not be less than 2.5%. The amount of fat may be easily determined with a Feser's lactoscope (Eimer and Amend, New York), directions for the use of which come with the instruments. It will generally vary from 3% to 4% in good milk. Should it fall below 2.5% the milk should be rejected as too poor for use. Such milk has probably been skimmed, or comes from unhealthy or poorly fed cows.

The specific gravity of milk should be from 1.027 to 1.033. This may be found with a Quevenne's lactometer. If it falls below 1.027, one has a right to claim that the milk has been watered or that the cows are in poor condition.[1]

The reaction of good milk varies from slightly alkaline to slightly acid or neutral. That from the same cow will be different on different days, even under the same apparent conditions of care, varying from one to the other, probably because of some difference in the nature of the food she has eaten. However, if the reaction is *decidedly* alkaline, and red litmus-paper becomes a distinct blue, the milk is not good, and possibly the animal is diseased. Should the reaction be decidedly acid, it shows that the milk has been contaminated, either from the air by long exposure, or from the vessels which held it, with those micro-organisms which by their growth produce an acid, a

---

[1] The following is the police order for milk, published in Darmstadt, 1879: (1) All milk must have a specific gravity of 1.029–1.033. (2) When skimmed it must have a specific gravity of 1.033. (3) All milk with a specific gravity under 1.027 is to be considered as watered and immediately confiscated. (4) All milk with specific gravity over 1.027, if after twenty-four hours standing and skimming the specific gravity is under 1.033, must also be confiscated, also all skimmed milk with a specific gravity under 1.033. (5) All milk must be considered skimmed which has less than 2.8 per cent. of fat.

certain amount of which causes what is known as "souring."

Milk from perfectly healthy and perfectly kept cows is *neutral,* leaving both red and blue litmus-paper unchanged; but as a general thing milk is slightly acid, even when transported directly from the producer to the consumer and handled by fairly clean workmen in fairly clean vessels. Such milk two or three hours old when examined microscopically is found to contain millions of organisms. Milk is one of the best of foods for bacteria, many of the ordinary forms growing in it with exceeding rapidity under favorable conditions of temperature. Now it has been found that such milk, although it may not contain the seeds of any certain disease, sometimes causes in young children, and the sick, very serious digestive disturbances, and may thus become indirectly the cause of fatal maladies.[1]

All milk, unless it is *positively known* to be given by healthy, well-nourished animals, and kept in thoroughly cleaned vessels free from contamination, should be sterilized before using. Often the organisms found in milk are of disease-giving nature. In Europe and America many cases of typhoid fever, scarlatina, and diphtheria have been traced to the milk-supply. In fact milk and water are two of the most fruitful food sources of disease. It therefore immediately becomes apparent that, unless these two liquids are above suspicion, they should be sterilized before using. Boiling water for half an hour will render it sterile, but milk would be injured by evaporation and other changes produced in its constituents by such long exposure to so high a degree of heat. A better method, and one which should be adopted by all who understand something of the nature of bacteria, is to expose the milk

[1] See article on the Feeding of Children.

for a longer time to a lower temperature than that of boiling.

To Sterilize Milk for Immediate Use. (1) Pour the milk into a granite-ware saucepan or a double boiler, raise the temperature to 190° Fahr., and keep it at that point for one hour. (2) As soon as done put it immediately into a pitcher, or other vessel, which has been thoroughly washed, and boiled in a bath of water, and cool quickly by placing in a pan of cold or iced water. A chemist's thermometer, for testing the temperature, may be bought at any pharmacy for a small sum, but if there is not one at hand, heat the milk until a scum forms over the top, and then keep it as nearly as possible at that temperature for one hour. Do not let it boil.

To Sterilize Milk which is not for Immediate Use. Put the milk into flasks or bottles with narrow mouths; plug them with a long stopper of cotton-wool, place the flasks in a wire frame to support them, in a kettle of cold water, heat gradually to 190° Fahr., and keep it at that temperature for one hour. Repeat this the second day, for although all organisms were probably destroyed during the first process, *spores* which may have escaped will have developed into bacteria. These will be killed by the second heating. Repeat again on the third day to destroy any life that may have escaped the first two.

Spores or resting-cells are the germinal cells from which new bacteria develop, and are capable of surviving a much higher temperature than the bacteria themselves, as well as desiccation and severe cold.[1] Some writers give a lower temperature than 190° Fahr. as safe for sterilization with one hour's exposure, but

---

[1] Spores may be further described as resistant forms which some organisms assume in times of danger, or lack of nourishment for the purpose of preserving their lives. Not all organisms form spores.

190 may be relied upon. Milk treated by the last or "fractional" method of sterilization, as it is called, should keep indefinitely, provided of course the cotton is not disturbed. Cotton-wool or cotton batting in thick masses acts as a strainer for bacteria, and although air will enter, organisms will not.

All persons who buy milk, or in any way control milk-supplies, should consider themselves in duty bound to (1) ascertain by personal investigation the condition in which the cows are kept. If there is any suspicion that they are diseased, a veterinary surgeon should be consulted to decide the case. If they are healthy and well fed, they cannot fail to give good milk, and nothing more is to be done except to see that it is transported in perfectly cleansed and scalded vessels. (2) If it is impossible to obtain milk directly from the producer, and one is obliged to buy that from unknown sources, it should be sterilized the moment it enters the house. There is no other means of being sure that it will not be a bearer of disease. Not all such milk contains disease-producing organisms, but it all may contain them, and there is no safety in its use until all bacteria have been deprived of life.

DIGESTION

Definition. Digestion is the breaking up, changing, and liquefying of the food in the various chambers of the alimentary canal designed for that purpose. The mechanical breaking up is done principally by the teeth in the mouth, the chemical changes and liquefying by the various digestive fluids.[1]

---

[1] It is supposed, but I think not yet demonstrated, that bacteria are among the transforming agents of our food, in the alimentary canal. Organisms in the saliva have been isolated and found to produce substances which will partially digest starch.

Digestive Fluids. The digestive fluids are true secretions. Each is formed from the blood by a special gland for the purpose which never does anything else; they do not exist in the blood as such. Their flow is intermittent, taking place only when they are needed. The liver, however, is an exception to all the others. It is both secretory and excretory, and bile is formed all the time, but is most abundant during digestion.[1]

Saliva. The fluid which is mixed with the food in the mouth is secreted by a considerable number and variety of glands, the principal of which are the parotid, submaxillary, and sublingual. Smaller glands in the roof and sides of the mouth, in the tongue, and in the mucous membrane of the pharynx contribute to the production of saliva, the digestive fluid of the mouth. The flow from the parotid gland is greatest. The flow from all the glands is greatly increased when food is taken, especially if it be of good flavor. Sometimes the amount is increased by smell alone, as when a nice steak is cooking, or a savory soup, and sometimes the saliva is made copious by thought, as when we remember the taste of dishes eaten in the past, and we say, "It makes the mouth water just to think of them."

Amount of Saliva. According to Dalton the amount of saliva secreted every twenty-four hours is $42\frac{1}{2}$ oz. Its reaction is almost constantly alkaline. It is composed of water, organic matter, and various mineral salts. Ptyalin is its active principle, and is called by some authors *animal diastase*, or starch converter.

Gastric Juice. Gastric juice is the digestive fluid of the stomach. It is acid. Its flow is intermittent, occurring only at times of digestion. Its active principle is pepsin.

It is worthy of notice here that the character of the

[1] Flint's "Physiology."

digestive fluids when food is taken is different from what it is when the organs are at rest. For instance, the gastric juice which flows in abundance under the stimulus of food, is not like the fluid secreted when the stomach is collapsed and empty.

Pancreatic Juice. Pancreatic juice is the digestive juice of the pancreas, and is poured into the small intestine a short distance below the pyloric opening. Its reaction is alkaline. Its flow is entirely suspended during the intervals of digestion.

Bile. Bile, the fourth in order of the digestive liquids, is the secretion of the largest gland of the body—the liver. It is poured into the small intestine by a duct which empties side by side with the duct from the pancreas. The flow of bile is constant, but is greatest during digestion.

Intestinal Juice. Intestinal juice has been to physiologists a difficult subject of study. It is mingled with the salivary and gastric juices at the times of digestion, when it is most desirable to notice its action. Nearly all authorities agree that it is alkaline, and that its function is to complete the digestion of substances which may reach it in an undigested condition.

Mucus of Large Intestine. The mucus secreted by the large intestine is for lubricating only.

Digestion in Different Parts of the Alimentary Tract. Different substances in food are digested in different portions of the alimentary canal, and by different means. Let us begin in the mouth. Taking the classes of foods, starch, one of the carbohydrates, is the one most affected by the ptyalin, or animal diastase, of the saliva. So energetic is the action of ptyalin on starch that 1 part is sufficient to change 1000 parts. Starch is not acted upon by the gastric juice of the stomach at all; however, the continued action of the saliva is not probably interrupted in the stomach. The digestion of starch is completed by the action of the pancreatic and intestinal juices, and consists in its being changed into soluble glucose, which is absorbed in solution.

Sugar. Cane-sugar, or common sugar (also called *sucrose*), passes through the mouth, unchanged, to the stomach, where it is converted into glucose by the slow action of the acid (hydrochloric) of the gastric juice. Dilute hydrochloric acid has the same action on sugar outside of the stomach.

The action of pancreatic juice on sugar is very marked; it immediately changes cane-sugar into glucose. The effect of intestinal fluid is not well understood, but there is the general agreement that it does not change cane-sugar, neither is cane-sugar, as such, absorbed in the intestine. Bile does not affect it, therefore cane-sugar is digested or converted into glucose either by the stomach or pancreas, or both. It will now be seen that ultimately the same substance, glucose, is obtained from both starch and sugar.

Protein. We now come to the consideration of the digestion of the protein compounds, of which albumen may be taken as a type. Possibly no action except breaking up and moistening takes place in the mouth.[1] Its digestion begins in the stomach, where its structure is broken up and a separation and dissolution of the little sacs which hold it take place. The same thing is partially accomplished outside of the stomach when white of egg is slightly beaten and strained through a cloth. Gastric juice further acts on the albumen itself, forming it into what is called albumen peptone. The digestion of raw and carefully cooked albumen has been found to be carried on very rapidly in the stomach, and the change is

---

[1] It is possible that albumen and fibrin are acted upon by some of the juices secreted in the mouth.

essentially the same in both cases, but in favor of the slightly coagulated. When the albumen is rendered hard, fine, and close in consistency by over-cooking, then it is less easy of digestion than when raw.

Absorption. It is probable that the greater portion of the process of digestion and absorption of albumen takes place in the stomach.

Fibrin. Fibrin is also digested in the stomach, and made into fibrin peptone.

Casein. Liquid casein is immediately coagulated by gastric juice, both by the action of free acid and organic matter.

Gelatin. Gelatin is quickly dissolved by gastric juice, and afterward no longer has the property of forming jelly on cooling. Gelatin is more rapidly disposed of than the tissue from which it is produced.

Vegetable Protein. The digestion of the vegetable protein compounds, such as the gluten of wheat and the protein of the various grains, such as corn, oatmeal, etc., is undoubtedly carried on in the stomach, but they must be well softened and prepared by the action of heat and water, or they will not be digested anywhere; and often corn, beans, and grains of oatmeal are rejected entirely unchanged. Partially or imperfectly digested proteins are affected by intestinal juice. It is probable that the function of this fluid is to complete digestive changes in food which have already begun in the stomach.

To summarize: The digestion and absorption of nitrogenous compounds take place in both the stomach and the intestines.

NUTRITION

One of the important points to bring to the notice of pupils in the study of cookery is the phenomenon of nutrition. It is astonishing how vague are the ideas that many people have of why they eat food, and vaguer still are their notions of the necessity of air, pure and plenty. Once instruct the mind that it is the air we breathe and the food we eat which nourish the body, giving material for its various processes, for nervous and muscular energy, and for maintaining the constant temperature which the body must always possess in order to be in a state of health, and there is much more likelihood that the dignity and importance of proper cooking and proper food will not be overlooked.

A knowledge that the health and strength of a person depend largely upon what passes through his mouth, that even the turn of his thinking is modified by what he eats, should lead all intelligent women to make food a conscientious subject of study.

In general, by the term "nutrition" is meant the building up and maintaining of the physical framework of the body with all its various functions, and ultimately the mental and moral faculties which are dependent upon it, by means of nutriment or food.

The word is derived from the Latin *nutrire*, to nourish. The word "nurse" is from the same root, and in its original sense means one who nourishes, a person who supplies food, tends, or brings up.

Anything which aids in sustaining the body is food; therefore, air and water, the two most immediate necessities of life, may be, and often are, so classed.

Nutriment exclusive of air is received into the body by means of the alimentary canal. The great receiver of air is the lungs, but it also penetrates the body through the pores of the skin, and at these points carbonic acid is given off as in the lungs. The body is often compared to a steam-engine, which takes in raw material in the form of fuel and converts it into force or power. Food, drink, and air are the fuel of the body,— the things consumed; heat, muscular and intellectual energy, and other forms of power are the products.

Food, during the various digestive processes, becomes reduced to a liquid, and is then absorbed and conveyed, by different channels constructed for the purpose, into the blood, which contains, after being acted upon by the oxygen of the air in the lungs, all those substances which are required to maintain the various tissues, secretions, and, in fact, the life of the system.

Some of the ways in which the different kinds of food nourish the body have been found out by chemists and physiologists from actual experiments on living animals, such as rabbits, dogs, pigs, sheep, goats, and horses, and also on man. Often a scientist becomes so enthusiastic in his search for knowledge about a certain food that he gives his own body for trial. Much valuable work has been done in this direction during the last decade by Voit, Pettenkofer, Moleschott, Ranke, Payen, and in this country by Atwater.

No one can explain all the different intricate changes which a particle of food undergoes from the moment it enters the mouth until its final transformation into tissue or some form of energy; but by comparing the income with the outgo, ideas may be gained of what goes on in the economy of the body, and of the proportion of nutrients used, and some of the intricate and complex chemical changes which the different food principles undergo in the various processes of digestion, assimilation, and use.[1] Probably

[1] The body loses each day, in the performance of its ordinary and usual functions, about nine pounds of matter (Martin); therefore, that amount of income of food, water, and air will be needed in every twenty-four hours.

hundreds of changes take place in the body, in its various nutritive functions, of which nothing is known, or they are entirely unsuspected, so that if we do our utmost with the present lights which we possess for guidance to health, we shall still fall far short of completeness. The subject of food and nutrition, viewed in the light of bacteriology and chemistry, is one of the most inviting subjects of study of the day, and is worthy of the wisest thought of the nation.

The body creates nothing of itself, either of material or of energy; all must come to it from without. Every atom of carbon, hydrogen, phosphorus, or other elements, every molecule of protein, carbohydrate, or other compounds of these elements, is brought to the body with the food and drink it consumes, and the air it breathes. Like the steam-engine, it uses the material supplied to it. Its chemical compounds and energy are the compounds and energy of the food transformed (Atwater). A proof of this is seen in the fact that when the supply from without is cut off, the body dies. The raw material which the body uses is the air and food which it consumes, the greater portion of which is digested and distributed, through the medium of the blood, to all parts of the body, to renew and nourish the various tissues and to supply the material for the different activities of life.

Ways in which Food Supplies the Wants of the Body. Food supplies the wants of the body in several ways — (1) it is used to form the tissues of the body — bones, flesh, tendons, skin, and nerves; (2) it is used to repair the waste of the tissues; (3) it is stored in the body for future use; (4) it is consumed as fuel to maintain the constant temperature which the body must always possess to be in a state of health; (5) it produces muscular and nervous energy.[1] The

[1] Prof. Atwater, in "The Century Magazine," 1887-88.

amount of energy of the body depends upon two things—the amount in the food eaten, and the ability of the body to use it, or free it for use.

With every motion, and every thought and feeling, material is consumed, hence the more rapid wearing out of persons who do severe work, and of the nervous — those who are keenly susceptible to every change in their surroundings, to change of weather, even to the thoughts and feelings of those about them.

We easily realize that muscular force or energy cannot be maintained without nutriment in proper quality and amount. An underfed or starving man has not the strength of a well-fed person. He cannot lift the same weight, cannot walk as far, cannot work as hard. We do not as easily comprehend the nervous organism, and generally have less sympathy with worn-out or ill-nourished nerves than muscles, but the sensibilities and the intellectual faculties, of which the nerves and brain are but the instruments, depend upon the right nutrition of the whole system for their proper and healthful exercise.

So many factors enter into the make-up of a thought that it cannot be said that any particular kind of food will ultimately produce a poem; but of this we may be sure, that the best work, the noblest thoughts, the most original ideas, will not come from a dyspeptic, underfed, or in any way ill-nourished individual.

The classification of foods has been usually based upon the deductions of Prout that milk contains all the necessary nutrients in the best form and proportions, viz., the nitrogenous matters, fat, sugar, water, and salts; the latter being combinations of magnesium, calcium, potassium, sodium, and iron, with chlorin, phosphoric acid, and, in smaller quantities, sulphuric acid.

These different classes seem to serve different purposes in the body, and are all necessary for perfect nutrition. Some of them closely resemble each other in composition, but are quite different in their physiological properties, and in the ends which they serve. For instance, starch ($C_6H_{10}O_5$) has almost the same chemical formula as sugar ($C_{12}H_{22}O_{11}$), and yet the one cannot replace the other to its entire exclusion.

The Protein Compounds. In general it may be said that the carbohydrates are changed into fats, and are used for the production of force, and that the fats are stored in the body as fat and used as fuel. The protein compounds do all that can be done by the fats and carbohydrates, and in addition something more; that is, they form the basis of blood, muscle, sinew, skin, and bone. They are, therefore, the most important of all the food compounds. The terms "power-givers" and "energy-formers" are sometimes applied to them, because wherever power and energy are developed they are present, though not by any means the only substances involved in the evolution of energy. Probably the fats and carbohydrates give most of the material for heat and the various other forces of the body. In case of emergency, where these are deficient, the proteins are used; but protein alone forms the basis of muscle, tendons, skin, and other tissues. This the fats and carbohydrates cannot do (Atwater). The different tissues are known from analysis to contain this complex nitrogenous compound, protein. Now, since the body cannot construct this substance out of the simpler chemical compounds which come to it, it becomes perfectly evident that the diet must have a due proportion of protein in order to maintain the strength of the body. We get most of our proteins from the flesh of animals, and they in turn get it from plants, which construct it from the crude materials of earth and air.

The Extractives, usually classed with the protein compounds, such as meat extract, beef tea, etc., are not generally regarded as direct nutrients, but, like tea and coffee, are valuable as accessory foods, lending savor to other foods and aiding their digestion by pleasantly exciting the flow of the digestive fluids. They also act as brain and nerve stimulants, and perhaps also in some slight degree as nutrients.

The principal proteins or nitrogenous substances are *albumen* in various forms, *casein* both animal and vegetable, *blood fibrin*, *muscle fibrin*, and *gelatin*. All except the last are very much alike, and probably can replace one another in nutrition.

Modern chemists agree that nitrogen is a necessary element in the various chemical and physiological actions which take place in the body to produce heat, muscular energy, and the other powers. Every structure in the body in which any form of energy is manifested is nitrogenous. The nerves, muscles, glands, and the floating cells[1] in the various liquids are nitrogenous. That nitrogen is necessary to the different processes of the system, is shown by the fact that if it be cut off, these processes languish. This may not occur immediately, for the body always has a store of nitrogen laid by for emergencies which will be consumed first, but it will occur as soon as these have been consumed. The energy of the body is measured by its consumption of oxygen. Motion and heat may be owing to the oxidation of fat, or of starch, or of nitrogenous substances; but whatever the source, the direction is given by the nitrogenous structure—in other words, nitrogen is necessary to all energy generated in the body.

Protein matter nourishes the organic framework, takes part in the generation of energy, and may be

---

[1] Hemoglobin, the red coloring matter of the blood, contains albumen.

converted into non-nitrogenous substances.[1] The necessity of the protein compounds is emphasized when we realize that about *one half* of the body is composed of muscle, *one fifth* of which is protein, and the nitrogen in this protein can be furnished only by protein, since neither fats nor carbohydrates contain it. It is therefore evident that the protein-containing foods, such as beef, mutton, fish, eggs, milk, and others, are our most valued nutrients. Our daily diet must contain a due proportion.

The proteins are all complex chemical compounds, which in nutrition become reduced to simple forms, and are then built up again into flesh. The animal foods are in the main the best of the protein compounds, for they are rich in nitrogenous matter, are easily digested, and from their composition and adaptability are most valuable in maintaining the life of the body.

A diet of lean meat alone serves to build up tissue. If nothing else be taken, the stored-up fat of the body will be consumed, and the person will become thin.[2] Athletes while in training take advantage of this fact, and are allowed to eat only such food as shall furnish the greatest amount of strength and muscular energy with a minimum of fat. The lean of beef and mutton, with a certain amount of bread, constitute the foundation of the diet.

Fats. Most of the fatty substances of food are

---

[1] Protein may be converted into fat; but although this will happen, it will not do to depend upon it for the supply in the nutrition of the body; for either it cannot be formed in sufficient quantity, or the excess of nitrogen acts as a poison. The body suffers unless a due amount of fat *as such* be taken. (Martin.)

[2] By regulating the amount of fat taken each day with food, so that a little less than is needed is consumed, one may reduce the amount of fat of the body and become thin, or reduce an excess of fat without injury to health. The process must be gradual, and continued for a number of months. Bismarck, by the advice of his physician, reduced himself in this way without loss of energy or any ill feeling.

liquefied at the temperature of the body. When eaten in the form of adipose tissue, as the fat of beef and mutton, the vesicles or cells in which the fat is held are dissociated or dissolved, the fat is set free, and mingles with the digesting mass. This is done in the stomach, and is a preparation for its further change in the intestines.

Fats are not dissolved — that is, in the sense in which meats and other foods are dissolved — in the process of digestion; the only change which they undergo is a minute subdivision caused principally by the action of the pancreatic juice. In this condition of fine emulsion they are taken up by the lacteals; they may also be absorbed by the blood-vessels.

It has been found that fat emulsions pass more easily through membranes which have been moistened with bile, and it is probable that the function of bile is partly to facilitate the absorption of fat. That the pancreatic juice is the chief agent in forming fats into emulsion was discovered in 1848. Bile is, however, essential to their perfect digestion, and we may therefore say that they are digested by the united action of the pancreatic juice and the bile.[1]

Fat forms in the body fatty tissues, and serves for muscular force and heat; it is also necessary to nourish nerves and other tissues, — in fact, without it healthy tissues cannot be formed. A proper amount of fat is also a sort of albumen sparer.

It is probable that the fat which is used in the body either to be stored away or for energy, is derived from other sources than directly from the fat eaten. From experiments made by Lawes and Gilbert on pigs, it is evident that the excess of fat stored in their bodies must be derived from some other source than the fat contained in their food, and must

[1] Flint's "Physiology."

be produced partly from nitrogenous matter and partly from carbohydrates, or, at least, that the latter play a part in its formation. It would appear from this that life might be maintained on starch, water, salts, and meat free from fat; but although the theory seems a good one, practically it is found in actual experiment[1] that nutrition is impaired by a lack of fat in the diet. The ill effects were soon seen, and immediate relief was given when fat was added to the food. Besides, in the food of all nations starch is constantly associated with some form of fat; bread with butter; potatoes with butter, cream, or gravy; macaroni and polenta with oil, and so forth. A man may live for a time and be healthy with a diet of albuminoids, fats, salts, and water, but it has not yet been proved that a similar result will be produced by a diet of albuminoids, carbohydrates, salts, and water without fat. Fat is necessary to perfect nutrition. Health cannot be maintained on albuminoids, salts, and water alone; but, on the other hand, cannot be maintained without them.

Probably the value of fats, as such, is dependent upon the ease with which they are digested. The fats eaten are not stored in the body directly, but the body constructs its fats from those eaten, and from other substances in food,—according to some authorities from the carbohydrates and proteids, and according to others from proteids alone.

Fats are *stored away* as fat, *furnish heat*, and are *used for energy;* at least, it is probable that at times they are put to the latter use. The fats laid by in the body for future use last in cases of starvation quite a long time, depending, of course, upon the amount. At such times a fat animal will live longer than a lean one.

[1] Parkes.

Doubtless in the fat of food the body finds material for its fats in the most easily convertible form. Of the various fatty substances taken, some are more easily assimilated than others. Dr. Fothergill, in "The Town Dweller," says that the reason that cod-liver oil is given to delicate children and invalids is, that it is more easily digested than ordinary fats, but it is an inferior form of fat; the next most easily digested is the fat of bacon. When a child can take bread crumbled in a little of this fat, it will not be necessary to give him cod-liver oil. Bacon fat is the much better fat for building tissues. Then comes cream, a natural emulsion, and butter. He further says there is one form of fat not commonly looked at in its proper dietetic value, and that is "toffee." It is made of butter, sugar, and sometimes a portion of molasses. A quantity of this, added to the ordinary meals, will enable a child in winter to keep up the bodily heat. The way in which butter in the form of toffee goes into the stomach is particularly agreeable.

Carbohydrates. The principal carbohydrates are *starch, dextrine, cane-sugar* or common table sugar, *grape-sugar*, the principal sugar in fruits, and *milk-sugar*, the natural sugar in milk. They are substances made up, as before stated, of carbon, hydrogen, and oxygen, but no nitrogen. They are important food substances, but are of themselves incapable of sustaining life.

The carbohydrates, both starch and sugar, in the process of digestion are converted into glucose. This is stored in the liver in the form of *glycogen*, which the liver has the power of manufacturing; it then passes into the circulation, and is distributed to the different parts of the body as it is needed. (The liver also has the power of forming glycogen out of other substances than sugar, and it is pretty conclusively proved that it is from proteids, and not from fats. Carnivorous animals, living upon flesh alone, are found to have glycogen in their bodies.)

It is impossible to assign any especial office to the different food principles; that is, it cannot be said that the carbohydrates perform a certain kind of work in the body and nothing else, or that the proteids or fats do. The human body is a highly complex and intricate organism, and its maintenance is carried on by complex and mysterious processes that cannot be followed, except imperfectly; consequently, we must regard the uses of foods in the body as more or less involved in obscurity. It is, however, generally understood that the proteids, fats, and carbohydrates each do an individual work of their own better than either of the others can do it. They are all necessary in due amount to the nutrition of the body, and doubtless work together as well as in their separate functions. They are, however, sometimes interchangeable, as, for instance, in the absence of the carbohydrates, proteids will do their work. The carbohydrates are eminently heat and energy formers, and they also act as albumen sparers.

The body always has a store of material laid by for future use. If it were not for this a person deprived of food would die immediately, as is the case when he is deprived of oxygen. (Air being ever about us, and obtainable without effort or price, there is no need for the body to lay by an amount of oxygen; consequently only a very little is stored, and that in the blood.)

The great reserve forces of the body are in the form of fatty tissues, and glycogen, or the stored-away carbohydrates of the liver; the latter is given out to the body as it is needed during the intervals of eating to supply material for the heat and energy of daily consumption, and in case of starvation. That they are true reserves is shown by the fact that they disappear during deprivation of food. The glycogen, or liver-supply, disappears first; then the fat (Martin). The heat of the body can be maintained on these substances, and a certain amount of work done, although no food except water be taken.

The principal function of the liver is to form glycogen to be stored away. It constantly manufactures it, and as constantly loses it to the circulation. Glycogen is chemically allied to starch, having the same formula ($C_6H_{10}O_5$), but differing in other ways. Its quantity is greatest about two hours after a full meal; then it gradually falls, but increases again when food is again taken. Its amount also varies with the *kind* of food eaten: fats and proteids by themselves give little, but starch and sugars give much, for it is found in greatest quantity when these form a part of the diet.

Inorganic Matter and Vegetable Acids. Water and other inorganic matter, as the salts of different kinds, and vegetable acids, as vinegar and lemon-juice, can scarcely be said to be digested. Water is absorbed, and salts are generally in solution in liquids and are absorbed with them.

Water is found in all parts of the body, even in the very solid portions, as the bones and the enamel of the teeth; it also constitutes a large proportion of its semisolids and fluids, some of which are nearly all water, as the perspiration and the tears.

Water usually is found combined with some of the salts, which seem to act as regulators of the amount which shall be incorporated into a tissue. Water is a necessary constituent of all tissues, giving them a proper consistency and elasticity. The power of resistance of the bones could not be maintained without it. It is also valuable as a food solvent, assisting in the liquefying of different substances, which are taken up by the various absorbent tubes, conveyed into the blood, and so circulated through the body. Most of the water of the body is taken into it from without, but it is also formed in the body by the union of hydrogen and oxygen.[1]

Sodium chlorid, or common salt, is found in the blood and other fluids, and in the solids of the body, except the enamel of the teeth; it occurs in greatest proportion in the fluids. The part that this salt plays in nutrition is not altogether understood. "Common salt is intermediate in certain general processes, and does not participate by its elements in the formation of organs" (Liebig). Salt is intimately associated with water, which plays an intermediate part also in nutrition, being a bearer or carrier of nutritious matters through the body.

Salt seems to regulate the absorption and use of nutrients. It is found in the greatest quantity in the blood and chyle. It doubtless facilitates digestion by rendering foods more savory, and thus causing the digestive juices to flow more freely. Sodium chlorid is contained in most if not all kinds of food, but not in sufficient quantity to supply the wants of the body; it therefore becomes a necessary part of a diet.

Potassium chlorid has similar uses to sodium chlorid, although not so generally distributed through the body. It is found in muscle, liver, milk, chyle, blood, mucus, saliva, bile, gastric juice, and one or two other fluids.

Calcium phosphate is found in all the fluids and solids of the body, held in solution in them by the presence of CO_2; both it and calcium carbonate enter largely into the structure of the bones.

Sodium carbonate, magnesium phosphate, and other salts play important parts in nutrition.

[1] Martin.

The various salts influence chemical change as well as act in rendering food soluble. For example, serum albumen, the chief proteid of the blood, is insoluble in pure water, but dissolves easily in water which has a little neutral salts in it.[1] Salts also help to give firmness to the teeth and bones.

To recapitulate, food is eaten, digested, assimilated, and consumed or transformed in the body by a series of highly intricate and complex processes. It is for the most part used for the different powers and activities of the system; there is, however, always a small portion which is rejected as waste. The first change is in the mouth, where the food is broken up and moistened and the digestion of starch begins; these changes continue in the stomach until the whole is reduced to a more or less liquid mass. As the contents of the stomach pass little by little into the duodenum, the mass becomes more fluid by the admixture of bile, pancreatic juice, and intestinal juice, and, as it passes along, absorption takes place; the mass grows darker in color and less fluid, until all good material is taken up and only waste left, which is rejected from the body.

That portion of the food which is not affected by the single or united action of the digestive fluids is chiefly of vegetable origin. Hard seeds, such as corn, and the outer coverings of grains, such as the husk of oatmeal and those parts which are composed largely of cellulose, pass through the intestinal canal without change.

It may be remarked here that since the digestive mechanism is so perfect a structure, and will try to dissolve anything given it, and select only that which is good, why should there be the necessity of giving any special attention to preparing food before it is eaten? The answer is that the absorptive vessels

[1] Martin.

cannot take up what is not there, neither can the digestive organs *supply* what the food lacks; therefore, the food must contain in suitable proportions all substances needed by the body. Also, food which contains a large proportion of waste, or is difficult of digestion from over or under cooking, or is unattractive by insipidity or unsavoriness, overworks these long-suffering organs (the extra power or force needed being drawn from the blood), and causes the whole system to suffer. Mal-nutrition, with the long line of evils which it entails, is the cause, direct or indirect, of most of the sickness in the world, for it reduces the powers of the system, and thus enfeebles its resistance to disease.

Ideal Diet. "The ideal diet is that combination of food which, while imposing the least burden upon the body, supplies it with exactly sufficient material to meet its wants" (Schuster).

In general the digestibility of foods may be summarized as follows:

1. The protein of ordinary animal foods is very readily and completely digestible.
2. The protein of vegetable foods is much less easily digested than that of animal foods.
3. The fat of animal foods may at times fail of digestion.
4. Sugar and starch are easy of digestion.
5. Animal foods have the advantage of vegetable foods in that they contain more protein, and that their protein is more easily digested. (Atwater.)

A diet largely of animal food leaves very little undigested matter. The albuminoids in all cases are completely transformed into nutriment. Fat enters the blood as a fine emulsion.

Absorption. The general rule of absorption is that food is taken into the circulation through the porous walls of the alimentary tract as rapidly as it is completely digested. A large portion of liquid is immediately absorbed by the blood-vessels of the stomach.

Adaptation of Foods to Particular Needs and Conditions. The demands of different individuals for nutrients in the daily food vary with age, occupation, and other conditions of life, including especially the peculiar characteristics of people. No two persons are exactly alike in their expenditure of muscular and nervous energy, so no two will need the same amount or kind of nutriment to repair the waste.

A man who digs in a field day after day expends a certain amount of muscular energy. A lawyer, statesman, or author who works with his brain instead of his hands uses nervous force, but very little muscular. Brain and muscle are not nourished exactly by the same materials; therefore, the demand in the way of nutriment of these two classes will not be the same.

The lawyer might find a feast in a box of sardines and some biscuit, while the field laborer would look with contempt upon such food, and turn from it to fat pork and cabbage. This is no mere difference in refinement of taste, but a real and instinctive difference in the demands of the two constitutions. Sardines supply to the brain-worker the material he needs, and the pork and cabbage to the laborer the heat and energy he expends.

In health the sense of taste is the best guide to what is demanded by the system, and may as a general rule be followed; but in sickness that will not do, as the sense of taste in particular is disturbed by most forms of disease.

When a patient is very ill only the simplest foods will be used, and those will be prescribed by the physician; but when a patient is out of danger, and the necessity for variety comes, then the nurse, by preparing or suggesting dishes, may do much toward restoring the person to health and strength.

As a very large percentage of diseases arise from imperfect nutrition (as large as eighty per cent. being given by some writers), the sense of taste is usually very much disturbed and dulled in illness; therefore those kinds of food which are savory, and at the same time easy of digestion and nutritious, should be selected. The savory quality is very important. A person in health may endure badly cooked food and monotony in diet; a person recovering from an illness cannot but suffer by it.

A nurse will find a pleasant field for the exercise of ingenuity in selecting and preparing such dishes as shall (1) be suited to the digestive powers of the patient; (2) shall be savory; (3) shall be sufficiently varied to supply all those materials which the depleted and exhausted body needs; and (4) shall be in such judicious quantity as shall increase nutrition, but never overtax the digestive powers.

The decision of No. 1 (food suited to the digestive powers) is the most difficult, and here again the doctor will advise for particular or peculiar diseases.

There are certain things which from their natural composition are more easy of digestion than others, such, for instance, as milk, eggs slightly coagulated and raw, beef tea with the *juices in solution*, cocoa milk, and cocoa, coffee, jellies, gruels, porridge from prepared grains (except oatmeal) when *thoroughly* cooked, oysters alive, rice, venison, and tripe.

No. 2, the *savory* quality, depends largely upon preparation, and is under the control of the nurse. A baked potato done in a *hot* oven, just to the point, and served immediately, is a delicious dish; overdone, or done in an oven of low temperature, and served lukewarm, it is very far from appetizing. A steak, if cut thin, salted, and broiled slowly, will be hard, dry, and lacking in flavor, but if it is cut thick, at least an inch and a half, better two inches, broiled for the first minute over very hot coals, and then slowly, that the heat may have time to penetrate to the center, and raise the whole to a temperature sufficiently high to cook it (about 160° Fahr.) without charring the outside, it will make a dish both wholesome and savory.

No. 3, the next consideration, is that of *variety*, and here the resources and judgment of the person in charge must come to the front. Only general hints can be given. Endeavor to supply some protein, some fat, some of the carbohydrates, and some mineral matter in each meal. Bread, grains, or potatoes will give the necessary starch. Sugar is usually supplied with drinks. Milk, eggs, meat, fish, and oysters will give protein; cream, butter, bacon, and the fat of other meats will furnish fat, and fruits and green salads give acids and mineral salts. For the latter, grapes, apples, carrots, onions, dandelions, and lettuce are very valuable. Grapes are composed of water with salts in solution, and glucose; both are absorbed with very little outlay from the system. The others are every-day foods, but science has taught that their instinctive use in the past has been a wise one.

No. 4, the *quantity* of food to offer to a sick person, will depend upon the individual. Give enough, but rather give to an invalid *too little* than too much, especially in the first days of using solid food; for after some forms of sickness there is great hunger, and one may injure himself by overeating at such a time. Furnish a little of each kind of food, but let that little be of *good quality* and *perfectly prepared*, so that every morsel is eatable. It is discouraging to any one to have set before him food such that much of it must be rejected uneaten. It is very encouraging, especially to an invalid, to be able to eat all that is brought him, and for this end cooking and serving are of great importance. It is necessary to adjust the *proportions* of the different kinds of foods to the needs of the consumer, otherwise all unnecessary material will be rejected from the body as waste, or will be accumulated in it to interfere with the workings of the different organs.

In general it may be said that the needs of no two individuals can be satisfied with exactly the same diet. In sickness it is the province of the physician to adjust the food to the condition of the patient. In convalescence the taste of the individual and the judgment of the nurse or attendant combined will usually not fail of good results. If an individual craves a certain dish, and there is no good reason why he should not have it, by all means procure it. Let only your judgment act. It may be something that you personally do not like. That should not influence a decision, provided, of course, that the food is not unwholesome.

We should bear in mind that a sick person is not in the same condition as ourselves, and that no matter how absurd his cravings may seem, they may be but perfectly natural longings for those substances which his depleted and exhausted system needs in order to be restored to health.

PART II
RECIPES

PART II

RECIPES

BEEF-JUICE, BEEF-TEA, AND BROTHS

Beef-Juice. The clear juice of beef, slightly diluted with water, is always excellent, being especially useful for its strong flavors. It is like concentrated beef-tea, and is often valuable in pleasantly exciting the action of the mouth and stomach after a long illness in which milk has been the chief article of diet.

Beef-juice is best made by broiling the beef. Prepared in this way, the flavor is superior, and it is a quick and easy method; but when a proper broiling fire cannot be had, then it may be made in a glass jar like beef-tea, except without the water.

Beef-Tea is valuable for its stimulating properties and for the warmth that it gives; it is also somewhat nutritious, containing as it does the albuminous juices of the meat, some salts, and the very important flavors. Beef-tea should be prepared in such a manner that the juices are held in solution in the water, not coagulated, to secure which the cooking temperature should never be allowed to exceed that of 160° Fahr.

Broths. Beef, mutton, and chicken broths are the most desirable forms of meat drinks for convalescents and those no longer dangerously ill. By slow cooking at a low temperature at first (the temperature should not exceed 150° Fahr. for the first hour), the extractives and albuminous juices are drawn out; then, by boiling, the gelatin of the bones, flesh, and tissues is dissolved. The nutritive qualities of these broths may be much increased by the addition of bread, rice, tapioca, barley, and sago, cooked during the whole time so that they may be completely dissolved in the liquid.

BEEF-JUICE

Bottled. Select a half pound of well-flavored beef, cut away everything except the lean fiber, divide it into small pieces, put them into a glass jar, cover, and place in a deep saucepan of cold water; heat gradually for one hour, but do not allow the temperature at any time to exceed 160° Fahr.; then strain out the juice and press the meat. The liquid should be clear red, not brown and flaky. Add a little salt, and it is ready to serve. A half pound will make three or four tablespoons of juice. If it is to be used constantly, a larger quantity may be made at once, as it will keep eighteen hours in a refrigerator. Beef-juice may be made into tea by diluting it with warm water.

Broiled. Prepare a fire of clear glowing coals from which all blue flames have disappeared. Cut a piece of lean beef (one half pound from the round or any good lean portion) one and one half inches thick, and remove from it all membranous tissues and fat. Put it into a wire broiler, and broil from six to eight minutes according to the intensity of the fire (see rules for broiling). The piece when done should be pink and full of juice, not dry and hard, nor, on the other hand, bluish-red in the middle. More juice will be obtained if the heat has penetrated to the center than if the meat is raw. When done, cut it into small pieces and squeeze out the juice with a meat-press or a lemon-squeezer. Add a little salt, and it is ready to serve. It should be given in spoonfuls, either warm or cold. If it is necessary to warm it, put a little into a cup and place it in a dish of warm water on the fire. Care should be taken that the water does not become hotter than 160° Fahr., for beyond that temperature the albuminous juices become coagulated and appear as brown flakes.

BEEF-TEA

Bottled. Select and prepare the meat in the same manner as for bottled beef-juice, except that for every half pound a cup of water should be used, poured over after it has been put into the jar. The liquid thus obtained will resemble beef-juice in every respect except in strength. Serve as a drink in a red wine-glass or a china cup.

With Hydrochloric Acid. Hydrochloric acid acts upon the fibers of meat in such a way that they become more easy of digestion. From a given portion of meat much more nutriment is extracted by the use of hydrochloric acid than without it; beef-tea made with it is recommended by physicians as the most easily absorbed form of beef drink, and for feeble children and patients much weakened by sickness it is especially useful.

To Prepare. Select a half pound of good beef; remove from it everything that is not clear meat,—that is, bone, gristle, connective tissue, and fat; chop it fine on a meat-board or in a chopping-tray. Put into a bowl one cup of water and five drops of dilute hydrochloric acid; stir into this the chopped meat, and set it in a refrigerator or any cool place for two hours to digest. Then strain, flavor with salt, and serve cold in a red wine-glass.

Should there be any objection to the taste or color, heat the tea until it steams and changes to a brownish hue; do not strain out the flakes of coagulated albumen and fibrin which appear, for they are the most nutritious portion of the tea.

Chemically pure hydrochloric acid may be obtained of a druggist (it is usually marked C. P.); from it a diluted solution may be made by mixing it in the proportion of five and one half fluidounces to fourteen ounces of water.

BEEF BROTH

Beef broth is the juice of beef extracted by the long application of heat in connection with some solvent, usually water.

To make beef broth, allow one pound of meat, or meat and bone, to every quart of water. Wash the meat with a cloth in cold water until it is clean, or wipe it with a wet cloth if it is apparently fresh cut; divide it into small pieces (half-inch cubes) in order to expose as great an extent of surface as possible to the dissolving action of the water. Put it into a granite-ware kettle with *cold* water, and cook it at a low temperature for two hours, then boil it for two hours to dissolve the gelatin. Remove it from the fire, and strain it, using a strainer so coarse that the flakes of albumen may go through (an ordinary wire strainer will do). Skim as much fat as possible from the surface with a spoon, and then remove the remaining small particles with a sheet of clean paper (unsized is best) drawn over the surface. Season the broth with salt and pepper, and serve it very hot. If not needed at once, it may be set away to cool, when the fat will rise to the top, and form into a cake which may be lifted off.

With Herbs. Make a broth according to the above rule, and flavor it with bay-leaves, mint, or with a bouquet of sweet herbs in the proportion of one teaspoon to a quart of liquid.

With Grains. One tablespoon of any of the following grains—rice, barley, oatmeal, or wheat—to one quart of liquid, gives a pleasant consistency and flavor to beef broth. Tapioca, sago, cold dry toast, or cuttings of bread may also be used. They should be put in when the broth is first set on the fire to cook, that they may be completely dissolved in the liquid.

With Vegetables. Celery, onion, carrot, turnip, or shredded cabbage may be used in broth in the proportion of one tablespoon to a quart. Cabbage is better in combination with onion than alone.

BROTH MADE FROM BEEFSTEAK

(A QUICK METHOD)

Scrape the pulp from a pound of round or of sirloin steak, or mince the meat in a chopping-tray until it is fine; put it into a saucepan with just enough cold water to cover it, and let it come to the boiling-point slowly; then simmer it for fifteen minutes (better half an hour if there is time). Strain it, take off the fat with a sheet of paper, and season it with salt. This is a somewhat expensive but savory broth, and may easily be made on a gas or alcohol stove.

A beef panada may be made by leaving the pulp in the broth and adding a little rolled cracker-crumbs or some bread softened and squeezed through a strainer.

SCOTCH BEEF BROTH

Put into a granite stew-pan a pint of prepared beef broth,—that is, broth which has been strained, cleared of fat, and seasoned. Add to it one tablespoon of rolled oats, or of ordinary oatmeal, and simmer it gently until the oatmeal is soft and jelly-like. The time required will be about two hours. Then strain it, and serve very hot. This makes a good dish for an invalid for whom oatmeal has not been forbidden. If the broth is reduced by the boiling, add enough water to restore the pint.

CHICKEN BROTH

Chicken broth should be made with fowl, not with young chicken; a good one weighing three pounds will make three pints of broth.

To Prepare. Singe the chicken with a piece of blazing newspaper to burn off the long hairs; remove all refuse or that which is not clear flesh, viz., pin-feathers, oil-bag, crop, lungs, kidneys, and, of course, the entrails if the fowl is not already drawn. If the pipes in the neck are not all drawn out with the crop, they may be easily taken away when the fowl is cut up. Scrub it well in cold water, and then disjoint and cut it into small pieces; wash each piece thoroughly, retaining the skin if it is clear and free from pin-feathers, otherwise removing it. Put the chicken into cold water and simmer it for two hours, then boil it for two hours. Finally strain it and remove the fat, season it with salt and a bit of white pepper, and serve very hot in pretty china cups, with or without a lunch-cracker or a bit of dry toast.

With Herbs. Parsley, bay-leaves, sage, thyme, or a bouquet of sweet herbs will give a pleasant flavor to chicken broth. A teaspoon to a pint is the right proportion.

With Grains or Vegetables. Rice may be used to advantage in chicken broth, and also pearl-barley, sago, tapioca, and bread. These are among the best additions of the kind that can be made, for with them one is able to preserve the light color so desirable in chicken broth. Onion, celery, and parsley in the proportion of one teaspoon to a pint are suitable vegetables. Celery is especially nice.

MUTTON BROTH

One pound of mutton from the neck, or, better, the loin, one quart of cold water, and one teaspoon of chopped onion will be needed for this broth. Remove from the mutton the tough skin, the fat, and all membranes, and cut the meat into small pieces; break the bone, and if it be a part of the spinal column, take out the spinal cord. Put the pieces of meat, the onion, and the water into a saucepan, and simmer them together for three hours; then strain out the meat, dip off the fat from the broth with a spoon, and remove the remaining small particles with paper; season it with salt and white pepper. Serve hot in a pretty cup, with a toasted cracker.

A little bunch of mint, a bouquet of herbs, a few bay-leaves, or a sprinkle of Cayenne pepper or curry-powder will vary the broth agreeably. Pearl-barley is a particularly good addition to make, or rice may be used in the proportion of one teaspoon to a pint.

OYSTER-TEA. No. 1

Select eight fresh oysters, chop them fine in a chopping-tray, and turn them into a saucepan with a cup of cold water; set the saucepan on the fire, and let the water come slowly to the boiling-point, then simmer for five minutes; strain the liquid into a bowl, flavor it with half a saltspoon of salt, and serve hot with or without a small piece of dry toast, or a toasted cream-cracker.

OYSTER-TEA. No. 2

Put a dozen large oysters with their liquor into a stew-pan; simmer for five minutes. Then strain the liquor, leaving out the oysters, and add to it one half cup of milk; set it back on the stove and heat it just to the boiling-point. Flavor with a sprinkle of white pepper and half a saltspoon of salt. Or make it according to rule No. 1, using milk instead of water.

CLAM BROTH

Six large clams in their shells and a cup of water will be needed for this broth. Wash the clams thoroughly with a brush, and place them with the water in a kettle over the fire. The broth is simply the juice of the clams with the water boiled for a minute. It does not require seasoning, as clam-juice is usually salt enough. As soon as the shells open, the broth is done.

This broth and oyster-tea No. 1 are good in cases of nausea, and will be retained on the stomach when almost everything else is rejected.

GRUELS

Gruels are cooked mixtures of grain or flour, with water, or with water and milk. They are best made with milk as a part of the liquid, but care must be taken not to put it into the gruel until the grain has been thoroughly cooked in water, and after that the mixture should not be allowed to boil, as so high a temperature changes the flavor and composition of the milk, and renders it a less desirable food than if it were cooked at a lower temperature,—for instance, 190° or 200° Fahr.

The largest ingredient of grains is starch, which is not easily digested unless well cooked; therefore the time for boiling gruels should be conscientiously kept by the clock. Should the water evaporate, restore to the original quantity before putting in the milk, which should be hot, though not *boiling*. It may, however, come just to the boiling-point without any special injury.

Gruels served with a cream- or a banquet-cracker or a square of toasted bread are excellent for a convalescent's lunch. They may be varied with flavorings of cinnamon, nutmeg, almond, or a little grated lemon-peel, and sugar. Sugar is mentioned with great hesitancy, for a sweet gruel is an abomination, and yet a gruel with a *very little* sugar has a pleasanter flavor than one without any.

Lacking color, gruels may be made attractive by

serving them in dainty-hued china. Gruels should be drunk slowly, that the starch, which is partially digested by the action of saliva, may be thoroughly mixed with it before it is swallowed.

BARLEY GRUEL

1 Tablespoon of Robinson's barley-flour.
1 Cup of boiling water.
1 Saltspoon of salt.
1 Scant teaspoon of sugar.
1 Cup of milk.

Mix the flour, salt, and sugar together with a little cold water, pour on the boiling water, and boil ten minutes; then add the milk, bring just to the boiling-point, strain, and serve very hot. This gruel may be made without the milk, but with a pint instead of a cup of water. Barley is a nutritious grain, rich in phosphates and protein.

ARROWROOT GRUEL

1 Tablespoon of arrowroot.
1 Saltspoon of salt.
1 Scant teaspoon of sugar.
1 Cup of hot water.
1 Cup of milk.

Wet the arrowroot with the sugar and salt in two tablespoons of cold water, then pour on the *hot* water, stirring constantly. Boil it for twenty minutes, then add the milk and bring just to the boiling-point. Strain it, and immediately serve.

Arrowroot is almost pure starch. Its grains burst at 140° Fahr.; therefore, if *boiling* water be poured upon it, it will form into lumps which will have to be strained out, and thus a part of the material will be lost; hence the necessity of wetting it in cold water to reduce the temperature so that it may be stirred smooth before the lumps form.

Milk is changed by long boiling, and loses some of its agreeable taste; it is better, therefore, not to put the milk into the gruel until after the flour has been thoroughly cooked in the water, thus preserving its natural flavor.

Arrowroot gruel may be flavored with cinnamon by boiling a half square inch of cinnamon bark in the water with which the gruel is made. Nutmeg, lemon juice or peel, and sherry wine may also be used; but the sherry should be avoided unless the gruel is to be served cold.

OATMEAL GRUEL FROM POUNDED GRAIN

Pound in a mortar or roll on a bread-board one cup of oatmeal until it is floury. Put it into a bowl, and fill the bowl with cold water; stir well and let it settle for a few seconds; then pour off the milky-looking water into a saucepan, fill again, mix and pour off the water, and so continue until the water no longer appears white, being careful at each pouring not to allow the brown cortex of the grain or any of the coarse portions to get out of the bowl; then boil the water for half an hour. For every pint put in a saltspoon of salt and half a cup of sweet cream, or, if that is not at hand, the same quantity of milk. Beef broth or wine may be used instead of cream. This is the best way to make oatmeal gruel, for by this method the coarse and irritating hulls are excluded, while the good flavor and nutritious properties are preserved.

OATMEAL GRUEL (Plain)

2 Tablespoons of oatmeal (rolled oats).
1 Saltspoon of salt.
1 Scant teaspoon of sugar.
1 Cupful of boiling water.
1 Cup of milk.

Mix the oatmeal, salt, and sugar together, and pour on the boiling water. Cook it in a saucepan for thirty minutes, or in a double boiler two hours; then strain it through a fine wire strainer to remove the hulls, put it again on the stove, add the milk, and allow it to heat just to the boiling-point. Serve it hot. Good oatmeal gruel may be made from cold porridge, by adding water, milk, and a little sugar and straining it, or it may be served unstrained. Many like it so, and it makes an excellent lunch.

FLOUR GRUEL

1 Tablespoon of flour.
1 Saltspoon of salt.
1 Teaspoon of sugar.
1 Cup of boiling water.
1 Cup of milk.
$\frac{1}{2}$ Square inch of cinnamon.

Mix the flour, salt, and sugar, as for other gruels, into a paste with a little cold water; add the piece of cinnamon and the hot water; boil it for twenty minutes, slowly, so that it may not stick to the bottom of the pan and burn; then put in the milk and bring to the boiling-point. Strain it, and serve it very hot. If the gruel is intended for a patient with fever, a little lemon-juice is good in place of the cinnamon. Other flavors may also be used, such as nutmeg, almond, and vanilla.

CRACKER GRUEL

2 Tablespoons of cracker-crumbs.
1 Scant saltspoon of salt.
1 Scant teaspoon of sugar.
1 Cup of boiling water.
1 Cup of milk.

To make the cracker-crumbs, roll some crackers on a board until they are fine. Bent's water-crackers are good, cream-crackers better; mix the salt and sugar with the crumbs, pour on the boiling water, put in the milk, and simmer it for two minutes. The gruel does not need long cooking, for the cracker-crumbs are already thoroughly cooked. Do not strain it.

FARINA GRUEL

Farina is a grain which is carefully prepared from the nitrogenous part of selected wheat, and is therefore a better nutrient than rice-flour or arrowroot.

1 Tablespoon of Hecker's farina.
1 Saltspoon of salt.
1 Teaspoon of sugar.
1 Cup of boiling water.
1 Cup of milk.

Mix the grain, salt, and sugar; pour on the boiling water, and cook ten minutes; then put in the milk, boil for a minute, and it is ready to serve. Farina, being partially prepared, does not need long cooking.

IMPERIAL GRANUM

Imperial Granum is a dainty, highly nutritious preparation of wheat, very useful for invalids and children.

    1 Tablespoon of Granum.
    1 Saltspoon of salt.
    1 Teaspoon of sugar.
    1 Cup of boiling water.
    1 Cup of milk.

Mix the meal, salt, and sugar in a saucepan, pour on the boiling water, and cook ten minutes; then add the milk, and let it again reach the boiling-point, when it is ready to serve.

Mush and porridge may also be made from this grain for the use of children, for whom it is an excellent food, being similar to farina, but more delicate and easier of digestion. Imperial Granum may be obtained at any pharmacy.

RACAHOUT DES ARABES

    1 Tablespoon of Racahout.
    1 Saltspoon of salt.
    1 Cup of hot water.
    1 Cup of milk.

Put the Racahout and salt into a saucepan, mix it into a paste with a little cold water, and then pour on the hot water; simmer for ten minutes. Have the milk scalding hot in another pan, and when the gruel has cooked the full time pour it in. Strain and serve.

Racahout is a compound consisting principally of sugar, arrowroot, rice-flour, and French chocolate. It makes a most appetizing gruel, and is quite nutritious. *Racahout des Arabes* is imported largely from France. It may be obtained at any first-class grocery store.

INDIAN-MEAL GRUEL

2 Tablespoons of corn-meal.
1 Tablespoon of flour.
1 Teaspoon of salt.
1 Teaspoon of sugar.
1 Quart of boiling water.
1 Cup of milk.

Mix the corn-meal, flour, salt, and sugar into a thin paste with cold water, and pour into it the boiling water. Cook it in a double boiler for three hours. No less time than that will cook the corn-meal thoroughly. Then add the milk, and it is ready to serve.

Use the fine granulated meal which comes in pasteboard packages, prepared for the table, and may be bought of almost any grocer.

MUSH AND PORRIDGE

Mush is meal or grain cooked in water to the consistency of rather thin pudding. *Porridge* is like mush, only thinner. The most important point connected with the preparation of these is thoroughness in the cooking. Made as they generally are of coarsely ground or of rolled grains, they need long boiling to soften the cellulose and to cook the starch properly.

Oatmeal. Oatmeal should be cooked for at least three hours in a double boiler. It is at its best prepared the day before it is needed, and then reheated as it is wanted. If it is done in this way, the flavor is fine, and there is no danger that the grains will be hard. When taken from the kettle, the oatmeal should be of the consistency to pour, and on cooling it ought to form into a tender, jelly-like pudding. Sometimes oatmeal is cooked so that the grains are whole and separate, but it is not easily digested so, and lacks the delicious flavor which long cooking gives.

Oatmeal for those for whom there is no objection to its use is a valuable nutrient, furnishing more for the money than almost any other food.[1]

---

[1] Composition of oatmeal:

Nitrogenous matter	12.6%
Carbohydrates, starch, etc.	63.8%
Fatty matter	5.6%
Mineral matter	3.0%
Water	15.0%
Total	100.00%

LETHERBY.

From Prof. Mott's Chart of the Composition, Digestibility, and Nutritive Value of Food.

Indian Meal. Indian meal also requires many hours' cooking. Even if it be in a single vessel and actually boiled, not less than an hour and a half of exposure to heat is safe.

Farina. Farina having been already subjected to a high degree of heat in its preparation, is thereby partially cooked, and does not require as long a time as the raw grains.

Mushes and porridges made from oatmeal, cracked wheat, or any grain on which the tough outside covering remains, are to be avoided in all cases of irritation or disease of the alimentary canal, particularly in diseases of the intestines, for the hard hulls are very irritating to the delicate lining membranes. Young children have exceedingly delicate digestive powers, and are often made ill by coarse, starchy food. For them it is always safest to use the prepared grains, such as farina, granula, and Imperial Granum.

All of the grains given in these recipes may be made into *porridges* by following the rules given for mushes, except that a larger proportion of water should be used. Porridges are like mushes, only thinner.

OATMEAL MUSH

½ Cup of rolled oats, or ½ cup of granulated oatmeal.
½ Teaspoon of salt.
1 Pint of boiling water.

Pick over the oatmeal, and put it into a double boiler with the salt. Pour on the boiling water, place the upper vessel of the boiler on the stove, and boil two minutes. This effectually starts the cooking. Then put the upper vessel into the lower, and cook for five hours. The water in the under boiler should *boil* during this time, and will occasionally need replenishing. Serve the mush steaming hot with sugar and cream, and baked apples, apple sauce, or tart jelly if one is fond of something acid.

If rolled oats be used, three hours are sufficient to cook it, but both kinds are best cooked the day before they are needed, as long cooking improves rather than injures the grain.

FARINA

Farina being a prepared grain and free from hulls and waste, so large a proportion will not be required to make a mush as of the raw grains.

> 3 Tablespoons of farina.
> ½ Saltspoon of salt.
> 1 Pint of boiling water.

Cook the mixture in a saucepan for twenty minutes after it actually boils, or in a double boiler for one hour. This is a delicious food for children, served with cream, or milk, and sugar.

WHEAT GERM

Wheat germ is a delicate and nutritious preparation of wheat. It is made so that by boiling for a short time it is ready for the table, and makes a delicious breakfast dish.

> ½ Cup of germ.
> ½ Teaspoonful of salt.
> 1½ Cups of boiling water.

Boil in a saucepan without a cover for half an hour, or cook in a double boiler twice as long. The directions on the packages give a shorter time, but it is extremely doubtful whether this grain can be wholesome with the few minutes' cooking usually advised.

IMPERIAL GRANUM

Imperial Granum, cooked according to the above rule, is always a wholesome and safe dish for children; or it may be made into a very thin gruel, and used as a drink instead of water.

GRANULA

Granula is a breakfast grain which has been partially prepared by dry heat, and is almost cooked enough to use. It is sometimes recommended that it be prepared by simply boiling a minute in milk. It is, however, both softened and improved in flavor by boiling from ten to fifteen minutes in one and one half times its bulk of water, with salt in the proportion of a teaspoon to a cup of grain.

CRACKED OR ROLLED WHEAT

1 Cup of cracked wheat.
1 Teaspoon of salt.
3 Cups of water.

Pick over the wheat, to remove any foreign substance that may be in it. Put it with the salt and the water (boiling) into a double boiler, and cook for two hours. Serve with cream and sugar, either hot or cold. If it is desirable to have it cold, it may be molded in cups or small round jelly-molds.

INDIAN-MEAL MUSH

1 Cup of corn-meal.
1 Teaspoon of salt.
1 Quart of boiling water.

No. 1. Make the corn-meal and salt into a paste with a little cold water, then pour in the boiling water and cook it in a double boiler for five hours.

No. 2. Put the salt into the water, and when the water reaches the boiling-point stir in the dry meal by taking a handful and sprinkling it slowly through the fingers. Use a wooden spoon for stirring. Boil an hour and a half. Or, wet the meal in a little cold water, and pour over it the boiling water. The most important point is thoroughness in the cooking, which should be done carefully so that the pudding may not burn on the bottom of the dish. If the temperature be regulated so that it just simmers, there will be little danger of this. Serve with maple syrup, or with cream.

HOMINY MUSH

1 Cup of hominy.
1 Teaspoon of salt.
$1\frac{1}{4}$ Quarts of water.

Put all together in a double boiler, and cook for three hours. Add more water if the mush seems stiff and thick; all preparations of corn absorb a great deal in cooking, and hominy usually needs a little more than four times its bulk. Hominy is exceedingly indigestible unless well cooked, but sweet and nutritious when subjected to a high temperature for a long time.

DRINKS

EGG-NOG

Break into a bowl one egg, add to it a saltspoon of salt and two teaspoons of sugar; beat it until it is light but not foamy; then add one cup of *slightly warm* milk — that is, milk from which the chill has been taken (for it is not well to use that which is ice-cold) — and one or two tablespoons of French brandy; mix and strain it into a tall slender glass, and serve at once. Egg-nog should not be allowed to stand after it is made, for both the egg and the milk lose some of their freshness by exposure to the air.

MILK-PUNCH

1 Cup of milk.
2 Tablespoons of brandy.
1 Teaspoon of sugar.
A little grated nutmeg.

Sweeten the milk with the sugar, stir into it the brandy, and mix thoroughly by pouring from one glass to another. Then grate a bit of nutmeg over the top.

Milk-punch is conveniently made with two tin cups; the mouth of one should be smaller than the mouth of the other, so that the one will fit into the other.

In these the milk should be shaken back and forth until a froth is formed. This does not add materially to the taste, but rather to the appearance, and thoroughly mixes in the sugar and brandy.

WINE WHEY

Warm one cup of milk to a little more than blood-heat, or 100° Fahr., then pour into it one half cup of sherry wine. The acid and alcohol of the wine will in a few minutes coagulate the albumen, which may be separated from the whey by straining. Do not squeeze the curd through the strainer, but let the liquid drip until it is all out. If it is necessary to make the whey quickly, heat the milk to the boiling-point before adding the wine.

WINE WHEY WITH RENNET
(SWEET WHEY)

1 Pint of milk heated to 100° Fahr.
1 Teaspoon of prepared rennet.
2 Tablespoons of wine.

Stir the rennet and wine into the milk quickly, so that the wine may not curdle the milk in blotches. Let it stand in a warm place (on the stove-hearth, for instance) for half an hour, and then separate the curd from the whey by straining. This whey is excellent for children with delicate digestion who need a little stimulant. It is very good also as a drink for invalids at any time.

Whey is the water of milk with the sugar and various salts of the milk in solution in it. The sugar furnishes some nutriment, and the salts supply some of the mineral matter needed in the body.

Whey may also be made with vinegar or lemon-juice. These acids will act more quickly when the milk is warmed before they are added.

LEMONADE

1 Lemon.
1½ Tablespoons of sugar.
1 Cup of boiling water.

Wash and wipe a lemon, cut a very thin slice from the middle, and squeeze the rest into a bowl; then put in the sugar, pour on the boiling water, and strain it. When it has become cold, serve it in a tumbler with the slice of lemon floating on the top.

Lemonade has a better flavor when made with boiling water, though it may be made with cold water. A few strawberries or raspberries may be put in, instead of the slice of lemon; or it may be colored pink with a little grape-jelly or carmine, and served with a straw.

MILK LEMONADE

1 Tablespoon of sugar.
1 Cup of boiling water.
¼ Cup of lemon-juice.
¼ Cup of sherry.
1¼ Cups of cold milk.

Pour the boiling water over the sugar, and then put in the lemon-juice and sherry. Stir it until the sugar dissolves, add the cold milk, and stir again until the milk curdles, then strain through a jelly-bag or napkin.

This is a cool and refreshing drink, especially for children.

BRANDY-MILK WITH EGG

Heat some milk in a granite saucepan for half an hour to sterilize it, but do not let it boil; then pour it into a pitcher, and set it aside to cool. When the milk is cold, beat one egg with one tablespoon of sugar until the sugar is well mixed; add to it two tablespoons of brandy and a cup of the cold milk. Strain it into a tall slender glass, and serve at once.

Heating the milk renders it perfectly wholesome and much safer for an invalid than raw milk, and also improves the flavor of the drink.

SHERRY AND EGG

Break an egg into a bowl, and put in a teaspoon of sugar; beat the two together until the sugar is thoroughly mixed with the egg, but not enough to make the egg froth; to this add two tablespoons of sherry wine, and a fourth of a cup of cold water, mixing them thoroughly. Strain all into a tumbler, and serve immediately.

STERILIZED MILK

The change which takes place in milk known as "souring" is caused by the growth of micro-organisms in it, which are killed by heat; therefore, to prevent souring, milk must be subjected to a temperature sufficiently high to insure their destruction. Some micro-organisms are killed at 136° Fahr., but this temperature cannot be said to destroy, or to inhibit the growth of all bacteria commonly found in milk. We must endeavor then to use such a degree of heat as shall accomplish this without seriously injuring the natural properties and flavors of the liquid. Authorities vary on this point, some putting the temperature as high as 212° Fahr., and others as low as 167° Fahr. The author has found, in an experience of two years in sterilizing milk every day, that 190° Fahr. is, under ordinary circumstances, a safe and easily practicable temperature to employ. With this degree of heat the flavor of the milk is excellent.

The process is as follows: The milk is put into clean glass flasks or bottles with small mouths which are stoppered with plugs of cotton batting, or, as it is sometimes called, "cotton-wool." These are placed in a wire basket, and the basket immersed in a kettle of warm water, the temperature of which is not allowed to exceed 190° Fahr. As soon as the heat is at or near that point the time is marked, and the milk is kept at that temperature for one hour. Then the bottles are removed, cooled quickly, and placed in the refrigerator. If it is desirable to keep the milk an indefinite time, the process should be repeated the second day, and again the third day, a third sterilization being necessary to insure success, since *spores* of organisms may escape the first and even the second heating.

For all ordinary household purposes, however, and as a safe food for the sick, heating once is all that is necessary. Milk thus treated will keep in the temperature of an ordinary room, even in warm weather, from twenty to thirty hours. By using the small-mouthed flasks very little scum is formed, and thus the valuable albuminous portion is preserved in the milk.

Also, a small quantity at a time may be used without disturbing the rest.

To Sterilize for Family Use. Milk may also be preserved by open sterilization in a saucepan or kettle by the following simple process: Heat the milk until a scum forms over it; keep it at, or near, the temperature it then has for one hour, then pour it into a thoroughly washed and scalded pitcher, cool it, and put it into a refrigerator or some cool place. It will remain sweet for twenty-four hours, and, unless the weather be very warm, it will be good at the end of thirty-six hours. Should it sour before the end of twenty-four hours, it indicates that the temperature was too low, or the time of exposure to the heat too short. A chemist's thermometer costs but little, and will be found very useful for testing milk. It should be borne in mind, in this connection, that milk is not rendered *absolutely* sterile,—that is, free from all possible organisms and spores which may occur in it,— except at a temperature of at least 212° Fahr., or even higher.

Sterilized milk diluted with water is a nutritious and wholesome drink for the sick. Of course the water with which it is diluted should be boiled.[1]

In hospital practice nurses have told me that patients suffering from sleeplessness will often fall into quiet slumber after drinking hot milk, and that not infrequently the ordered hypodermic of morphine is not needed when hot milk is used.

MILK AND SELTZER

Mix equal quantities of sterilized milk and seltzer-water. Drink immediately.

---

[1] For a further account of micro-organisms in milk, see the chapter on Milk.

MILK AND SODA-WATER

Into a glass half full of fresh milk put an equal quantity of soda-water. Use at once. This is an agreeable way to take milk, and is a nutritious and refreshing drink.

TOAST-WATER

Cut three slices of bread each a third of an inch thick, and toast them slowly until very brown and dry throughout; break them into small pieces, put them into a bowl with a pint of cold water, and set aside to soak for an hour; at the end of that time turn it into a strainer or napkin, and squeeze out the liquid with the back of a spoon. To the water thus obtained add a little cream and sugar, and serve it cold in a tumbler. It may also be served without the cream.

BARLEY-WATER

1 Tablespoon of barley flour.
1 Teaspoon of sugar.
1 Teaspoon of lemon-juice.
1 Quart of water.

Boil the flour, water, and sugar together fifteen minutes, then add the lemon-juice, and strain.

Tamarinds may be used instead of lemon-juice for flavor—two or three boiled with the water. Barley-water may also be made by boiling two tablespoons of barley (the grain) in a quart of water for one hour.

RICE-WATER

Pick over and wash two tablespoons of rice; put it into a granite saucepan with a quart of boiling water; simmer it for two hours, when the rice should be softened and partially dissolved; then strain the liquid through a fine wire strainer into a bowl or pitcher, add to it a saltspoon of salt, and serve it either warm or cold.

If a patient may take or needs stimulants, two tablespoons of sherry or of port wine is an agreeable addition, especially if the drink be taken cold.

FRUIT-SODA. No. 1

From Strawberries. Remove the stems from one quart of strawberries, and pick them over carefully. Wash them under a stream of water in a colander, gently, so that they may not be crushed; then put them into a double boiler with half their bulk of sugar, and heat for an hour or more until the berries are soft. When this is accomplished, turn them into a jelly-bag and drain until the juice has completely oozed out, which will require two or more hours. Do not squeeze them. Then put the juice into a saucepan and, returning to the fire, heat it to a temperature of 200° Fahr., and keep it at that temperature for one hour. If a thermometer is not at hand, heat the juice until it steams a little, but do not let it boil, for the flavor is not nearly so delicate with the high temperature. Then it may be canned or bottled for future use. If the bottle be scalded and carefully sealed as in preserving fruits, the juice will keep indefinitely.

The length of time that it remains at 200° is important, as it is a process of sterilization which takes place, and the temperature must be maintained for a given time or the desired result will not be accomplished. The condition of the bottle also must be carefully considered, as the thorough cleaning and scalding is for the purpose of rendering it sterile. This is most easily and thoroughly done by filling the bottle with hot water and placing it in a kettle of boiling water for half an hour.

To Use. Dilute the juice with *cool* water (not iced water) or soda-water in the proportion of one half juice to one half water.

From Oranges. The oranges should be peeled and the seeds removed, and then treated in the same way as the strawberries in the preceding rule, except that to every quart of fruit the juice of two lemons should be added.

From Raspberries. Employ the same method as for strawberries.

From Currants. The same as for strawberries, except that three fourths of the bulk of the fruit of sugar should be used instead of one half.

With Other Fruits. Other fruits, such as apricots, peaches, cranberries, apples, etc., may be used for syrups, varying the water and sugar according to the kind of fruit used. Apples, apricots, and peaches will require half their bulk of water.

FRUIT-SODA. No. 2

Sprinkle two cups of sugar over one box of ripe strawberries, which, of course, have been hulled and washed, and set them away for three hours, or until the juice has oozed out of the fruit and made a thick syrup with the sugar. Strain the juice, bottle it, and put it in a cool place. It will keep for three days.

To Use. Pour one third of a cup into a tumbler, add two tablespoons of cream, and fill the tumbler with soda-water from a siphon. This makes a delicious and cooling drink.

Oranges, raspberries, currants, or any other juicy fruit may be used for syrup, which is very palatable when made from fresh uncooked fruits. These syrups are useful not only for drinks, but for flavoring ice-creams and pudding sauces.

COFFEE SYRUP

Make some strong coffee with two tablespoons of the ground berry (Mocha and Java mixed), a little white of egg, and one cup of boiling water. Simmer together one cup of sugar and one third of a cup of water for five minutes, then add to it one half of a cup of the coffee. Strain and bottle it for use. This is delicious with soda-water and cream.

VANILLA SYRUP

Make a sugar syrup by boiling together one cup of sugar and one half of a cup of water for five minutes. Add to it two or three tablespoons of vanilla extract. It is to be used, like coffee syrup, with soda-water and sweet cream.

OTHER SYRUPS

A variety of syrups may be made, besides those mentioned, by using a sugar syrup like that in the above recipe, and flavoring it with cinnamon, lemon, almond, rose-water, chocolate, etc. All of the cooked syrups will keep indefinitely.

GRAPE JUICE

Grape juice mixed with cold water or with soda-water makes a pleasant and invigorating drink for a sick person. The best grapes for the purpose are the blue varieties, such as Isabellas, Concords, or Black Hamburgs.

To Make a Bottle of Juice. Pick over (and wash if they need it) one quart of grapes. Remove them from the stems, and put them into a double boiler with just enough cold water to cover them. Heat them slowly until the juice oozes out and the fruit becomes soft, which will take two or three hours. Then turn the fruit into a jelly-bag made like a long pointed pocket, draw the string at the top and hang it to drain. Do not squeeze or press the bag, and use only the juice which drips out, which will practically be all that the grapes contain. To this add one fourth of the quantity of sugar—that is, if there is a quart of juice, put in one cup of sugar—and heat it until it is quite hot, or to a temperature of 200° Fahr., and keep it at that temperature for one hour, but do not let it boil. Then pour it into thoroughly cleaned and scalded hot bottles,—in other words, those which are sterile. Seal the bottles with wax, and set them away in a cool place.

To Use. Mix equal quantities of juice and cold water, and serve at once.

FLAXSEED TEA WITH LEMON

1 Tablespoon of flaxseed.
1 Pint of water.
1 Tablespoon of sugar.
Juice of one lemon.

Boil the flaxseed one hour in the water; strain it, and add the lemon-juice and sugar. The flaxseed should be examined for little black grains which often occur in it, and which injure the delicate flavor of the drink. Serve this tea either cold or warm. It is excellent for croup, or for any irritated condition of the throat or lungs.

APPLE TEA

Wash and wipe a good sour apple, cut it into small pieces, and boil it in a cup of water until it is soft. Then strain the water into a bowl, add a bit of sugar, and serve when cold.

If the apple is of good flavor this is a pleasant drink, and may be given to fever patients, children with measles, or whenever there is much thirst.

KUMISS

1 Quart of perfectly fresh milk.
$\frac{1}{8}$ of a two-cent cake of Fleischmann's yeast.
1 Tablespoon of sugar.

Dissolve the yeast in a little water and mix it with the sugar and milk. Put the mixture into strong bottles,—beer-bottles are good,—cork them with tightly fitting stoppers, and tie down securely with stout twine. Shake the bottles for a full minute to mix thoroughly the ingredients, then place them on end in a refrigerator, or some equally cool place, to ferment slowly. At the end of three days lay the bottles on their sides; turn them occasionally. Five days will be required to perfect the fermentation, and then kumiss is at its best. It will keep indefinitely in a refrigerator.

To Make Sweet Kumiss. Ferment the kumiss mixture for twelve hours in a temperature of 70° Fahr.,— that is, the same degree of heat that is required for raising bread.

Do not attempt to open a bottle of kumiss without a champagne-tap, for the carbonic acid generated in the fermenting liquid has enormous expansive force, and will throw the contents all over the room if the bottle be opened in the ordinary way.

In an emergency, however, the cork may be punctured with a stout needle to let the gas escape. The mouth of the bottle may then be held in a large bowl or dish and the cords cut, when the kumiss will rush out, usually, however, without so much force but that it may nearly all be caught. It should look like thick, foamy cream.

Kumiss is highly recommended as an article of sick diet, being especially valuable for many forms of indigestion and for nausea. Often it will be retained in the stomach when almost anything else would be rejected. It is partially predigested milk, containing carbonic acid and a little alcohol, both of which have a tonic effect.

True kumiss is an Eastern product made from mare's milk, but in this country cow's milk is always employed. Sometimes the term *kefer* is given to it, to distinguish it from that made from mare's milk. It may be obtained in nearly all pharmacies, but a better quality can be made at home at slight expense.

Sometimes patients will object to taking kumiss, on account of the odor, which is not pleasant to every one, but it leaves a peculiarly agreeable after-taste in the mouth, and one who has once taken a glass of it will seldom refuse a second offer. The kumiss of commerce sold under the name of "Cream Koumyss" is an excellent preparation.

THE COCOA-BEAN

The cocoa-bean is a product of the tropics. It is dried, roasted like coffee, and cracked, or ground into powder, for use. It is one of our best foods, containing in good proportions nearly all the elements necessary to nourish the body.

There are many preparations of the bean. The most common, and those usually found in our markets, are *shells, cracked cocoa, chocolate,* and *various forms of powder*.

Shells are the outer husk or covering of the bean, and from them a delicate drink may be made with long, slow boiling.

Cracked cocoa, or *cocoa-nibs* as it is sometimes called, is made by breaking the beans into small pieces.

Chocolate is prepared by grinding the cocoa-bean into powder, mixing it with sugar, and molding it into blocks. There is some temptation on the part of manufacturers to substitute foreign fats, corn-starch, and other cheap materials for the natural ingredients of the bean in the making of chocolate.

The powdered forms of cocoa generally contain a good percentage of the bean except the fat, which is always extracted. All Dutch brands are excellent. Weight for weight, they cost more than some other kinds, but so much less is needed to make a cup of drink that they are really the least expensive.

COCOA

½ Teaspoon of any Dutch cocoa.
1 Cup of boiling water.
1 Cup of boiling milk.
1 Tablespoon of sugar.

Put the cocoa and sugar into a saucepan, and pour in the boiling water; cook for two minutes, then add the milk, and let it heat just to the boiling-point. When most other brands are used, as a general thing a larger proportion of powder will be necessary. It is therefore important to experiment with each until it is found what amount will make a drink equal in strength to the above. This valuable food is often made so strong that ill persons cannot digest it.

COCOA-SHELLS

Put a tablespoon of shells into a pint of water, and simmer for two hours; add one tablespoon of sugar and a cup of milk, then strain out the shells, and it is ready to serve. This is a mild and delicately flavored drink, and may be used freely in cases of great thirst.

COCOA-NIBS

Boil one teaspoon of cracked cocoa in a pint of water one hour; then add a cup of milk and a tablespoon of sugar, let it heat to the boiling-point again, strain out the nibs, and it is ready to serve.

It is necessary to *boil* cracked cocoa, otherwise you will have a bitter infusion, lacking the good flavor which is extracted by the higher degree of heat. This is an instance in which a few degrees more or less of heat make a great difference in the result.

CHOCOLATE

Put *one third* of a square (one ounce) of Baker's chocolate, with one cup of boiling water and a tablespoon of sugar, into a saucepan. Set the saucepan on the fire, and stir for a while, moving the piece of chocolate through the water occasionally until it is melted. *As soon as it boils* add a cup of milk, and when it again reaches the boiling-point it will be ready to serve. If chocolate is allowed to boil for a length of time, separation of the fat from the other ingredients takes place, rendering it indigestible. Chocolate, if delicately and carefully made, is as nice as cocoa, much more nutritious, on account of the fat which it contains, and less expensive.

TEA

Tea has refreshing and invigorating properties very comforting to one spent with toil. Its active principle is theine, a crystalline alkaloid found in both tea and coffee. Theine and caffeine were once supposed to be different substances, but have recently been found to be identical.

Tea is a valuable article of diet, though not a direct nutrient. It is classed with the so-called "accessory" foods, and, although not itself nutritious, aids, by its good flavor and stimulating properties, the digestion of other things. It is a nerve tonic, and is quite valuable as a curative agent for headache and some forms of indigestion. The slight stimulation resulting from its use is unattended by any after ill effects.

It is good for soldiers, hard-working people, travelers, and others who are much exposed to the rigors of climate.[1]

[1] George Kennan, in his accounts of his perilous journeyings through Siberia, bears ample testimony to the comforting effects of hot tea. Often when he and his companion were chilled through, and almost dead with cold and fatigue, after many hours' travel over the frozen snows, they were revived by draughts of hot tea provided at the stations.

COMPOSITION OF TEA

	Black.	Green.
Essential oil	.60	.79
Chlorophyl	1.84	2.22
Wax		.28
Resin	3.64	2.22
Gum	7.28	8.56
Tannin	12.88	17.80
Theine	.46	.43
Extractive matter	21.36	22.80
Coloring substances	19.19	23.60
Albumen	2.80	3.00
Fiber	28.33	17.80
Ash[1]	5.24	5.56

MULDEN.

From Prof. Mott's Chart on the Composition, Digestibility, and Nutritive Value of Food.

Two of the most important points suggested by a study of tea are the few adulterations and the great difference between different varieties, comparing weight and bulk. Some kinds of very cheap tea are adulterated with sage and raspberry leaves, and leaves of other plants dried to simulate tea, and often flavored with essences to give an agreeable taste, but a vast amount of the tea which is sold is pure. Adulterations with chemicals are now rare, on account of the extensive cultivation of tea and the large quantities sold.

Teas vary greatly in weight,— that is, a given bulk of one tea weighs very differently from the same bulk of another. This is especially marked in the comparison of Oolong and Gunpowder.

Below are given the weights of a moderate-sized caddy-spoon of each of these teas.

KINDS OF TEA.	Grains.	No. of spoons to the pound.
Oolong	39	179
Hyson	66	106
Gunpowder	123	57

[1] The ash of tea contains potash, soda, magnesia, phosphoric acid, chlorin, carbonic acid, iron, silica, and traces of manganese.

From this it appears that Gunpowder tea, bulk for bulk, is more than three times as heavy as Oolong; consequently in using it only about one third as much should be taken for a given amount of water. In making the infusion teas should be weighed, not measured, but it is not easily practicable in all households to do so; however, it can always be borne in mind that the closely rolled teas, such as Gunpowder, Young Hyson, and Japan, should be used in smaller proportion than those which are loosely rolled, like Oolong, English Breakfast, and other black teas.

There is a popular notion that green teas are dried on copper, but according to unquestionable authorities it is an erroneous one. Green teas are dried quickly so that the natural color of the leaves is preserved. Black teas are dried slowly for many hours until a sort of fermentation sets in, which causes the difference in color, as pickings from the same plant may, in the process of curing, become either green or black tea, according to the method employed. Also, different varieties of tea may be made from the same branch by difference of treatment in curing, the aromatic flavors, which did not exist in the leaves before, being produced by the drying. Different varieties or kinds of tea are also made from the same plant by gathering the leaves at different ages.

Black tea should be black, but not dead black,—rather of a grayish hue. No red leaves should be mixed with it. It should be regular in appearance, each leaf with a uniform twist, that is, in all except the "broken" teas. The leaves of tea are gathered four times a year by hand, and the finest kind is made from the tender young buds. Young Hyson is made from the early buds of April, and is noted for its mild, delicate flavor.

The principle most to be avoided in tea is the tannin, which in any considerable quantity is injurious to health. It dissolves easily when tea is either *steeped for a length of time,* or *boiled.* The important point, therefore, is not to make tea more than a few minutes before it is to be drunk, and not to boil it.

The principal kinds of tea in common use are Oolong, Japan, English Breakfast, Imperial, Gunpowder, and Young Hyson. Gunpowder, Japan, Young Hyson, and Imperial are green teas; the others are black.

To Prepare Tea.

1 Teaspoon of tea.
1 Cup of boiling water.

Fill a cup with boiling water, and let it stand a minute, or until the cup is heated through. Then empty it, put the teaspoon of tea into a tea-ball, place it in the hot cup, and pour on the boiling water slowly until it is full, leaving the tea-ball in for three minutes. This will give you a delicious and fragrant drink. If there is not a tea-ball at hand, use a small strainer, holding it so that the tea is under water for the required time.

The same principle is to be followed in making a pot of tea, except that the time of steeping should be somewhat longer. Scald the pot, which should be either of silver, granite-ware, or earthenware, not tin. Put into it the tea, in the proportion of one teaspoon to a cup of water (one half pint), and let it infuse for five minutes, but by no means allow it to boil, for boiling dissipates the aroma, and extracts the tannin, which is the injurious principle. Serve it in hot tea-cups with loaf-sugar and cold cream or milk. I think it is Miss Lincoln who says: "Never disgrace yourself by serving that abomination, boiled lukewarm tea in a cold cup."

Water for tea should be fresh, and soft water—that is, water which is free from lime—is to be preferred; by taking *one teaspoon of tea* and *a cup of water* as the unit, any amount may be made; for instance, for a pot of tea for five or six persons, six teaspoons of tea and a quart and a half (6 cups) of water will be required. The time of exposure to the heat is, of course, not multiplied, the same number of minutes being enough for a greater or a lesser amount.

In connection with the study of tea, it is a very interesting fact that most authorities agree as to the time of steeping. There seems to be the unanimous opinion that *it should not exceed fifteen* minutes. Five minutes is the usual time given for the average kinds of tea, but for the fine, pure teas from eight to ten is a wise rule to follow.

COFFEE

Coffee is a product of the East, where it has been used since very ancient times. It grows on trees, the fruit in clusters which singly look somewhat like cherries, each containing two beans. Unroasted coffee-beans are tough, and a drink made from them is bitter, acrid, and very unpleasant. Coffee was brought to western Europe in the seventeenth century, where it seems to have immediately become a popular drink. When coffee-houses were first opened in England, they were opposed by the liquor-dealers, who claimed that their trade would be spoiled. Its introduction was also bitterly opposed by others, and even denounced from the pulpit. It was regarded somewhat in the light of a dangerous Eastern drug. From western Europe it was brought to America, and at the present time is the most extensively used food beverage in the world.

The kinds in common use in this country are Java and Mocha from the East, and the South American coffees Rio, Santos, and Maracaibo. The soil and method of cultivation influence the quality of coffee, as does also the age of the beans. The longer the beans are kept (unbrowned) the finer the flavor.

Coffee is adulterated with grains of different kinds, chicory, caramel, carrots and some other roots, and with pastes made to resemble the coffee-bean. The use of chicory is prohibited by law, unless the mixture be labeled "Mixture of coffee and chicory." Nevertheless, its use is common, and in nearly all hotels and restaurants coffee is flavored with it.

"The detection of the presence of chicory, caramel, and some sweet roots, as turnips, carrots, and parsnips, is quite easy. If a few grains of the suspected sample are placed on the surface of water in a glass vessel, beaker, or tumbler, each particle of chicory, etc., will become surrounded by a yellow-brown cloud which rapidly diffuses through the water until the whole becomes colored. Pure coffee under the same conditions gives no sensible color until after the lapse of about fifteen minutes. Caramel (burnt sugar) of course colors the water very deeply. Dandelion root gives a deeper color than coffee, but not as deep as chicory. The same is true of bread raspings. Beans and pease give much less color to the water than pure coffee. They can be readily detected by the microscope, as can roasted figs and dates or date-stones." (Mrs. Richards, in "Food Materials and Their Adulterations.")

Coffee is said to owe its refreshing properties to (*a*) caffeine, (*b*) a volatile oil developed by heat, not contained in the unroasted bean, and to (*c*) astringent acids.

Coffee diminishes the sensation of hunger, exhilarates and refreshes, and decreases the amount of wear and tear of the system.

Its composition, according to Payen, is as follows:

Cellulose	34.000
Water	12.000
Fatty matter	13.000
Glucose, dextrine, and undetermined vegetable acids	15.500
Legumin, casein, etc.	10.000
Chlorogenate of potash and caffeine	3 to 5.000
Nitrogenized structure	3.000
Caffeine	.800
Essential oil	.001
Aromatic essence	.002
Mineral substances	6.970

It is difficult to determine whether coffee may be classed as a food, but that it has value as an adjunct to true nutrients there can be no doubt. There is a general agreement among physiologists that coffee is invigorating, that it aids digestion both in the sick and the well, that it is capable of allaying or retarding waste and thereby acting indirectly as a food. But the mistake should not be made that coffee will *replace* food. Coffee may be compared in its effects on the system to beef-tea—it is valuable for its flavors rather than for actual nutritious principles.

It is a curious fact that coffee is most frequently made in such a way that its valuable flavors are undeveloped or destroyed. Care must be taken that the roasting be not carried so far as to char the coffee-beans, yet far enough to convert the sugar into caramel, and to change the nature of the volatile oil, so that the highest point of flavor will be reached. This can be best accomplished in regular roasting-houses, where the temperature and time may be accurately measured.

It is best to get a supply of fresh roasted coffee every day, but when this is not practicable, once in three days, or once a week, will do. Although theoretically the roasting of coffee should be a part of its preparation — that is, it should be roasted, immediately ground, and made into drink — practically it is very seldom done.

COFFEE. No. 1

A favorite mixed coffee is made with two thirds Java and one third Mocha. It should be ground just before it is needed. For a pot of coffee use the proportions of one heaped tablespoon to a cup of water. It is well to calculate the number of persons there are to be served, and allow one cup (one half pint) for each; this amount, with the milk or cream used, will make two ordinary china cups of coffee. To the ground coffee add a little yolk or white of egg, with a spoonful of water to dilute it; mix thoroughly until all the grains are coated over with albumen, then pour on the boiling water, simmer for five minutes, and steep at a temperature just short of simmering for ten minutes more. The coffee is then done. It should be served at once with *loaf-sugar*, and either hot or cold cream, or hot milk. The coffee should be perfectly clear and of fine color and flavor.

There are many methods of making coffee, but the above, everything considered, seems the most desirable for family use. One egg is enough to clear three quarts of coffee, and both yolk and white are of equal value for the purpose.

COFFEE. No. 2

For every cup of water use a heaped tablespoon of coffee; soak the coffee overnight or for several hours in cold water, then bring it to the boiling-point, and let it simmer for a few minutes just before using.

This is said to be the most economical method of making, as more is obtained from the coffee by this treatment. The flavor is certainly fine.

Long boiling dissipates the delicious aromatic oils, and as probably these are the most valuable properties of the coffee, the necessity of preserving them is easily seen. Care should be taken not to boil coffee for more than from three to five minutes, and simmer rather than boil, so as to preserve as much as possible the fine flavors which are so quickly dissipated by boiling; yet the high temperature seems to be necessary to extract the desirable properties of the bean. One must therefore ever bear in mind the seeming paradox that coffee should reach the boiling-point, and yet not boil.

We do not estimate highly enough the value of flavors. It is a well-demonstrated fact among a few persons that many dishes containing actual nutritious principles are but partially or imperfectly digested, because of their lack of good flavor, either from want of proper preparation, lack of seasoning, or poor cooking. There is no doubt that many people suffer from indigestion after eating such food.

Use in coffee-making either silver, granite-ware, or earthenware urns or pots, never tin. They should be made *perfectly clean* before using, especial attention being necessary for the spout.

MULLED WINE

1 Egg.
1 Tablespoon of sugar.
1 Clove.
$\frac{1}{4}$ Square inch of cinnamon.
$\frac{1}{2}$ Cup of wine.
$\frac{1}{2}$ Cup of water.

Put the water and spice together in a saucepan, and boil for ten minutes; then add the wine, and let the liquid just reach the boiling-point; meanwhile beat the egg and sugar in a bowl, and just at the moment when the wine begins to boil, pour it slowly into the egg, stirring constantly to distribute the heat throughout the whole. Unless the weather is very cold, there is usually enough heat in the boiling liquid to coagulate the albumen of the egg slightly, but should this not be accomplished, set it on the fire for a minute to finish. When done it should be of the consistency of cream. Do not let the wine and water boil for any appreciable time, for boiling dissipates some of the pleasant flavor of the wine.

Beer, ale, and porter are excellent, mulled in the same way.

COCOA CORDIAL

½ Teaspoon of Dutch cocoa.
Some boiling water.
2 Blocks of loaf-sugar.
2 Tablespoons of port wine.

Put the cocoa and sugar into a china cup, and pour directly upon them some boiling water, then add the wine, making in all the usual amount called a cupful. Serve at once. This is an excellent drink for those who are chilled or exhausted, or to take after a bath.

JELLIES

(FROM GELATINE)

Gelatin is always of animal origin. The gelatinous substance obtained from apples, grapes, cranberries, and other fruits is not gelatin; it is a different material, derived by the action of heat from pectose, a substance which occurs in plants and is closely associated with cellulose. Unprepared *gelatin* is sometimes distinguished in writing from the *gelatine* of commerce by the difference of an *e* in spelling.

Gelatin enters into the composition of all, or nearly all, the tissues of the body. The walls of the microscopic cells of flesh are composed of it. It is found also in cartilage, tendons, connective tissue, bone, and in the larynx and joints. Spiders' webs and the thread of silkworms are gelatin in a liquid state, which solidifies upon exposure to the air. Another kind of gelatin forms the framework of insects, such as the locusts on which John the Baptist fed. It also forms the true skeleton of lobsters, crabs, and shrimps. The edible birds' nests of the Chinese are a delicate kind of gelatin more digestible than some other kinds, for it is made from the saliva of a swallow, and probably contains pepsin. (M. Williams.)

The part which gelatin plays as a food is not well understood. Many experiments have recently been made by scientists on dogs and other animals, to test the value of gelatin in this respect. From these experiments the following conclusions have been drawn:

1. That gelatin alone is not **sufficient** as a food. 2. That although insufficient it is not worthless. 3. That gelatin is sufficient to sustain life when combined with other substances which would themselves be wholly insufficient if given alone. 4. That gelatin must always be flavored to render it digestible and nutritious.

Mattieu Williams says: "It would seem that gelatin alone, although containing the elements required for nutrition, needs something more to render it digestible. We shall probably not be far from the truth if we picture it to the mind as something too smooth, too neutral, too inert, to set the digestive organs at work, and that therefore it requires the addition of a decidedly sapid something that shall make these organs act."

Gelatin dissolves easily in warm liquid. Albumen coagulates under similar circumstances.

The gelatine of commerce is made from the tissues of animals, particularly from the thick skin of certain portions of the body and from the head and feet. When well flavored and in a liquid state as in broths, or of a tender consistency as in well-made jelly, it is a most desirable food for the sick. Lemon and orange juice, strawberry, raspberry, grape, and indeed any fruit syrup, coffee, cocoa, vanilla, wine, brandy, and Jamaica rum, and strong meat broths which have been cleared, may be used for flavoring. The jelly should not be made hard and tenacious, but tender and jelly-like, though firm.

The phosphated gelatine which may be bought of any grocer is delicious for wine jelly made according to the usual rule for jelly, with the exception of omitting the lemon. Chalmer's and Nelson's are other well-known brands. All jellies made with gelatine are excellent for invalids. They are especially valuable in cases of disease of the intestines, such as typhoid fever and inflammation of the bowels, because, being digested and absorbed, for the most part or entirely, in the stomach, those organs are relieved of effort, at the same time that the system is supplied with a nutritious form of solid food.

WINE JELLY. No. 1

¼ Box of Nelson's gelatine.
¼ Cup of cold water.
1¼ Cups of boiling water.
½ Cup of sugar.
½ Square inch of cinnamon.
1 Clove.
½ Cup of sherry wine.

Put the gelatine and cold water together in a dish large enough to hold the whole mixture; let it soak for half an hour; then pour the boiling water, in which the clove and cinnamon have been simmering, over the softened gelatine, add the sugar and wine, and stir until the sugar and gelatine are perfectly dissolved; then strain through a fine napkin into a granite-ware or earthenware pan or mold, and cool it in a refrigerator or in a pan of iced water. Wine jelly made from phosphated gelatine, omitting the spice, is delicious.

WINE JELLY (No. 2) WITH LEMON

The same proportions and ingredients are to be used as in the above recipe, except that the juice of half a lemon should be substituted for the spice.

LEMON JELLY

¼ Box of gelatine.
⅓ Cup of cold water.
1¼ Cups of boiling water.
½ Cup of sugar.
¼ Cup of lemon-juice.
1 Tablespoon of brandy.

Put the gelatine and water together in a dish, and let them soak half an hour; then pour on the boiling water, and stir until the gelatine is dissolved. Do not put in the sugar and then pour on the boiling water, as there may not be heat enough in making a small quantity of jelly to dissolve both, but add the sugar after the water, then the lemon-juice and brandy. Strain it through a napkin and cool it in a refrigerator or in a pan of iced water. Use china or granite-ware molds, never tin, for the acid of lemon acts chemically upon it, forming compounds that are injurious to health.

ORANGE JELLY

¼ Box of gelatine.
¼ Cup of cold water.
½ Cup of boiling water.
½ Cup of sugar.
1 Cup of orange-juice.
Juice of half a lemon.

Soften the gelatine in the cold water by soaking it for half an hour; then pour in the boiling water, stirring as previously directed until the gelatine is dissolved; add the sugar, orange-juice, and lemon-juice, in the order in which they are given, stir for a moment, and then strain the liquid through a napkin into molds, and set it to cool. Use earthenware or graniteware molds, not tin. The point most to be observed in making this jelly is getting the juice from the oranges. The most natural way for one to do would be to cut the oranges in halves, and squeeze them in a lemon-squeezer, but that will not do, for the orange-oil of the rind is extracted in such large quantities as to destroy the delicate flavor of the jelly. The proper way to do is to peel the fruit, cut it in pieces, put them in a jelly-bag, and squeeze out the juice with the hand.

COFFEE JELLY

$\frac{1}{4}$ Box of gelatine.
$\frac{1}{4}$ Cup of cold water.
1 Cup of boiling water.
$\frac{1}{2}$ Cup of strong coffee.
$\frac{1}{2}$ Teaspoon of vanilla.
$\frac{1}{2}$ Cup of sugar.

Soak the gelatine in the cold water for half an hour; then pour on the boiling water, and put in the sugar, coffee, and vanilla. Strain it through a napkin into a glass dish in which it may be served, and cool it as jellies are usually cooled, either in a refrigerator or in cold water, unless of course it is winter, when the jelly quickly becomes firm in any cool place, or it may be molded. Serve it with sweet cream and sugar, or, if it be molded, with whipped cream arranged around the form. The coffee should be strong, made with the proportion of two tablespoons of coffee to a cup of water.

This delicious jelly is acceptable to most invalids.

FRENCH JELLY WITH FRESH FRUITS

Make a wine jelly according to the recipe on page 122. When it has lost some of its heat, but before it begins to thicken, pour into it a pint of carefully picked and cleaned raspberries, distributing them evenly through the liquid; then set it away in a cool place, or in a refrigerator, to harden. This makes a nice dessert when served with sugar and cream. Other fruits and other jellies may be combined at the discretion of the maker. Orange jelly with oranges and bananas is very good.

RESTORATIVE JELLY

½ Box of gelatine.
1 Cup of port wine.
1 Tablespoon of powdered gum arabic.
2 Tablespoons of lemon-juice.
3 Tablespoons of sugar.
2 Cloves.
½ Square inch of cinnamon.

Put the gelatine, wine, and spice into a double boiler, or if one is not at hand, improvise one by placing a bowl in a pan of water. Set the boiler on the fire, and when the gelatine is dissolved, put in the gum arabic, lemon, and sugar. Stir thoroughly; strain it quickly through a fine napkin, and cool it in a shallow dish, so that the layer of jelly shall be an inch thick. It is to be cut into cubes, which may be served two or three at a time, to be held in the mouth until melted.

CHICKEN JELLY

Clean a small chicken, disjoint it, and cut the meat into small pieces; remove the fat, break or pound the bones, and put all into cold water, using the following proportion: *A pint for every pound of chicken.* Heat the water very slowly at first, and then simmer it until the meat is tender; it will require three or four hours. Boil down to one half the quantity. Strain it and remove the fat; then clear it with an egg, and season it with salt, pepper, and lemon. Strain it through a fine napkin, pour into small cups, and cool. Parsley, celery, and bay-leaves give a good flavor. A suspicion of red pepper is also an addition.

PUNCHEON JELLY

$\frac{1}{4}$ Box of phosphated gelatine.
1 Cup of cold water.
$\frac{1}{2}$ Cup of hot tea.
$\frac{1}{2}$ Cup of sugar.
$\frac{1}{4}$ Cup of Jamaica rum.
1 Tablespoon of brandy.
5 Drops of almond extract.

Put the gelatine to soak in the cold water, and at the end of thirty minutes pour on the hot tea; then add the sugar, rum, brandy, and almond: strain it through a fine napkin, and set it in a cool place to become firm.

Phosphated gelatine is a delicate acidulated preparation, very nice for wine, lemon, or puncheon jelly, but it cannot be used for creams on account of the acid, which curdles them. Some of the directions indicate that it may be neutralized with soda; that, however, should not be done, since there is no accurate means of ascertaining how much acid there is in a given amount, or how strong it is; consequently there is no guide to the amount of soda required.

TOAST

The principal constituent of ordinary wheaten bread is starch.

When starch is subjected to a high temperature, it is changed into the easily digested substance dextrine. In the ordinary cooking of a loaf of bread, the starch in the outer layers is changed into dextrine, which helps to give the crust of bread that peculiar, agreeable flavor which we call "sweet." Slices of bread undergo a similar change when toast is made.

To make toast successfully, one should endeavor to convert as much as possible of the starch into dextrine. To do this, cut the bread one third of an inch thick, place the slices in a toaster, or wire broiler, and dry them slowly, either in a moderate oven, or by holding the broiler some distance from the fire. The object is to give the heat time to penetrate to the center of the slice before the outside has begun to change color. If a sheath be formed over the outside at once, the moisture will be shut in, and the middle of the slice will be prevented from becoming sufficiently heated to change its starch, for the temperature will not rise much above 212° Fahr. until the water is dried out. (Starch is changed into dextrine at 401° Fahr.)

Toast that is clammy in the middle and blackened on the outside is less wholesome than untoasted bread. Great care should therefore be taken with the drying. When this has been accomplished, lower the broiler a little nearer the coals, when the toast will quickly turn a golden brown. An ideal piece of toast is crisp and golden throughout. But many will say that they prefer toast that is soft inside, and that they cannot eat hard, dry toast. The ideal piece of toast is not really so hard as it seems. It breaks and crumbles very easily, and is quickly moistened by the saliva. If one would persevere with a slice, he would soon learn to prefer it to any other kind; at all events, that which is soft inside should not be given to the sick. It is better to make the toast dry, and then moisten it, if need be, by dipping the slices into hot water for an instant, but *do not soak them.*

Dry toast should be served directly from the fire, if possible. When this is not practicable, pile it on a platter, cover it with a napkin, and put it on the hearth or in the oven.

Toast is given in all slight cases of illness, because it is so easily digested. The more thorough the conversion of the starch, the more easily and perfectly the system will manage it, for the change of starch into dextrine, by the action of heat, is simply doing outside of the body that which takes place in it in the ordinary course of digestion, by the action of the digestive fluids. Therefore, when this is accomplished by artificial means, nature is spared so much energy.

BUTTERED WATER TOAST

Toast four thin slices of bread. Put into a shallow pan a pint of water with half a teaspoon of salt. Dip each slice quickly into the water, place it in a covered dish, and spread it with butter, piling one slice above another.

Do not let the bread *soak* in the water. Endeavor to keep a suggestion of crispness in it, for sloppy, sodden toast is not nice. Serve it *very* hot, with apple sauce, sweet baked apples, or tart jelly. Water toast is really delicious if care is taken to have it hot. It will be eaten with relish much longer than that made with milk.

MILK TOAST

Put a cup of rich milk into a saucepan, and place it on the stove. While it is heating, toast three slices of bread a delicate brown. Put them one at a time into a covered dish, and when the milk is boiling hot season it with a saltspoon of salt and pour it over the bread. A little butter may be spread upon each slice before the milk is poured over, but it is a more delicate dish without it.

CREAM TOAST

1 Pint of milk.
1 Tablespoon of flour.
1 Tablespoon of butter.
1 Saltspoon of salt.
4 Large or 6 small slices of bread.

Make a white sauce with the milk, flour, and butter according to the following directions. Pour the milk into a saucepan, and set it on the fire to heat. Put the butter and flour together in another saucepan, place it on the fire, and stir gently until the butter melts; let them bubble together two or three minutes. The high temperature which the butter quickly attains will thoroughly cook the flour in a short time. Then pour in a little of the milk, and stir until the two are mixed; add a little more milk, and stir again until it bubbles; if at this point the mixture does not seem smooth, lift it from the fire, and beat it until it is waxy and perfectly free from lumps. Then add more milk, stir again, and so continue until all the milk is in. Let it simmer slowly until the toast is ready, which should be made according to the rule for dry toast. Then soak the slices in boiling salted milk (four if from a large, and six if from a small loaf of bread), arrange them in a covered dish, and pour the cream, salted, between and over them. Irregular pieces and odds and ends of bread may be used instead of whole slices, and are very nice toasted in a tin pan in the oven.

One precaution is necessary in making this dish; that is, to soak the bread *thoroughly* in the boiling milk, for the sauce or cream is too thick to soften it. On account of the high temperature to which the butter rises, the starch is more perfectly cooked in it than if the flour were mixed with cold water and poured into the boiling milk, as is sometimes done.

FRENCH OR EGG TOAST

1 Egg.
1 Cup of milk or cream.
1 Saltspoon of salt.
3 Slices of bread.

Break the egg on a plate, and beat it with a fork for a minute, or until the viscousness is destroyed. Then mix in the milk and salt. In this mixture soak the slices of bread until they are soft, lay them in a buttered omelet-pan, and fry them slowly until a golden brown. Then place a bit of butter on the upper side of each slice, turn and brown that side. Spread a little butter, powdered cinnamon, and sugar on each slice and arrange them one above another in a covered dish. Serve very hot.

CROUTONS

Crouton is a French word which in English means *crust*. The term was first applied to the paste of sawdust, flour, and water in which the peasants of southern France used long ago to inclose their pieces of meat before roasting. After the meat was done the crust was broken open and thrown away. The word with us is applied to little cubes of buttered bread which have been browned in the oven. They are used in soups and stews, sprinkled in just before serving.

To Make Croutons. Butter a slice of evenly cut bread. Divide it into cubes that will be one third of an inch on a side. This will necessitate cutting the slice of bread exactly a third of an inch thick. Place these little cubes on a tin plate, or shallow dish, and put the dish on the grate in a moderate oven for fifteen minutes. When done they should be light golden brown throughout, crisp and brittle. Sometimes cubes of bread are fried in fat to resemble croutons, but unless done by a skilful hand they are usually soaked with fat. Even at the best they lack the delicate flavor of those which are buttered, and browned in an oven.

SIPPETS

Sippets are evenly cut oblongs of bread delicately toasted. They may be served as dry toast, or with broiled birds or broiled oysters. They are also nice for a lunch with a cup of tea or cocoa.

To Make Sippets. Cut thin slices of bread, and from them make oblongs one inch wide by four inches long. Toast carefully so that they will not break, and pile on a small bread-plate if they are to be served dry.

VERMICELLI TOAST

Prepare a cream toast according to the rule on page 130, except arrange the slices on a platter and pour the sauce evenly over them. Press through a coarse wire strainer enough hard-boiled yolk of egg to lightly cover it. It will fall in irregular, broken, crinkled threads, somewhat resembling vermicelli, hence the name.

SOUPS

OYSTER SOUP

1 Cup of fresh oysters.
1 Cup of milk.
1 Saltspoon of salt.
2 Tablespoons of rolled cracker-crumbs.
A sprinkle of pepper.
¼ Teaspoon of butter.

Put the milk with the cracker-crumbs into a saucepan on the stove; while it is heating pick over the oysters on a plate, and remove any bits of shell that may be among them. Have a hot omelet-pan ready to receive them, and when the milk reaches the boiling-point, put the oysters into the omelet-pan. Stir and turn them until they become plump, or while about sixty can be *slowly counted;* then drop the oysters into the boiling milk, take it immediately from the fire, add the salt, pepper, and butter, and serve at once. The point which requires the most attention is the cooking of the oysters in the omelet-pan. Do not let them cook *quite enough*, as the milk has sufficient heat to finish them. If too long exposed to the heat, the albuminous juice becomes overcooked, and the oysters consequently tough and leathery. For thickening oyster soup, two tablespoons of white sauce may be substituted for the cracker-crumbs.

CHICKEN SOUP

Thoroughly clean a good fowl. Separate it at the joints and cut it into small pieces. Put the meat into a saucepan with three pints of water, and stew it for two and one half or three hours, or until it becomes very tender. Then take out the meat, let the liquor continue to boil, and to it add one tablespoon of rice, one tablespoon of finely cut onion which has been fried with a bit of butter until soft, but not brown, and three peppercorns. Cut the nicer portions of the meat into small pieces, after removing all the skin, gristle, and bone. Put these pieces, with one teaspoon of salt, into the soup, and let all simmer until the rice is very soft. Then take out the peppercorns. A very little white pepper and a little celery-salt or curry-powder may be added. Serve hot with croutons. If the water boils away during the cooking, which it will do unless the simmering is very gentle, restore the quantity.

MOCK-BISQUE SOUP

1 Pint of tomatoes, measured after they have been stewed and strained.
1 Pint of white sauce.
1 Teaspoon of salt.
¼ Saltspoon of pepper.
½ Saltspoon of soda.

Although mock-bisque soup is better made with fresh tomatoes, the canned fruit may be used, with the precaution that it be allowed to stew only just long enough to soften it through, for long boiling develops in it a very strong acid. When the tomatoes are soft, strain them through a soup-strainer, or other coarse wire strainer, until there is nothing left but the seeds. Measure a pint of the liquid, add the soda, salt, and pepper, and set it on the stove to heat slowly. Meanwhile make a white sauce with one tablespoon of butter, one of flour, and a pint of milk, according to the rule on page 130. Add this sauce to the tomato, strain all into a double boiler, return to the fire, and serve as soon as it becomes steaming hot.

If fresh tomatoes can be obtained, wash and wipe them, cut out the green part near the stem, divide them into small pieces without taking off the skins, and stew without water until the fruit is just soft enough to mash. If the tomatoes are fully ripe and carefully cooked, they will not require the soda, but when soda is necessary, fresh tomatoes need only half the amount used for canned fruit.

This is an appetizing and delicate soup, and may be freely used by most invalids.

POTATO SOUP

3 Medium-sized potatoes.
1 Teaspoon of chopped onion.
2 Saltspoons of celery-salt, or 3 stalks
1 Teaspoon of salt.   [of celery.
A little white pepper.
A speck of cayenne.
1 Teaspoon of flour.
2 Teaspoons of butter.
1 Pint of milk.

Pare and boil the potatoes. Cook the onion and celery in the milk, with which make a white sauce with the flour and butter. When the potatoes are done, drain off the water and dry them over the fire by moving the pan back and forth on the stove to keep them from sticking. Then, without removing the pan from the fire, mash them thoroughly with a potato-masher, and put in the sauce, pepper, cayenne, and salt; strain all through a soup-strainer, and if the consistency be not perfectly smooth and even, strain it again. Put it into a double boiler, set back on the stove, and when hot it is ready to serve. If the soup seems very thick, add a little more milk, for some potatoes are drier than others, and will consequently absorb more moisture. It should be like a *thin purée*.

This soup may be varied by using a quart instead of a pint of milk, and the whites of two eggs well beaten, the latter to be added just two minutes before it is removed from the fire, which will be sufficient time for the egg to cook. Care should be taken not to allow the egg to harden, or the soup will have a curdled appearance.

CREAM-OF-CELERY SOUP

1 Head of celery.
1 Pint of water.
1 Pint of milk.
1 Tablespoon of butter.
1 Tablespoon of flour.
½ Teaspoon of salt.
½ Saltspoon of white pepper.

Wash and scrape the celery, cut it into half-inch pieces, put it into the pint of boiling water, and cook until it is very soft. When done mash it in the water in which it was boiled, and add the salt and pepper.

Cook the onion in the milk, and with it make a white sauce with the butter and flour; add this to the celery, and strain it through a soup-strainer, pressing and mashing with the back of a spoon until all but a few tough fibers of the celery are squeezed through. Return the soup, in a double boiler, to the fire, and heat it until it is steaming, when it is ready to serve.

By substituting chicken broth for water, and using celery-salt instead of fresh celery when it is not in season, a very acceptable variation of this soup may be made.

CREAM-OF-RICE SOUP

$\frac{1}{4}$ Cup of rice.
1 Pint of chicken broth or stock.
1 Pint of sweet cream.
1 Teaspoon of chopped onion.
1 Stalk of celery.
3 Saltspoons of salt.
A little white pepper.
$\frac{1}{2}$ Saltspoon of curry-powder.

Pick over and wash the rice, and put it into the chicken broth in a saucepan to cook. Simmer it slowly until the rice is very soft. It will require two hours' cooking to accomplish this. Half an hour before the rice is done put the cream into a saucepan with the onion, celery, pepper, and curry, and let them simmer slowly for twenty minutes; then pour the mixture into the rice; press all through a soup-strainer; add the salt, and set it back on the stove to heat to the boiling-point It should be a rather thin soup, not a *purée*. Should the broth boil away while the rice is cooking, or should the soup be too thick, add more broth, or some water.

QUEEN VICTORIA'S FAVORITE SOUP

1 Cup of chopped chicken meat.
1 Pint of strong chicken broth.
1 Pint of sweet cream.
½ Cup of cracker- or bread-crumbs.
3 Yolks of eggs.
1 Teaspoon of salt.
½ Saltspoon of pepper.

The chicken may be obtained from what remains of a roast, in which case the bones, skin, tendons, and all the scraps left should be boiled for the broth. It is better, however, to use a fowl which has been cooked on purpose, as the broth from such a one is of finer flavor. Soak the cracker-crumbs in a little of the cream. Break three eggs, separate the whites from the yolks, and carefully drop the yolks into hot water; boil them until they are hard. Chop the chicken in a chopping-tray until it is as fine as meal, previously having removed everything except the clear meat; mix the soaked cracker with it; press the hard egg-yolks through a coarse wire strainer and put them in, and also the salt, pepper, and broth. Then strain the whole through a colander, adding the cream a little at a time, and pressing through all of the meat. Boil it for five minutes in a saucepan, or cook it in a double boiler for half an hour. This makes a delicious soup.

CHICKEN-TAPIOCA SOUP

2 Tablespoons of tapioca.
½ Cup of cold water.
1 Pint of strong chicken broth or white stock.

1 Pint of milk.
1 Stalk of celery, or some celery-salt.
1 Tablespoon of chopped onion.
½ Square inch of mace.
1 Scant teaspoon of salt.
½ Saltspoon of white pepper.
½ Teaspoon of butter.

The broth for this dish may be made by boiling the bones of a roast with the left-over pieces of meat, and then reducing the liquor until it is strong enough. Put the tapioca to soak in the cold water, overnight if it be the common, coarse kind, but if pearl or granulated tapioca is used, twenty minutes will do. Then add the chicken stock, and simmer it until the tapioca is completely softened. It will require two or three hours. About half an hour before the tapioca will be done, put the milk, celery, onion, and mace into a saucepan to cook, and as soon as the tapioca becomes soft pour it in; remove from the fire, and strain the whole through a wire strainer, forcing through with a spoon all the grains of tapioca. Then add the salt, pepper, and butter; set it back on the stove, and heat it just to the boiling-point, when it is ready to serve.

BEEF-TAPIOCA SOUP

¼ Cup of granulated tapioca.
1½ Cups of water.
1 Pint of strong beef broth.
½ Teaspoon of salt.
½ Teaspoon of mixed sweet herbs.
1 Teaspoon of minced onion.
A little black pepper.

Soak the tapioca for twenty minutes in a half cup of cold water, then set it to cook in a double boiler with the rest of the water (one cupful). When the grains become soft and begin to look transparent, put in all the other ingredients and cook until the tapioca is completely dissolved. This will require two or three hours. Strain it, and return it to the fire to boil for five minutes, when it is ready to serve. This soup may be made with the ordinary stock from a stock-kettle. A little chicken broth is an improving addition, and really makes a most savory soup.

CHICKEN PANADA

A panada is a dish the foundation of which is bread. For chicken panada there will be needed:

- 1 Cup of chicken meat.
- ½ Cup of bread soaked in milk.
- 1 Pint of chicken liquor or broth.
- ½ Teaspoon of salt.
- ¼ Saltspoon of pepper.

The chicken may be obtained from a cold roast, the bones, gristle, and tendons of which should be boiled for the broth, or a fowl may be used on purpose for it.

Put the bread-crumbs to soak in enough milk to cover them. Cut the chicken into small pieces, leaving out everything which is not clear meat, and chop it in a chopping-tray until it is very fine. Press the bread-crumbs through a coarse wire strainer into it, pour in the broth (from which the fat has been removed by skimming with a spoon), and add the pepper and salt. Boil for one minute. The panada should be about the consistency of thick gruel. It may be varied by seasoning it with either celery-salt or curry-powder. Two tablespoons of sweet cream is also a desirable addition.

CONSOMMÉ

3 Quarts of cold water.
½ of a good fowl.
2 Pounds of lean beef, or 2½ pounds of beef and bone.
¼ Pound of lean ham.
1 Tablespoon of chopped carrot.
1 Tablespoon of chopped turnip.
1 Teaspoon of minced onion.
1 Tablespoon of celery.
3 Cloves.
3 Peppercorns.
1 Tablespoon of mixed sweet herbs.

Wipe but do not wash the beef, unless, of course, it is very dirty. Cut it into small slices, and fry it in a hot frying-pan to brown it and to develop the flavor of the meat. Then divide the slices into small pieces, so as to expose as large a surface as possible to the action of the water. Put it, with the chicken (after it has been cleaned and cut into small pieces), into a porcelain-lined or granite-ware soup-digester, with the piece of ham and three quarts of cold water. Let it slowly reach the boiling-point, and simmer it gently for six hours. Boiling briskly dissipates the flavors by separating certain subtle substances which are perceptible to the sense of smell, and if they are in the air they cannot also be in the broth.

When it has been cooking for three hours, fry the

carrot, turnip, and onion together in a little butter until they are brown, and put them with the cloves, sweet herbs, peppercorns, and celery into the soup. If these are cooked with the meat from the beginning, the flavor is not so good.

At the end of the six hours, when the meat is in rags, strain the liquid into a china bowl, and set it away to cool until all the fat rises and forms in a cake on the top. It is a good plan to cool it overnight when there is plenty of time. Every particle of fat must be removed, and it is not possible to do this unless the soup is cooled. *To clear consommé* return it to the fire, and as soon as it becomes liquid break into it two eggs, and stir slowly until the soup begins to steam and the albumen of the eggs is coagulated. The coagulum will entangle all the insoluble matter; then strain the liquid through a napkin, salt it, and heat it just to the boiling-point, when it is ready to serve.

It should be perfectly clear, and of a golden-brown color like sherry wine. If the color is not dark enough, a little caramel (burnt sugar) may be added.

The above quantity of meats and flavoring should give a quart of consommé.

BOUILLON

Make a plain beef broth according to the rule on page 78. To a quart of this add a pinch each of thyme, sage, sweet marjoram, and mint (or enough to make in all what will fill a teaspoon), and a teaspoon each of chopped onion and carrot. Boil all together until the broth is reduced to one pint. Strain, season with salt and pepper, and serve very hot in covered cups.

APPLE SOUP

2 Cups of apple.
2 Cups of water.
2 Teaspoons of corn-starch.
1½ Tablespoons of sugar.
1 Saltspoon of cinnamon.
A bit of salt.

Stew the apple in the water until it is very soft. Then mix together into a smooth paste the cornstarch, sugar, salt, and cinnamon with a little cold water. Pour this into the apple, and boil for five minutes. Strain it into a soup-tureen, and keep hot until ready to serve. This is very good eaten with hot buttered sippets.

OYSTERS

Oysters are a highly prized food, though why it is difficult to say, as they are neither very easy of digestion nor very nutritious. But they possess a delicate insinuating flavor that is generally acceptable to most palates, and probably are really valuable for the salts which they contain.

The composition of oysters (Payen's analysis) is as follows:

Nitrogenous matter	14.010%
Fat	1.515%
Saline substances	2.695%
Water	80.385%
Non-nitrogenous matter and waste	1.395%
Total	100.000

According to Professor Mott's Chart of the Composition, Digestibility, and Nutritive Value of Foods, from actual experiment the time required for the digestion of oysters is as follows:

	Hours.	Minutes.
Raw oysters	2	55
Roasted oysters	3	15
Stewed oysters	3	30

This shows that they require a longer time than do most kinds of fish, venison, beefsteak, tripe, soused pig's feet, eggs, and roast beef, all of which are digested in varying times less than those mentioned.

Oysters are found in greatest perfection in the Eastern States, and in the cooler waters of the western Atlantic. The choicest varieties in the world come from the shores of Long Island, and from the Providence River. Chesapeake Bay is noted for the abundance of its oysters.

Oysters are in season from September to May; during the rest of the year they are insipid and unfit for food, although they are sometimes used.

Convalescents often begin with fresh, sound oysters, before they venture to try other kinds of solid animal food.

Oysters may be used in a variety of ways, but served raw and broiled slightly in the shells are perhaps the two most desirable ways with which to begin. Afterward stews and soups are recommended on account of their liquid form and warmth, warm foods being always so much more desirable than cold.

There are some points to be carefully observed in preparing oysters for the sick. (1) Make every effort to have the oysters alive when used. If this is impossible, buy salt-water oysters as fresh as they can be obtained of a reliable dealer. Many serious cases of illness, and even death, have been caused by eating oysters so long dead that poisonous substances had formed in them. (2) Remember that oysters contain an albuminous juice which increases in hardness with an increase of temperature, just as the albumen of an egg does. When oysters are cooked with reference to this juice alone, they are also cooked in the best possible manner with reference to their other ingredients; therefore subject them to a low temperature, and for a short time, bearing in mind that 160° Fahr. is the cooking temperature of albumen.

RAW OYSTERS

Wash and scrub the shells well under a stream of water, with a vegetable brush. With a hammer break the thin edges of the shell so that a knife may be inserted to sever the muscle which holds the two parts of the shell together; when this is cut remove the upper half, and wipe the edges free from any grains of sand. Then sever the muscle which joins the oyster to the other half, so that it may be easily lifted out, without the necessity of cutting. Arrange them on an oyster-plate, and serve with salt, black pepper, and lemon-juice. A half or a quarter of a lemon may be placed in the center of the plate, which usually has a groove on purpose for it.

OYSTERS ROASTED IN THE SHELL

Wash the shells very carefully with a brush. Put them in a wire broiler over glowing coals, the round side of the shell down so as to hold the juice. Cook them quickly, turning once or twice until the shells open. They may also be done in a hot oven. When done, remove the upper half of the shell; season them quickly with salt, pepper, and a tiny bit of butter, and vinegar, if liked, and serve them while they are very hot. The true oyster flavor is delightfully developed by preparing in this way. They may also be served with melted butter, seasoned with salt, pepper, and lemon-juice.

OYSTER SOUP

See recipe under **Soups**, on page 134.

OYSTER STEW

1 Cup of oysters.
1 Cup of rich milk.
2 Saltspoons of salt.
A little white pepper.
¼ Teaspoon of butter.

Set the milk in a saucepan on the fire to heat. Prepare the oysters by pouring over them a cup of cold water to wash them, from which lift them out with a fork, and search for bits of shell which sometimes adhere when they are opened. Then lay them on a napkin or a piece of clean cloth, to drain off as much as possible of the water. Unless oysters are just taken from the shells, the liquor is not of much value. Just as the milk reaches the boiling-point, put the oysters into an omelet-pan, which has been previously set on the stove to heat, and cook them for a minute, or until they become plump, turning them every ten seconds with a fork. The moment the edges or frills begin to curl, drop them into the milk and remove it immediately from the fire. Now add the seasoning and butter, and the stew is ready to serve—which should be done as soon as possible.

Oyster stew may also be made by preparing the oysters as above and then dropping them into boiling-hot milk, which should remain for one or two minutes on the fire before removal.

CREAMED OYSTERS

Clean a pint of oysters according to the directions in the previous rule. After drying them on a napkin, spread them on a plate and season them with salt, pepper, and a suspicion of cayenne.

Make a rich cream sauce with *one pint* of cream, *one tablespoon* of butter, and *two tablespoons* of flour.

When the sauce is cooked, roll into it the seasoned oysters, put them in individual scallop-dishes, or a dish such as might be used for scalloped oysters, or any shallow baking-dish that is good enough to serve; then bake them in a hot oven, on the grate, for ten minutes if in small dishes, or for fifteen if in a single large one. This gives time enough for the oysters to become cooked but not hardened. The mixing of the oysters and sauce should be done quickly, so that the sauce may not become cold before they are put into the oven; for if there is much delay, it will take longer to cook them than the time given.

This is a good way to cook oysters for the sick, for the sauce made according to the rule for such sauces (page 130) is easily digested, nutritious, and of good flavor.

BROILED OYSTERS

Select large oysters. Drain them on a cloth or napkin, turning them from one side to the other, to make them as dry as possible. Meanwhile soften some butter, and season some cracker-crumbs with salt and pepper. Then, holding each oyster on a fork, dip it into the crumbs, then into the melted butter, and again into the crumbs. Arrange them in an oyster-broiler (which differs from ordinary broilers by having the wires closer together), and broil over a hot fire for about two minutes, turning the broiler every few seconds. They should not be shriveled, but plump, soft, tender, and juicy. The salt and pepper in the crumbs will sufficiently season them.

FANCY ROAST OR PAN-BROILED OYSTERS

Eight oysters will be enough for one person. Drain the oysters on a cloth or napkin, making them as free from moisture as possible. Heat an omelet-pan, with a small piece of butter in it, very hot; then drop the oysters one by one into the pan, turning each before the next is put in. One should work quickly, otherwise the first will be overdone before the last is put in. When the pan is full, shake it a moment, lift it from the fire, and turn the oysters quickly into a square covered dish, with toast-points in the corners. Season them with salt, pepper, and a bit of butter, and serve them as quickly as convenient.

Each oyster should be cooked so quickly that its juices are shut into itself and do not ooze out into the pan. There is usually a very little juice with the butter, but if it is considerable, one may know that the oysters have not been cooked in a sufficiently high temperature. Oysters are very nice done in this way, but it takes a skilful worker to do them without letting the juice ooze out, or, on the other hand, overcooking them. The toast-points are made by cutting small squares of bread diagonally across.

OYSTER BROTH

Chop a dozen oysters in a chopping-tray until they are quite fine. Turn them into a small saucepan with a cup of cold water, and let them slowly approach the boiling-point, and then simmer them for five minutes, the object being to get as much as possible of the flavor of the oysters into the water. Then strain out the oysters, season the liquor with a bit of salt, and serve.

A broth with milk may be made by putting in less water, and adding milk three or four minutes before the broth is taken from the fire.

OYSTERS COOKED IN A CHAFING-DISH

Chafing-dishes are generally made of silver, and are much used just at present for cooking oysters at the table. A chafing-dish consists of a covered dish resting in a frame, and heated from below with an alcohol lamp. It is brought to the table with the lamp lighted and the raw oysters ready to be cooked. Some member of the family takes it in charge, and the result is a much more satisfactory dish than could be otherwise obtained, for it requires intelligence and a cultivated taste to cook and season these delicious bivalves.

Uses of the Chafing-dish. It may be used for broth, stew, soup, and fancy roast, the treatment being exactly the same as with a saucepan or an omelet-pan on a stove.

EGGS

Eggs, next to milk, are the most valuable form of food for those who are very ill. They contain in excellent proportion most of the elements necessary to nourish the body; but being a concentrated form of food, it is well to associate with them milk or some other liquid, and such starchy foods as bread, potatoes, etc.

According to Laws and Gilbert the composition of egg is as follows:

SHELL	Carbonate of lime	10.00%
YOLK	Nitrogenous matter	16.00%
	Fatty matter	30.70%
	Saline matter	1.30%
	Water	52.00%
	Total	100.00%
WHITE	Nitrogenous matter	20.40%
	Saline matter	1.60%
	Water	78.00%
	Total	100.00%

A large proportion of both yolk and white is *albumen*.[1] It has been found by experiment (page 25) that when white of egg is subjected to a temperature

[1] Egg whole	Water	74.00%
	Nitrogenous matter	14.00%
	Fat	10.50%
	Inorganic matter	1.50%
		PAVY.

of 134°–140° Fahr. little white threads appear in it; that if the temperature be increased to 160° Fahr., the whole mass becomes a white, but tender, easily divided substance; that if the heat be raised to 200° Fahr. it loses its tender, jelly-like consistency, and becomes firm and tenacious; and that with continued rise of temperature the toughness increases until at from 300°–350° Fahr. it becomes so hard that it is used as a cement for marble.

From these statements it will at once be inferred that the proper cooking temperature of eggs is not that of boiling water, but 52° lower. Eggs cooked the customary three minutes in boiling water will be overdone in the part nearest the shell, and not cooked at all in the center of the yolk, as three minutes is not long enough for the heat to penetrate to that point. The yolk, though not injurious in this condition, is not as palatable as when it is cooked. The condition of the white, however, is of grave importance, as even well persons are sometimes made ill by eating it.

It is generally agreed that although albumen will coagulate at a temperature somewhat lower than 160° Fahr., the degree of firmness obtained by exposing it to this temperature is the most desirable for food. Therefore we speak of 160° Fahr. as its *cooking temperature*. An egg cooked ideally would be subjected to that temperature for a sufficient time to allow the heat to penetrate and act upon all portions of it. The time required is half an hour. Cooked according to this method, the white would be opaque and firm, but tender and delicate, the yolk not liquid and lukewarm, but thick and almost firm. The flavor of both is delicious.

A knowledge of the proper temperature necessary to bring about this change is absolutely essential to any one who would cook eggs, and dishes which contain them, such as creams, puddings, etc., as they should be cooked. A great deal of the philosophy of cooking depends upon this knowledge, for nearly all kinds of meat, fish, oysters, milk, and other albuminous foods contain as one of their most valuable nutrients the substance known as albumen. When they are cooked with reference to this *alone*, we find that they are also done in the best-known way with reference to their other ingredients.

Practically with our present kitchen appliances it is exceedingly difficult to maintain for half an hour a steady temperature of 160°, but excellent results may be obtained by the following method.

SOFT-COOKED EGGS

Pour enough boiling water into a saucepan to more than cover whatever number of eggs are to be cooked; then put in the eggs, and let them stand for ten minutes on the hearth or any place where the water will not lose its warmth too quickly. Remember that it is the heat in the water which is to do the cooking. The saucepan should remain uncovered. Practically this is an excellent way to do, for the amount of heat in the water will not fall below 160° Fahr. in the ten minutes, and that time is sufficient for it to penetrate to the center of the egg. Moreover, if the egg be forgotten, and remains in the water for a longer time, it will not become hard unless the temperature of the water be raised.

Theoretically an egg should be cooked at 160° Fahr., but practically this would involve a considerable waste of time and necessitate the use of a thermometer. Almost the same result is obtained in an easy and convenient way by the above method, although it is not an exact one. The proportion of boiling water for each egg which will insure cooking in the time given is one pint, but somewhat less will do if many are to be cooked; for instance, eight eggs will do in six pints, as comparatively less heat is lost in warming the pan.

POACHED OR DROPPED EGGS

From a thin, even slice of home-made bread cut out a round piece with a biscuit-cutter; toast it a delicate brown.

Pour some boiling water into a small saucepan and salt it, using a saltspoon of salt to a cup of water; place it on the stove to boil. Break a fresh egg into a cup, and when the water is boiling slip it gently into the pan. At first the egg will cool the water below the boiling-point, but should the water again begin to boil, withdraw the pan to a cooler part of the stove. When the white is firm, or at the end of about two minutes, lift out the egg by means of two spoons or a skimmer (being careful not to break the yolk), and place it on the round of toast. The egg should not be trimmed. Season it with a speck of salt, a little pepper, and a bit of butter placed on the middle of the yolk. This is a dainty and easy way of preparing eggs for the sick, and one is always sure of the condition of the eggs, which is not the case when they are cooked in the shell.

A layer of minced ham or of minced chicken laid on the toast makes a palatable variation.

Egg-poachers, or little tin cups with perforated bottoms set in a frame, may be bought for poaching eggs, but in those that the author has seen the raw albumen runs into the little holes and makes it difficult to remove the egg after it is done without breaking it. Muffin-rings may also be used.

SCRAMBLED EGGS. No. 1

Break two eggs into a plate, and sprinkle on a little pepper and a saltspoon of salt; beat them with a fork for one minute, add two tablespoons of milk or, better, thin sweet cream; beat again and pour the mixture into a buttered pan; stir it gently, letting it cook slowly for about two minutes, or until the albumen of the egg is coagulated. It should be soft and tender, not hardened. Serve it on toast, or in a small, square covered dish.

SCRAMBLED EGGS. No. 2

Beat two eggs, a saltspoon of salt, and a sprinkle of white pepper in a bowl with a Dover egg-beater until quite light; add two tablespoons of sweet cream or of milk, and turn the mixture into a double boiler to cook, stirring it constantly until the albumen is just coagulated. A delicate and easily digested dish is the result. It is a safer way to use the double boiler rather than an omelet-pan. If no double boiler is at hand, one may be improvised with a bowl or dish set into a kettle of hot water.

OMELETS

Omelets may be made in a great variety of ways, the kind depending not upon a difference in mixing the eggs, but upon the ingredients which are added. *Spanish* omelet is ordinary omelet with onion. *Truffles, mushrooms, chopped oysters, rum,* and *tomato* make other varieties. Flour should never be used in them, as it cannot be properly cooked in the short time that should be given to the eggs. If it should happen that an omelet is to be made, and there is no milk at hand, water may be substituted, but an omelet should never be made without one or the other.

CREAMY OMELET

Beat four eggs slightly with a fork until you can take up a spoonful; add two saltspoons of salt, half a saltspoon of pepper, four tablespoons of milk or cream, and mix well. Butter an omelet-pan, and before the butter browns turn in the mixture. Then with the point of a fork pick or lift up the cooked egg from the center, and let the uncooked egg run under. This leaves the butter on the pan, and is better than stirring. Continue the lifting until the whole is of a soft creamy consistency, then place it over a hotter part of the fire and brown slightly, fold and turn out as usual. (Adapted from Mrs. D. A. Lincoln's "Boston Cook Book.")

For an invalid's use take half the quantities mentioned above — that is, use two eggs, two tablespoons of milk or cream, a saltspoon of salt, and a bit of pepper; and instead of having the omelet-pan hot, have it just warm enough to melt the butter; otherwise the first layer of egg which is cooked may be overdone and hardened.

FOAMY OMELET

Separate the yolks from the whites of two eggs, and put them into bowls. To the yolks add a saltspoon of salt and one fourth of a saltspoon of pepper. Beat with a Dover egg-beater until light. Then add two tablespoons of milk. Beat the whites until stiff, but not as stiff as possible, and *fold*, not *beat* them into the yolks, so that the whole shall be very light and puffy. Pour the mixture into a buttered omelet-pan, and cook slowly until the under side begins to change color and become brown, or for about *two minutes*. Then put the pan on the grate in the oven for about *one minute*, to cook the upper surface. One must endeavor to avoid both over and under cooking. If the omelet is not done enough, the raw egg will ooze out after it is folded; on the other hand, if it is cooked too much, it will be dry and tough. When it seems to be coagulated on the upper surface, run a case-knife under it to separate it from the pan, and fold one half over the other. Take the platter which is to receive it in the right hand, lay it against the edge of the pan, and tip the omelet out. Serve immediately.

An omelet is a dainty and delicate way of serving eggs, and may be well made by any one who will bear in mind that the cooking temperature of albumen is 160° Fahr., and that if exposed to a very much higher degree of heat for many minutes, it will be spoiled,—rendered both unpalatable and indigestible.

OMELET WITH HAM. No. 1

Broil a thin, small slice of ham until thoroughly

well done. Lay it between the folds of an omelet. Either creamy or foamy omelets may be used.

OMELET WITH HAM. No. 2

Mince a piece of cooked ham until it is fine. Stir it into an omelet in the proportion of one teaspoon to an egg, or it may be sprinkled over the surface just before folding. When seasoned with a little mustard, it makes a very piquant addition. Either creamy or foamy omelets may be used.

OMELET WITH JELLY

Spread a tablespoon of grape or currant jelly over the middle of the upper surface of a two-egg omelet just before folding it.

OMELET WITH CHICKEN

Chop fine the cooked white meat of a piece of chicken. Season it with salt and pepper, and sprinkle it over an omelet, or stir it into the egg before cooking, in the proportion of one teaspoon to an egg, as is done with ham.

OMELET WITH TOMATO

Prepare thin slices of very ripe tomatoes, by removing the skin and seasoning slightly with salt.

Lay them on that part of the omelet which is to be the lower half, and fold; or the tomato may be tucked into the omelet after folding.

OMELET WITH PARSLEY

Wash some parsley. Break off the stems and roll the rest into a little ball; then, holding it firmly in the left hand, cut slices from it, or chop it on a board. Stir it into the omelet mixture before it is cooked, in the proportion of one teaspoon for each egg.

SPANISH OMELET

To an omelet mixture add two drops of onion-juice for each egg, or half a teaspoon of very finely minced onion.

ORANGE OMELET

"The thinly grated rind of one orange and three tablespoons of the juice, three eggs, and three teaspoons of powdered sugar. Beat the yolks, add the sugar, rind, and juice, fold in the beaten whites, and cook. Fold, turn out, sprinkle thickly with powdered sugar, and score in diagonal lines with a clean red-hot poker. The burnt sugar gives to the omelet a delicious flavor.

"This is a convenient dessert for an emergency, and may be prepared in ten minutes if one has the oranges." (From Mrs. D. A. Lincoln's "Boston Cook Book.")

POTATOES

Next to wheat flour, potatoes are our most common form of starch food. The potato is a tuber, a native of America, and may be said to have been discovered to the civilized world by the Spaniards, who found it growing in Chili and Peru. Thence it was carried to Spain, and from there to other parts of Europe, some time in the sixteenth century. Potatoes were at first used as luxuries, but are now almost ranked among the necessities of life.

The composition of potatoes (Letherby) is as follows:

Water	75.00%
Starch	18.80%
Nitrogenous matter	2.00%
Sugar	3.00%
Fat	.20%
Salts	1.00% [1]

From this we see that starch is the principal nutrient, therefore potatoes in use for food should be associated with nitrogenous substances, such as eggs, meat, fish, and milk. The potash salts which potatoes contain are very valuable. According to Letherby, an

---

[1] Another analysis is that of Payen, the distinguished French chemist.

Water	74.4%
Starch, sugar, pectose	21.2%
Nitrogenous matter	1.7%
Fat	.1%
Cellulose and epidermis	1.5%
Inorganic matter	1.1%
Total	100.00%

Pohl found the proportion of starch, judging by specific gravity in different varieties, to be as follows: 16.38%, 17.11%, 18.43%, 18.95%, 20.45%, 21.32%, 24.14%.   Dr. SMITH's "Food."

average of thirty-one analyses of the ash of potatoes gave 59.8 per cent. of potash, 19.1 per cent. of phosphoric acid, the other ingredients being in exceedingly small proportions. These salts are necessary to a healthy condition of the blood. Potatoes are a valuable antiscorbutic.

According to Mattieu Williams, scurvy prevailed in Norway to a very serious extent until the introduction of the potato; and Lang, with other good authorities, testifies that its disappearance is due to the use of potatoes by a people who formerly were insufficiently supplied with salts-giving vegetable food.

The salts of the potato are most abundant in or near the skin, and the decision of the question as to whether potatoes shall be pared or not before cooking is somewhat aided by this fact. For persons who eat but few other fresh vegetables by all means leave the skins on, but for those who have access to a good kitchen garden and have plenty of other vegetables and fruits from which to get their salts, it makes no important difference whether the skins are removed.

The potato is eminently a starch food, and this knowledge indicates the method of treatment in cooking. Since starch is its principal ingredient (the amount of nitrogenous matter being very small), if it is cooked with reference to that alone, it will be done in the best possible manner.

Starch, in order to be rendered most digestible and acceptable to the human system, must be subjected to a high temperature in the presence of some liquid. At 401° Fahr. (see pages 33 and 34) it is converted into dextrine. This change, if not performed outside the body, will be done in the ordinary processes of digestion after the starch is eaten; therefore the nearer we approach to it in cooking, the more perfectly is the food prepared which contains it.

Usually the first vegetable prescribed by the physician for a sick person who is beginning to use solids, is a baked potato. A baked potato, however, may be no better than a boiled potato unless it is cooked in so high a temperature that the starch is affected. Boiled potatoes cannot be subjected to a higher temperature than 212° Fahr. Baked potatoes may be done in such a way that they are but little better than boiled—for instance, done in a slow oven. On the other hand, if they are put into a temperature of 380° or 400° Fahr., or a hot oven, they will be done in such a manner that the conversion of starch will in a degree take place, and they will be consequently both palatable and easily digested.

Potatoes roasted in hot ashes or embers are delicious, and for the same reason. But it must not be understood that by cooking potatoes in a high temperature the starch which they contain is *all* changed into dextrine. This does not usually take place except in slight degree, but by the high temperature it is better prepared for this change in the processes of digestion. Probably what does take place is a sort of hydration of the starch, resulting in the complete swelling and final bursting of the granules, with possibly an intermediate change between this and dextrine. Just at the moment when potatoes are done they should be immediately taken from the fire and served at once. The potato is capable of being made into a variety of dishes, and when properly prepared has a delicate flavor which is very acceptable to most people. *It is one of the most easily digested forms of starch-containing food.*

BOILED POTATOES

For boiled potatoes, if they are to be served whole, select those of the same shape and size. Wash them under a stream of water with a vegetable brush. Pare carefully so as not to waste the potato, and evenly, that they may look smooth and shapely. Cook them in a granite-ware kettle or covered saucepan, in enough salted boiling water to just cover them. If cold water is used, there is a greater loss of potash salts by solution, because of the longer time of exposure to the action of the liquid. The proportion of salt should be one teaspoon to a quart of water.

Potatoes being already hydrated, it makes no great difference whether they are put into hot or cold water, except in the time which will be required to boil them and the slight loss of salts. For medium-sized potatoes from thirty to forty minutes will be necessary after they begin to boil. The moment they feel soft when pierced with a fork they are done. Take them at once from the fire, drain off all the water, and dry them by gently moving the pan back and forth over the top of the stove for a minute. Serve as quickly as possible. Unless they are to be eaten at once, it is better to mash them, and keep them in the oven until needed.

MASHED POTATOES

For mashed potatoes the uneven sizes may be used; the large ones should be cut into small pieces. Prepare according to the foregoing rule, and when they are cooked and dried, add salt, butter, pepper, and cream, in the following proportions:

1 Pint of potatoes.
1 Teaspoon of butter.
$\frac{1}{2}$ Teaspoon of salt.
$\frac{1}{2}$ Saltspoon of pepper (white).
2 Tablespoons of sweet cream or of milk.

Put into the potatoes the butter, salt, and pepper, and mash them on the stove, in the dish in which they were boiled, to keep them hot. Use an open wire potato-masher, and mash quickly so that they may be light and dry, not "gummy." Last put in the cream, mix for a moment, and serve immediately in a covered vegetable-dish. If it is necessary to keep them for a time, arrange them like a cake in the dish in which they are to be served, smooth over the top, dot it with little bits of butter, or brush it over with milk or the beaten white of egg, and brown them a delicate golden color by placing the dish on the grate in the oven.

BAKED POTATOES

For baked potatoes, select those which are of uniform size and not very large. Scrub them thoroughly in a stream of water from the faucet, to wash off every particle of sand, for many like to eat the outside. Bake them in a hot oven for from forty-five to fifty minutes. If the potatoes are of *medium* size, and do not cook in that time, it indicates that the oven is not of the proper temperature.

Baked potatoes, not being exposed to the solvent action of a liquid, lose none of their potash salts in cooking, as boiled potatoes do. The same is true of those roasted, and of those fried raw in deep fat.

ROASTED POTATOES

Bury medium-sized potatoes in the embers or ashes of an open fire for a half hour or more, according to their size. At the end of that time dust off the ashes with a brush. Burst the shells by squeezing them in the hand, and serve at once with salt, and butter or cream. Either baked or roasted potatoes are delicious eaten with sweet cream, salt, and pepper.

CREAMED POTATOES

Left-over potatoes may be used for this dish, or potatoes may be boiled on purpose for it. Whichever is used, cut them into half-inch dice, put them in an omelet-pan, season them with salt and pepper, and pour in milk until it is even with the surface of the potato; then simmer gently until all the milk is absorbed, or for about half an hour. For every pint of potatoes make a pint of white sauce, season it with a saltspoon of salt and a teaspoon of chopped parsley, and pour it over. Potatoes are very nice done in this way, if care is taken in simmering them in the milk. Unless this is done according to the rule, they will have the cold-potato taste, which is not at all palatable.

A little chopped onion may replace the parsley with good effect.

DUCHESS POTATOES

1 Pint of potatoes.
1 Teaspoon of butter.
$\frac{1}{2}$ Teaspoon of salt.
1 Egg.
$\frac{1}{4}$ Teaspoon of white pepper.

Wash, pare, and boil the potatoes. Drain out every drop of water, and dry them in the usual way. When dry and mealy, put in the butter, salt, and pepper, and mash them thoroughly and quickly. If potatoes are mashed for a long time slowly, they become waxy, so endeavor to do it quickly and as lightly as possible. Then add the egg, well beaten, and the cream; mix, and form it into a flat cake (on a board) about half an inch thick. Cut it into oblongs or squares, or shape it into rounds or balls, brush over with the beaten white of egg, or milk, and bake in a hot oven until a delicate brown. Serve the cakes on a platter as soon as they are done.

MEATS

(BROILED)

Of the different ways of cooking the flesh of animals, especially for the sick, broiling is at once the most delicious and the most difficult.

The difference between broiled meat and meat cooked in water is that the broiled meat is cooked in its own juices, while the other is not. The albumen is coagulated in both cases, and the gelatinous and fibrinous tissues are softened by being heated in a liquid. In broiling or roasting meat the juices are retained, while in stewing they go more or less into the water, and the loosening of the fibers and solution of the gelatin and fibrin may be carried further, on account of the longer exposure to heat and the larger amount of solvent. In broiling, as the meat is to be cooked in its own juices, it is evident that these must be retained as completely as possible; and in order to succeed in this, we have to struggle with a dry heat, which may not only cause rapid evaporation, but may volatilize or decompose some of the flavoring principles.[1]

We should, therefore, endeavor to have such a temperature as shall at first be sufficiently high to quickly coagulate, even harden, the albumen in the outside surface, and thus form a layer or protecting coat over the whole, and then to so modify and regulate the

[1] Mattieu Williams.

heat afterward that the interior shall be raised to such a temperature as shall properly cook it without loss of its nutritive properties.

The time of exposure will be different for different kinds of meat—beef and mutton requiring a shorter time than lamb, chicken, or game. Beef and mutton are best when cooked rare; lamb, chicken, and some kinds of game are best when well done. Game with *white flesh* should be *well done; all other kinds*, generally speaking, may be *rare*.

Much of the science of cooking depends upon a knowledge of the effects of heat; and as many changes in food are due to the dissociation caused by heat, the degree of change depending upon the temperature, the value of a sound knowledge of the subject cannot fail to be seen.

To illustrate: aside from the evaporation of juices and coagulation of albumen in a piece of steak, the chemical separation of its constituents, especially of the outside shell or sheath, will vary with the degree of heat in which it is cooked.

Not only for meats, but for most animal foods, a cooking temperature less than 212° but above 160° is most advisable. This applies particularly to milk, eggs, oysters, meats, and fish. Of course in broiling we partially sacrifice the outside by cooking in a high temperature for the sake of preserving the inner portions.

BEEF

Beef is, without doubt, our most valuable kind of meat. It is nutritious, of excellent flavor, and comparatively easy of digestion. It contains many of the substances necessary to nourish the body—water, fat, albumen, gelatin, fibrin, salts, and flavoring properties. The direct nutrients which it contains are fat and protein.

The quality of beef varies with the age of the animal and the manner in which it has been fattened. It requires a considerable amount of study to be able to select a good roast or steak. If the fat be of light, golden color, firm and thick, and the lean be streaked with fine lines of fat, it is one indication of a well-nourished animal. A reliable dealer may be of great service in aiding one to distinguish between good and poor qualities.

The best portions for steak are from the loin, top of the round, and rump. The cut called "porterhouse" is from near the middle of the loin, and is the best portion of the animal. It has a rich, fine flavor, and contains a section of tenderloin. Sirloin steak is from the loin, and is also very nice. The first and second cuts from the top of the round are excellent, containing much well-flavored juice. The composition of a round steak free from bones is as follows (in 100 parts):

Nutrients..	Protein, gelatin, fibrin, etc.......	23.00%
	Fats...........................	9.00%
	Mineral matters	1.30%
Water		66.70%
	Total	100.00%

ATWATER.

The time given below for the digestion of beef is taken from calculations by Dr. Beaumont:

	Hours.	Minutes.
Beefsteak broiled................	3	
Beef, fresh, lean, roasted	3	30
Beef fried	4	

VALUE OF BEEF

As material for muscle	19
As heat-giver	14
As food for brain and nervous system	2
Water	65

ATWATER.

To Broil Steak. Select a steak from the loin, top of the round, or rump. Have it cut an inch and a half (or, better, two inches) thick. If there is a great deal of fat, trim off part of it, and wipe the steak with a clean, wet cloth. A fire of glowing red coals is necessary to do broiling well. Place the steak in a wire broiler, and put it as near the coals as possible (one writer says plunge it into the hottest part of the fire), *count ten* and turn it, count again and turn again until it has been turned *five* or *six times* so as to quickly cook a thin layer all over the outside, to shut in the juices of the meat, and to form a protecting sheath of coagulated albumen over the whole. Then lift the broiler away from the coals and do the rest of the process *slowly*,—that is, in a lower temperature, that the heat may have time to penetrate to the center of the piece and raise the juices to a sufficiently high temperature to soften the fibers, but not so high as to hornify the albumen or char the outside. Turn it every half minute until done.

If the fat melts and flames, do not lift up the broiler; it will do no harm, and the black deposit which results is only carbon. This carbon is not injurious; the color is not especially attractive, but the taste will be good. The cautious cook who does not appreciate this will lift up the broiler, thus cooling the meat, and will perhaps blow out the flame, a proceeding which is open to question as a point of neatness.

As coal fires are never twice alike, and the amount of heat sent out is variable, it is constantly necessary to judge anew as to where the broiler shall be placed. A certain amount of practice is required to be able to broil with even fair success. When done a steak should be brown on the outside, pink and juicy inside, and plump, not shriveled. Steak should be at least an inch thick, otherwise the proportion of surface exposed to the heat will be so great in proportion to the amount of meat as to cause the loss by evaporation of most of the juice, thus making the steak tough and dry.

From *five* to *seven* minutes will be required to cook a steak an inch thick; if an inch and a half thick, from *eight* to *ten* minutes. Serve the steak on a hot platter after having seasoned *both* sides of it with salt and pepper, but no butter. If it is desirable to use butter, serve it with the steak rather than on it.

HAMBURG STEAK. No. 1

(SCRAPED BEEF)

Cut a piece of tender steak half an inch thick. Lay it on a meat-board, and with a sharp knife scrape off the soft part until there is nothing left but the tough, stringy fibers. Season this pulp with salt and pepper, make it into little flat, round cakes half an inch thick, and broil them two minutes. Serve on rounds of buttered toast. This is a safe and dainty way to prepare steak for one who is just beginning to eat meat. When it is not convenient to have glowing coals, these meat-cakes may be broiled in a very hot omelet-pan.

HAMBURG STEAK. No. 2

Pound a thin piece of beefsteak until the fibers are broken; season it with salt and pepper, fold and pound again; then broil it three or four minutes over a clear hot fire. Serve at once.

TENDERLOIN STEAK

Broil a tenderloin steak, and at the same time a small piece of round steak, which usually contains a great deal of well-flavored juice. Cut the round steak into small pieces, and squeeze the juice from it over the tenderloin. Tenderloin steak is tender, but usually neither juicy nor particularly well flavored. By this method one gets a delicious steak.

BEEFSTEAK À LA MAÎTRE D'HÔTEL

Broil a steak, place it on a platter, and season it with salt and pepper; sprinkle it with finely chopped parsley, drops of lemon-juice, and some little bits of butter. Set it in the oven long enough to soften the butter. A steak done in this way may be made quite attractive by garnishing it with hot mashed and seasoned potatoes which have been squeezed through a potato-strainer. A colander may be used in lieu of a strainer. The potato loses some of its heat in the process, so care must be taken to have the dish very hot or to place it in the oven until it becomes so.

A steak may always be garnished with parsley, water-cress, or slices of lemon.

CHICKEN
(BROILED)

For broiling, select a young chicken — one from three to eight months old. Singe it. Split it down the back, and free it from all refuse, such as pinfeathers, lungs, kidneys, oil-bag, windpipe, and crop (the latter is sometimes left in when the chicken is drawn). Wash it quickly in cold water, fold it in a clean cloth kept for the purpose, and clap gently between the hands until all the water is absorbed. Separate the joints — the *lower joint of the leg* and the *upper joint of the wing* — by cutting the flesh on the under side and severing the white tough tendons. Soften some butter until it runs, then dip the chicken into it, season it with salt and pepper, dredge with flour, and broil it in a wire broiler for from fifteen to twenty minutes, according to the size.

The same principle holds in broiling chicken as in steak. The first part of the process should be done in a high temperature to coagulate the juices of the outer layers, and the last part very slowly. Care must be taken that it is thoroughly done at the thick joints of the wing and leg. Serve hot.

To Buy a Chicken. The best chickens have yellow skin, but one may be deceived if guided by this alone, for *fowls* often have yellow skin also. The flexibility of the end of the breast-bone is always a sure means of deciding as to the age of the bird. If it be soft, easily bent, and if it feels like cartilage, the chicken is young. Sometimes dealers break the bone for the purpose of deceiving buyers, but it does not take a great deal of intelligence to decide between a broken bone and one that is easily bent. If the bone be hard and firm, it is an indication of age. For broiling, of course, the chicken should be young, the flesh of good color and well nourished, and, as in the buying of beef, one may rely upon the judgment of a good dealer. The way in which chickens are fed has much to do with the flavor of the meat.

BIRDS

Various kinds of birds, such as squab, partridge, plover, snipe, pheasant, etc., are particularly appropriate food for the sick, partly because we associate them with the dainty things of life, but more on account of the valuable nutrient properties which they contain. They are especially rich in salts (particularly the phosphates), which are so much needed by a system exhausted by disease.

Birds which feed mostly on grains, such as the partridge and the pheasant, will bear transportation, and will keep, in cold weather, a long time. Birds with dark flesh, which live mostly on animal food, decay quickly.

A general rule for the cooking of game is this: that with white flesh should be well done, that with dark should be rare, and usually is only properly cooked when served so, as in the case of woodcock, duck, and snipe.

When in Season. Some birds, such as reed-birds, partridge, and plover, have a season which varies slightly in different parts of the country, according to the game laws of different States. In Maryland, the following birds may be found in market according to the time stated:

Squabs	All the year.
Partridge	November 1 — December 25.
Snipe	September — December.
Plover	September — November.

Pheasants ....October — January.
Woodcock ....August — February.
Rice- or reed-birds ....September — Middle October.
Field-larks......................Summer and early autumn.
Grouse (prairie-hen)...........All the year.
Pigeons ....All the year.

The cleansing and preparation of birds is in general carried out in the same manner as with chickens. When there is any variation from this, it will be mentioned under the rule for each.

SQUABS

Squabs are young domestic pigeons. The Philadelphia market supplies nearly all of those used in the eastern part of the United States.

Remove the feathers, and all pin-feathers; cut off the head and legs, and split the bird down the back carefully with a sharp knife. Lift out carefully the contents of the body, which are contained in a little sac or delicate membrane; they should be taken out without breaking. Do not forget the windpipe, crop, lungs, and kidneys. Wash, and prepare the squab in the same manner that chicken is done, except the dipping in butter and dredging with flour; this may be omitted, as squabs are generally fat and do not require it. Broil from twelve to fifteen minutes, according to the size of the bird and the intensity of the fire. It should be well done. Serve on hot buttered toast.

PARTRIDGE

The partridge is a white-fleshed bird. It may be broiled or roasted.

To Broil. Follow the same rule as that given for squab, except dip in melted butter and dredge with flour.

To Roast. Prepare in the same manner as for broiling, except dip in butter and dredge twice. Do not forget the salt and pepper. Then skewer the body so that it will resemble a whole bird, and look as if it had not been split down the back. Spread a teaspoon of butter on the breast, and bake it in a hot oven for twenty to thirty minutes. Partridge done in this way is delicious, for the butter enriches the meat, which is naturally dry. It should be served well done, not rare, on hot buttered toast, with currant jelly.

The season for partridges is in most States during the last part of the autumn, and generally the laws in regard to them are rigid. Nevertheless, they can be bought from the middle of October until May, or the beginning of warm weather. The partridge is a bird that keeps well bears transportation, and is sent from one part of the country to another, many coming from the West when the season is over in the Eastern States. It is a medium-sized bird, with mottled brown feathers, which are black at the ends, especially those on the back, and mottled brown and silver-gray on the breast.

SNIPE

Snipe may be both prepared and cooked as partridges are—that is, broiled and roasted. The snipe has rich, dark meat, and therefore will not need to be dipped in butter for either broiling or roasting. It is about the same size as a squab, but as it is to be cooked rare (it is more tender and of nicer flavor so), ten minutes is sufficient time for broiling, and from twelve to fifteen minutes for roasting in a hot oven. Serve it with currant jelly on hot buttered toast.

The snipe has a long bill, from two to two and a half inches in length. It is about the size of a squab, with dark, almost black, wing-feathers tipped with white, and the feathers of the back are intermingled with flecks of golden brown. The under sides of the wings are pearl-gray, and the breast is white.

PHEASANTS

Pheasants may be broiled or roasted. As the meat is dry, they should be well rubbed with soft butter and dredged with flour. It is a good way, after putting on the salt and pepper, to dip the bird into melted butter, then dredge it with flour, then lay on soft butter and dredge a second time; or, when it is skewered and ready for the oven, it may be spread thickly over the breast with softened butter. Care must be taken that the very thick portion of the breast be cooked through, as pheasant should be well done, and from one half to three quarters of an hour will be necessary for this.

WOODCOCK

The woodcock is about the size of a partridge, with mottled dark brown and gray feathers, except on the breast, where they are a sort of light salmon brown. It has a long slender beak, somewhat like that of a snipe.

Prepare woodcock like squab, only do not cut off the head, as the brain is considered a dainty by epicures. Remove the skin from the head, and tie or skewer it back against the body. Use salt and pepper for seasoning, but neither flour nor butter, as the woodcock has dark, rich flesh. Broil from eight to ten minutes. Serve rare on toast.

REED-BIRDS

Reed-birds are to be prepared after the general rule for dressing birds. Although they are sometimes cooked whole, it is better to draw them. Split them down the back, remove the contents of the body, and after washing and wiping them, string three or four on a skewer, pulling it through their sides, so that they shall appear whole. Roast in a shallow pan in a hot oven, from *eight* to *ten* minutes; or, before roasting, wrap each one in a very thin slice of fat pork and pin it on with a skewer (wire).

Broiled. Prepare as for roasting, except peel off the skin, taking the feathers with it. Broil from two to four minutes. Serve on toast.

It is a good plan to skin all small birds.

The reed-bird is the bobolink of New England, the reed-bird of Pennsylvania, and the rice-bird of the Carolinas.

GROUSE

The grouse or prairie-hen is in season all the year, but is at its best during the fall and winter.

To Prepare. Clean, wash, and wipe it. Lard the breast, or fasten to it with slender skewers a thin slice of salt pork. Grouse has dry flesh, consequently it will be improved by rubbing softened butter over it, as well as by using pork. Sprinkle on a little salt, dredge it with flour, and cook in a quick oven for thirty minutes.

Grouse are also very nice potted. After they are made ready for cooking, fry a little fat pork and some chopped onion together in a large deep spider for a few minutes, then lay in the grouse, cover the spider, and fry until the outside of each bird is somewhat browned, or for twenty minutes, slowly. Then put them into a granite-ware kettle and stew until tender, which will take from one to two hours. When they are done, lift them out, thicken the liquid slightly with flour, and season it with salt and pepper for a gravy. Serve the grouse on a deep platter with the gravy poured around, or simply season the liquid and cook tiny dumplings in it, which may be served around the birds. Then thicken the liquid and pour over. The amount of onion to be fried with the pork should not exceed half a teaspoon for each bird, and of pork the proportion of a cubic inch to a bird is enough.

Pigeons potted according to these directions for grouse are excellent.

FIELD-LARKS

Field-larks and robins may be prepared and cooked in exactly the same way that reed-birds are done. Robins are good in autumn.

VENISON

Venison is in season during the late autumn and winter. When "hung" for a proper length of time, it is the most easily digested of all meats. For this reason it is a favorite with epicures who eat late suppers. According to Dr. Beaumont it is digested in *one hour and thirty-five minutes.*[1]

Steaks may be taken either from the loin or the round. Broil them according to the rule for beefsteak, and serve very hot with a slice of lemon or a little claret poured over.

Venison will not please an epicure unless it is hot and rare when served. To accomplish this in a perfectly satisfactory manner, it has become the fashion in families to have the broiling done on the table, in a chafing-dish, each person attending to his own steak, and cooking it according to his particular fancy.

MUTTON

A good piece of meat freed from refuse,—that is, indigestible portions such as bone, etc.,—if neatly prepared and *properly cooked*, is practically entirely digested. If carelessly handled and cooked so that its juices are evaporated, and its natural flavors undeveloped or destroyed, there will be more or less waste in the process of digestion.

Mutton requires more care in cooking than beef, or, in other words, it is more easily spoiled in that process; but when done with due consideration, it is a most acceptable meat. A thick, carefully broiled, hot, juicy mutton chop just from the coals is a very delicious morsel. The same piece with the adjectives reversed,—that is, done without thought, perhaps raw in the middle, charred on the outside, and cold,—is far from being acceptable to even a healthy person.

Just inside of the outer skin of the sheep there is

[1] From actual experiment.

a thick, tough membrane enveloping the whole animal; the peculiar flavor called "woolly," which makes mutton disagreeable to many, is given to the meat largely by this covering. It is supposed that the oil from the wool strikes through. An important point in the preparation of the meat for cooking is the removal of this skin, for otherwise the unpleasant taste will be very strong, and the chop or roast consequently far from as delicate as it might be.

The value of mutton as a nutrient is practically the same as that of beef, as may be seen by comparing the following table with that of beef previously given.

As material for muscle	21
As heat-giver	14
As food for brain and nervous system	2
Water	63

DIGESTIBILITY OF MUTTON

	Hours.	Minutes.
Broiled	3	
Boiled	3	
Roasted	3	15

MUTTON CHOPS

For the same reason that is given in the rule for beefsteak, mutton chops should be thick. When the fat is abundant and little lines of fat run through the flesh, it is an indication of a good quality of meat.

To prepare the chops for broiling, cut away the tough outside skin, trim off a part of the fat, but not all, and any portion of the spinal cord which may be attached. Broil in the same manner that steak is done — that is, close to the glowing coals — for about one minute, turning often, and at a distance from them for the rest of the time, which should be from *four* to *six* minutes for a chop an *inch thick*.

Mutton, like beef, should be served rare. Season chops with salt and pepper, but no butter, as the meat is rich in fat and does not require it. Tomato-sauce is an old-fashioned accompaniment of a chop, and may or may not be served with it. For breakfast it is better omitted.

CHOPS, PAN-BROILED

Chops are fairly good pan-broiled. The same principle is to be followed as in cooking over coals — that is, a high degree of heat at first, to sear over the outside before the juices escape, and a low temperature afterward; therefore heat the pan or spider *exceedingly* hot (use no fat), drop in the chop, count ten and turn, count again and turn again for about one minute, then draw the pan to the side or back of the stove and finish slowly. A chop one inch thick will be perfectly done in from *five* to *seven* minutes. If the pan is hot enough at first, there will be no loss of juice or flavor. Season and serve in the same manner as broiled chops.

FRENCH CHOPS

Trim a chop until there is nothing left but the round muscle at the thick end, with a little fat about it. Cut away all the meat from the bone, which will then look like a handle with a neat morsel at one end. Broil.

CHOPS IN PAPER

Spread a piece of paper evenly and thickly with butter. Lay upon it a nicely trimmed chop, and double the paper with the edges together. Fold and crease these edges on the three sides; then fold and crease again, so that the butter cannot run out. These folds should be *half an inch* wide. It will be necessary to have the sheet of paper (note-paper or thick brown paper will do) considerably more than twice as large as the chop. Broil over coals, not too near, turning often so that the temperature shall not get so high as to ignite the paper. A chop broiled in this way is basted in the butter and its own juices, and is very delicate. Be careful not to let the paper ignite, and yet do not have it so far from the coals that the meat will not cook. This is best accomplished by holding the broiler near the coals and turning often: that is, about once in twenty seconds. There is no danger that the paper will catch fire if the broiler is turned often enough. A chop three quarters of an inch thick will cook in *five* minutes, one an inch thick in *eight*. Should the paper catch fire, it need not destroy the chop. Take it out, put it into a fresh paper, and try again. The chop should be served very hot, seasoned with salt and pepper.

LAMB CHOPS

Lamb chops are very delicate and tender. They may be known by the lighter color of the flesh as compared with mutton chops, and by the whiteness of the fat. Prepare and broil them in the same way that mutton chops are broiled, except that they are to be *well done* instead of rare, and to accomplish this longer cooking by about three minutes will be required: for a chop an inch thick, from *eight* to *ten* minutes, instead of from four to six as for mutton.

STEWS

CHICKEN STEW

1 Cup of chicken meat.
1 Teaspoon of chopped onion.
2 Tablespoons of white turnip.
1 Saltspoon of curry-powder.
½ Teaspoon of salt.
A little white pepper.
1 Tablespoon of rice.

Left-over broiled chicken or the cuttings from a cold roast will do for this dish. Divide the meat into small pieces, excluding all skin, gristle, tendons, and bone. Boil the bones and scraps, in water enough to cover them, for an hour. Then strain the liquor, skim off the fat, and put into it the chicken, onion, turnip (which should be cut in small cubes), curry-powder, salt, pepper, and rice. Simmer all together for an hour. Serve. The vegetables and curry flavor the meat, and a most easily digested and palatable dish is the result.

Potatoes may be substituted for the rice, and celery-salt, bay-leaves, or sweet marjoram for the curry. If herbs be used, tie them in a bag and drop it into the stew, of course removing it before carrying the dish to the table.

The above rule will make enough stew for two persons. By multiplying each item in it, any amount may be made.

BEEF STEW

Use for beef stew either cold beefsteak, the portions left from a roast, or uncooked meat.

1 Cup of beef cut into small pieces.
1 Teaspoon of minced onion.
2 Tablespoons of turnip.
2 Tablespoons of carrot.
½ Teaspoon of salt.
½ Cup of cut potatoes.
A little black pepper.

If beefsteak is selected, free it from fat, gristle, and bone, and cut it into small pieces. Fry the onion, carrot, and turnip (which should be cut into small cubes) in a little butter, slowly, until they are brown. Add them to the meat, cover it with water, and simmer for one hour. Then skim off the fat, put in the potatoes (cut in half-inch cubes) and the salt and pepper. Boil for half an hour more. Serve in a covered dish with croutons.

The vegetables are fried partly to give the desirable brown color to the stew, and partly because their flavor is finer done that way. A beefsteak stew is a very savory and satisfactory dish. If fresh, uncooked meat is used, cut it into small pieces and fry it in a hot buttered pan for a few minutes, to brown the outside and thus obtain the agreeable flavor that is developed in all meats by a high temperature. Simmer two and a half hours before putting in the potatoes.

When the left-over portions of a roast are used, the meat should be freed from all gristle, bone, and fat; these may be boiled separately for additional broth.

MUTTON STEW

Exactly the same rule may be followed for mutton stew as for beef. Do not forget to trim the meat carefully. Use only clear pieces of the lean. If a roast is used and there are bones, boil them in water with the scraps for additional broth. Mutton stew is good made with pearl-barley instead of potatoes, in the proportion of one teaspoon of grain to a cup of meat; it should be put in at the beginning of the cooking. A half teaspoon of chopped parsley is a nice addition, or a few tablespoons of stewed and strained tomato.

SWEETBREADS

Sweetbreads are the pancreatic glands of the calf. They are good while the animal lives on milk, but change their nature when it begins to eat grass and hay, and are then no longer useful for food. The gland consists of two parts, the long, slender portion called the "neck" sweetbread, and the round, thick part known as the "heart" sweetbread. These are sometimes sold separately, but they should be together. Among epicures sweetbreads are considered a dainty, and are certainly a most acceptable form of food for the sick.

To Prepare. As soon as sweetbreads come from market, they should be cleaned and parboiled. Cut off any refuse,—such as pipes, fat, and all bruised portions,—and wash them quickly in cold water. Pour into a saucepan some boiling water, salt it, and add a little lemon-juice or vinegar (not more than a teaspoon to a pint of water); boil the sweetbreads in this for fifteen minutes if they are to be creamed, broiled, or baked, or again cooked in any way; but if they are to be served plain with peas, they should remain on twenty-five or thirty minutes. When done, drain off the water and set them aside to cool. Sweetbreads must always be parboiled as soon as possible after being taken from the animal, as they decay quickly. Sweetbreads may be made white by soaking them in cold water for half an hour; the flavor, however, is said to be injured by so doing.

CREAMED SWEETBREADS

Make a *cream sauce* with a cup of sweet cream, a tablespoon of flour, and half a tablespoon of butter. Then cut a sweetbread into half-inch cubes, salt it slightly, and sprinkle on a little white pepper. Mix equal quantities of it and the cream sauce together, put the mixture into individual porcelain patty-dishes or scallop-dishes, sprinkle the top with buttered crumbs, and bake on the grate in a hot oven for ten minutes. This will give sufficient time to finish the cooking of the parboiled sweetbread without hardening it.

The sauce may be made quite acceptably with milk, by using a tablespoon of butter instead of half that quantity. This is a good way to prepare sweetbreads, and one particularly desirable for the sick. They will be tender and delicate if care is taken not to overcook them in either the boiling or the baking.

FRICASSEED SWEETBREADS

Cut a parboiled sweetbread into half-inch cubes. Then make a sauce with half a teaspoon of flour, a teaspoon of butter, three fourths of a cup of strong chicken broth, and one fourth of a cup of sweet cream. Heat the broth. Cook the flour in the butter, letting the two simmer together until brown, then add the hot broth, a little at a time, stirring constantly, and last put in the cream. Season the sauce with a bit of salt, a little black pepper, half a teaspoon of lemon-juice, and a speck of curry-powder. Roll the cut sweetbread into it, simmer for five minutes, and serve on sippets, or on squares of dry toast in a covered dish. The chicken broth may be made by boiling the bones and cuttings of a roast, and milk may be substituted for the cream.

SWEETBREADS WITH PEAS

A favorite way of serving sweetbreads is with fresh peas. They should be boiled in salted water and arranged in the middle of a platter with the peas (cooked and seasoned) around them. Serve them with a cream sauce. Or the peas may be piled in the middle of a platter, the sweetbreads arranged as a border, and the sauce poured around the whole. Sweetbreads larded and baked may also be served in this way.

FISH

Fish fresh from the lakes or sea is excellent food. The point of freshness is a very important one, for all kinds spoil quickly, and, unless you can be quite sure how long they have been out of the water, it is better to find some other food for your invalid. Some shell-fish, such as crabs and lobsters, are especially dangerous, and should not be eaten by either sick or well, unless they are *known* to be in perfect condition. For the sick they had better not be used at all.

"The flesh of good fresh fish is *firm* and *hard*, and will rise at once when pressed with the finger. If the eyes be dull or sunken, the gills pale, and the flesh soft and flabby, the fish is not fresh." (Mrs. Lincoln.)

Fish with red blood, such for instance as *salmon*, are highly nutritious but not easily digested, partly because of the amount of fat distributed through the flesh. *Herring* and *mackerel* belong to this class. White fish, such as *cod, haddock, turbot, halibut,* and *flounder*, contain comparatively little fat, and that mostly in the liver. They are easy of digestion, and possess a delicate flavor. When in season and just from their native element, these fish are delicious, and make excellent food for the sick, on account of the ease with which they are digested.

To Prepare. If fish be brought from market with the scales on, as is usually the case, it is a very easy matter to remove them. A large sheet of brown paper, or a newspaper, and a knife not very sharp, are all that are necessary. Spread the paper on the table, lay the fish upon it, and then with the blade of the knife held *parallel* with the body of the fish, or nearly so, not at right angles to it, push off the scales. They will come off easily, and will not fly unless you turn the edge of the knife too much. Should this happen, the paper will catch the scales, and when the fish is finished all the refuse can be rolled up in the paper and burned. After removing the scales, cut off the head, fins, and tail. Make a slit on the under side, and take out the contents of the cavity, clearing out everything that is not flesh. Then wash the fish quickly in a stream of cold water, wipe it, and set it in a cool place (a refrigerator if you have it) until it is required for cooking. Do not lay it directly on ice, for the juices of the fish are dissolved by the water which is formed as the ice melts, and its delicate flavor is thus impaired.

WHEN IN SEASON

Cod	All the year.
Haddock	All the year.
Cusk	Winter.
Halibut	All the year.
Flounders	All the year.
Salmon	May to September.
Shad	Spring.
Bluefish	June to October.
Whitefish	Winter.
Swordfish	July to September.
Smelts	September to March.
Perch	Spring and summer.
Mackerel	April to October.
Oysters	September to May.
Clams	All the year.

BROILED FISH

Small fish, such as perch, scrod (young cod), etc., are excellent broiled. After the fish is cleaned, washed out, and wiped, split it lengthwise if it be thick, sprinkle on salt and pepper, squeeze over it some drops of lemon-juice, dip it in melted butter, and broil over clear coals, quickly at first and then very slowly, allowing ten minutes for each inch of thickness. Serve with butter cream.

To Make Butter Cream. Cream some butter in a cup or bowl, season it with salt, Cayenne pepper, lemon-juice, and vinegar. A teaspoon of butter is enough for an ordinary small fish such as a perch, and to season it a speck of cayenne, a speck of salt, and a teaspoon of vinegar and lemon-juice (half of each), will be good proportions. Spread it on the fish, and let it melt and run over it, or serve it separately in a little ball on a glass butter-plate. A nice addition to the butter is a little finely minced parsley, or chopped pickle, such as cucumbers or olives, or the three mixed, if they are at hand.

CREAMED FISH

To make creamed fish, any white fish which flakes easily may be used. Cusk, cod, and haddock are especially recommended. Cook the fish fifteen or twenty minutes by gentle boiling. Then remove the flesh carefully from the bones, letting it separate into flakes; season it with pepper and salt, and a few drops of lemon-juice sprinkled over. For every pint of prepared fish make a rich cream sauce with four tablespoons of butter, two of flour, and a pint of milk in which a small slice of onion has been boiled. Pour the sauce over the seasoned fish, rolling them together gently so that the flakes may not be broken, arrange on a platter, sprinkle the top with buttered crumbs, and bake in a hot oven from twenty minutes to half an hour. A speck of cayenne is a good addition to make to the sauce. This is a delicious and wholesome dish. The butter is so thoroughly incorporated with the flour of the sauce that it becomes one of the few very easily digested forms of cooked fat.

BOILED FISH

Select any white fish — fresh cod for instance. Prepare it according to the directions given for cleaning fish, put it into a wire vegetable-basket, drop the basket into a dish of boiling salted water, and let it simmer for from fifteen minutes to three quarters of an hour according to the size of the fish (a cod weighing three pounds will require cooking a half hour). Do not allow it to boil rapidly at any time, or it will break. When it is done lift it out of the basket and serve it at once with drawn butter made in the following manner:

Put two tablespoons of butter and one of flour into a saucepan; let them simmer together for two minutes (count the time); then add, a little at a time, a pint of boiling water or of chicken broth, stirring constantly. This will give a smooth cream-like sauce which will be enough for two pounds of fish. Season it with parsley, grated yolks of hard-boiled eggs, a few drops of lemon-juice, a bit each of cayenne and mustard, and a few drops of onion-juice.

CUSTARDS, CREAMS, PUDDINGS, AND BLANC-MANGE

SOFT CUSTARD
(BOILED)

Soft custard is a nutritious dish made of yolk of egg and milk. It is frequently used as a sauce for puddings, but is very good, eaten by itself, for one who is confined to light or liquid diet.

> 1 Pint of milk.
> Yolks of two eggs.
> 2 Tablespoons of sugar.
> 1 Saltspoon of salt.

Put the milk into a saucepan, and set it on the stove to boil. Beat together the yolks of the eggs, the salt, and the sugar, in a bowl, and when the milk just reaches the boiling-point, pour it in slowly, stirring until all is mixed. Return it to the saucepan without delay, and cook for *three minutes*, meanwhile stirring it slowly. Carefully endeavor not to either overcook or undercook the custard, for if it is not cooked enough, it will have a raw, unpleasant, "eggy" taste, and if it is cooked too much, it will have the appearance of being curdled. If there is no unnecessary delay in pouring the milk into the egg so that not much of its heat is lost, and if it is returned immediately to the fire, three minutes' exposure to the heat will usually be long enough, but of course the time will vary according to the condition of the fire and the kind of pan used. When done, strain it at once into a cool dish, and flavor it with a teaspoon of vanilla. Soft custard may also be flavored with sherry wine, almond extract, cinnamon-bark, caramel, and nutmeg. It should be of a smooth and even consistency, and as thick as rich cream.

BAKED CUSTARD
(IN CUPS)

1 Pint of milk.
2 Eggs.
1 Saltspoon of salt.
2 Tablespoons of sugar.
½ Square inch of cinnamon-bark.

Put the cinnamon and milk together in a saucepan, and set on the stove to heat. Break the eggs into a bowl, add the salt and sugar, and beat them until well mixed, but not light. When the milk boils, pour it on the beaten egg, stir slowly for a minute to dissolve the sugar, and then strain it into custard-cups. Place the cups in a deep iron baking-pan, and pour *boiling* water around, until it reaches almost to their tops. Bake in a hot oven twenty minutes.

The blue baking-cups which are small at the bottom and widen toward the top are good ones to use. They bear the fire well, and are pretty enough to serve.

By baking the custards in a dish of boiling water, the temperature cannot rise higher than 212° Fahr., and there is less danger of hardening the albumen in the more exposed portions before the middle is cooked enough, than if water is not used. The top is sacrificed—somewhat overcooked—for the sake of the pretty brown color which they should always have. Custards, when done, should be of a perfectly smooth, even, velvety consistence throughout, not curdled or wheyey.

To test them after they have been cooking twenty minutes, dip a pointed knife into water, and plunge it into the middle of the custard. If it comes out clean, the custard is done; if milky, it is not cooked enough, and should be put into the oven for five minutes longer. Do not try every one unless the cups are of different sizes, and make a small, narrow slit, so that their appearance will not be too much injured. This mixture may also be baked in a pudding-dish. Baked custards may be flavored with a variety of substances, among the best of which are grated nutmeg, almond extract, vanilla, and caramel.

To Make Caramel. Boil together one cup of sugar and one third of a cup of water until the color is a rich reddish brown, then add one cup of water, and bottle for use. Two tablespoons of this syrup will be required to flavor a pint of custard.

FRENCH CUSTARD

Make a custard mixture according to the above rule, omitting the cinnamon. Put into the bottom of the custard-cups in which it is to be baked, a teaspoon of raspberry jam. Then with a tunnel pour the custard in slowly. Bake twenty minutes. The jam, if firm, will not mix with the custard. It imparts a nice flavor to the whole, and is an interesting dish to many, who wonder how the jam can be kept from dissolving.

RENNET CUSTARD OR SLIP

Put into a glass pudding-dish a pint of milk, a tablespoon of sugar, and a teaspoon of rennet. Stir to dissolve the sugar, cover it and place it on the stove-hearth, or any warm place, to heat sufficiently for the rennet to act upon the casein of the milk—that is, to about 98° Fahr. As soon as it is "set," or becomes solid, remove to a cool place, so that the separation of the casein shall not go too far and whey appear. When it is cool, serve it in glass dishes. Rennet custard may be flavored with nutmeg grated over the surface, or by stirring in with the rennet a teaspoon of vanilla, or of rose-water, or a tablespoon of wine. When brandy is added, it is called *junket*.

Liquid rennet is an extract of the inner lining of the stomach of the calf. It has the power of freeing the albuminous part of milk from its solution,— in other words, of coagulating it. Rennet custard is not of course strictly a custard; it is also called slip, and in Cape Cod it bears the graphic name of "Gap-and-swallow."

EGG CREAM

2 Eggs.
2 Tablespoons of sugar.
Juice and grated rind of half a lemon.

Separate the yolks of the eggs from the whites, and beat them with the sugar in a bowl until both are well mixed. Then put in the lemon-juice and rind, and place the bowl in a dish of boiling water on the fire. Stir slowly until the mixture begins to thicken; then add the beaten whites of the eggs and stir for two minutes, or until the whole resembles *very thick* cream; then remove it from the fire, pour into a small pudding-dish, and set it away to cool. Serve in small pretty china cups, or small glass dishes, for a mid-afternoon lunch or for tea.

VELVET CREAM

¼ Box of gelatine.
¼ Cup of cold water.
¼ Cup of sherry wine.
1 Teaspoon of lemon-juice.
½ Cup of sugar.
1¼ Cups of creamy milk, or
1½ Cups of sweet cream.

Soak the gelatine in the cold water in a bowl for half an hour; then pour in the wine, and set the bowl in a dish of boiling water on the fire. When the gelatine is dissolved, put in the lemon-juice and sugar, stir for a minute to dissolve the sugar, and then strain it through a fine wire strainer into a granite or other metal pan. Set the pan in a dish of ice and water to cool. As soon as it begins to thicken, or is about the consistency of molasses on a warm day, turn in the cream and stir regularly and constantly until it begins to thicken. Before it is quite as hard as it will become, turn it into a glass or pretty china dish, in which it may be served, and set it away in the refrigerator or back in the dish of ice and water until perfectly firm. Serve it in small glass or china dishes, with sweet cream poured over. This cream should be of a perfectly smooth, even consistency, hence the name "velvet cream."

COFFEE CREAM

¼ Box of gelatine.
¼ Cup of cold water.
½ Cup of strong coffee.

½ Cup of sugar.
1½ Cups of sweet cream, or
1¼ Cups of creamy milk.

Soak the gelatine in the cold water for half an hour. Then pour on the coffee, boiling hot, to dissolve it; add the sugar, stir until it is dissolved, and strain the liquid into a granite pan. Set it in iced water to cool; when it has become so, and is beginning to thicken, or is about the consistency of syrup or a little thinner, pour in the cream; stir regularly and evenly for about ten minutes, or until it is thick, but not hard; then turn it into a glass dish while it is still slightly soft, and it will settle into a smooth, even mass. It may be returned to the iced water, or put into a refrigerator, to stiffen.

Coffee cream is similar to velvet cream and the process is exactly the same for both. They are delicious creams, very nutritious, and to be recommended for their excellent nourishing properties and flavors.

To Make the Coffee. Mix two tablespoons of ground fresh Java, or Java and Mocha coffee mixed, with a little cold water and raw egg (either white or yolk) in a coffee-pot. Stir it to thoroughly mix the egg and coffee. Pour in a cup of boiling water, and set it to boil for five minutes. Then move the pot to a less hot part of the stove, where the coffee will barely simmer, for ten minutes, when it will be ready for use.

CHOCOLATE CREAM

2 Tablespoons of sugar.
½ Ounce (½ square) of Baker's chocolate.
1 Pint of cream.
Whites of four eggs.

Cook the sugar, chocolate, and cream (sweet cream or, if that cannot be had, rich milk) together in a double boiler until the chocolate is perfectly dissolved. It will require occasional stirring, and should be, when done, entirely free from specks or flakes of chocolate. Then stir in, pouring slowly, the well-beaten whites of the eggs while the cream is still on the stove. Cook for three minutes, or until the albumen is coagulated, but not hardened. It should look creamy and smooth, not curdled. Turn into a pudding-dish and cool.

TAPIOCA CREAM

¼ Cup of granulated tapioca.
¼ Cup of cold water.
1 Pint of milk.
3 Tablespoons of sugar.
1 Saltspoon of salt.
2 Eggs.

After the tapioca is picked over and washed, put it into a double boiler with the cold water, and let it stand until the water is absorbed. Then pour in the pint of milk, and cook until each grain is transparent and soft. It will take an hour. At this point, beat the eggs, sugar, and salt together until very light, and pour them slowly into the hot pudding, at the same time stirring rapidly, so that the two will be perfectly mixed. After the egg is in, continue to stir for about three minutes, or long enough to cook the egg as it is done in soft custard. The pudding should have the appearance of cream, as the name indicates, with flecks of tapioca all through it. Turn it into a china dish. Serve either hot or cold.

RICE CREAM

2 Tablespoons of rice.
2 Cups of milk.
1 Saltspoon of salt.
2 Tablespoons of sugar.
2 Eggs.

Cleanse the rice by washing it several times in cold water; cook it in a double boiler with the milk until the grains will mash. Three hours will generally be required to do this. Should the milk evaporate, restore the amount lost. When the rice is perfectly soft, press it through a coarse soup-strainer or colander into a saucepan, return it to the fire, and while it is heating beat the eggs, sugar, and salt together until very light. When the rice boils, pour the egg in rather slowly, stirring lightly with a spoon for three or four minutes, or until it coagulates and the whole is like a thick, soft pudding; then remove from the fire, and pour it into a pretty dish. By omitting the yolks and using the whites of the eggs only, a delicate white cream is obtained.

PEACH FOAM
(DELICIOUS)

Peel and cut into small pieces three or four choice and very ripe peaches (White Heaths are good), so that when done there will be a cupful. Put them into a bowl, with half a cup of powdered sugar, and the white of one egg. Beat with a fork for *half an hour*, when it will be a thick, perfectly smooth, velvety cream, with a delightful peach flavor, and may be eaten *ad libitum* by an invalid.

SNOW PUDDING

¼ Box of gelatine.
¼ Cup of cold water.
1 Cup of boiling water.
1 Cup of sugar.
¼ Cup of lemon-juice.
Whites of three eggs.[1]

For the sauce :

Yolks of two eggs.
2 Tablespoons of sugar.
½ Saltspoon of salt.
1 Pint of milk.
½ Teaspoon of vanilla.

Divide a box of gelatine into fourths by notching one of the upright edges. Cut off one fourth of the box for a measure, which can afterward be used as a cover. When taking out a fourth, be sure to pack the measure as closely as it was packed in the box. Soak the gelatine in the cold water for half an hour. Then pour on the boiling water, add the sugar and lemon-juice, stir for a minute, and strain through a fine wire strainer into a granite pan; place the pan in iced water to cool. Meanwhile beat the eggs as light as possible, and as soon as the gelatine mixture begins to thicken, or is about as thick as honey, turn in the eggs, and stir slowly and regularly, with the back of the bowl of the spoon against the bottom of the pan, until the egg is mixed completely with the gelatine and the whole nearly stiff. Just before it becomes firm turn it into a melon-mold, and return it to the iced water to harden. It should be perfectly white, *literally,* like snow.

[1] From Mrs. Lincoln's "Boston Cook Book."

With the materials for the sauce make a soft custard, cool it, and serve with the pudding either in a pitcher, or poured around it in an ice-cream dish, or other shallow pudding-dish.

PRINCESS PUDDING

¼ Box of gelatine.
¼ Cup of cold water.
¾ Cup of boiling water.
1 Cup of sugar.
½ Cup of white wine (sherry).
Juice of one lemon.
Whites of three eggs.

For the sauce:

1 Pint of milk.
Yolks of two eggs.
3 Tablespoons of sugar.
1 Saltspoon of salt.
1 Teaspoon of rose-water.

The process is exactly the same as for *snow pudding*, and it is served in the same manner, with the soft custard for a sauce. Ordinary sherry wine may be used, although white sherry is better.

CORN-STARCH PUDDING

1½ Tablespoons of corn-starch.
1 Tablespoon of sugar.
1 Saltspoon of salt.
2 Tablespoons of cold water.
1 Pint of milk.

Put the milk on the stove to heat. Mix in a saucepan the corn-starch, sugar, and salt with the cold water, and when the milk has just begun to boil pour it in, slowly at first, stirring all the while. The corn-starch should become thick at once, when it may be poured into a clean double boiler and cooked thirty minutes. The time should be faithfully kept, as corn-starch is an unpalatable and indigestible substance unless thoroughly cooked. See to it that the water in the under boiler *actually boils* during the thirty minutes. At the end of that time beat one egg very light, and stir it in, pouring slowly, so that it may be mixed all through the hot pudding and puff it up. Then cook for one minute, turn it into a china pudding-dish, or into individual molds, and cool. Serve with cream.

Corn-starch pudding should have a tender consistency and a sweet and wholesome taste. The difficulty with many is that they are not thoroughly cooked, and are too stiff and hard when cool. When you find this to be the case, lessen the amount of corn-starch used. The proportion in this recipe may always be relied upon.

Other similar puddings may be made by substituting in the above recipe arrowroot, flour, or farina for the corn-starch.

BARLEY PUDDING

2 Tablespoons of Robinson's barley flour.
1 Tablespoon of sugar.
1 Saltspoon of salt.
1 Cup of water (boiling).
½ Cup of rich milk.
Whites of three eggs.

Mix the flour, sugar, and salt in a saucepan with a little cold water. When smooth and free from lumps pour in the boiling water, slowly stirring meanwhile to keep it smooth; then set it on the fire to simmer for ten minutes, continuing the stirring until it is thick. To prevent burning, draw the pan to the side of the stove, unless the fire is very slow, for barley is a grain which sticks and burns easily. At the end of the ten minutes put in the milk, and strain all into a clean saucepan, through a coarse strainer, to make the consistency even. Beat the whites of the eggs until light but not stiff, and stir, not beat, them into the pudding, making it thoroughly smooth before returning it to the fire. Cook for five minutes, stirring and folding the pudding lightly until the egg is coagulated. Then pour it into a china pudding-dish. Serve cold with sweet cream. This is good for one who is just beginning to eat solid food.

CREAM-OF-RICE PUDDING

1 Quart of milk.
½ Cup of rice.
2 Tablespoons of sugar.
1 Saltspoon of salt.

Put the milk, rice, sugar, and salt together in a pudding-dish, stir until the sugar is dissolved, then place the dish in a pan of water, and bake in a slow oven for three hours, cutting in the crust which forms on the top once during the time. Should the pudding become dry, pour over it a little more milk, but this will not happen unless the fire is too hot. When done it ought to be creamy inside, with the grains of rice almost dissolved in the milk. The long exposure to heat changes both the sugar and the starch, and gives them an agreeable flavor.

FRUIT TAPIOCA

Wash half a cup of tapioca, put it into a double boiler with a pint of water, and cook until the grains are soft and transparent. If granulated tapioca is used, one hour is sufficient time. Then add to it half a cup of grape or currant jelly, and mix until the jelly is dissolved; turn it into a pudding-dish. Serve cold, with sugar and cream. Any well-flavored fruit jelly may be used instead of the grape or currant.

TAPIOCA JELLY

½ Cup of tapioca.
2 Cups of water.
½ Cup of sugar.
Juice and grated rind of half a lemon.
¼ Cup of sherry wine, or
¼ Cup of brandy (French).

Pick over and wash the tapioca. Put it into a double boiler with the water, and cook it for one hour, or until the grains are transparent and soft. Then add to it the sugar, juice and grated rind of the lemon, the sherry and the brandy, mixing them thoroughly. Press all through a wire strainer into a glass pudding-dish, and set it in a cool place to become a jelly. It should be served cold, and with cream.

ORANGE LAYERS

4 Oranges.
3 Bananas.
1 Cup of sugar.
⅓ Cup of water.
1 Cup of claret wine.

Peel the oranges, slice them in thin slices, and remove the seeds. Peel and slice the bananas. Arrange both in alternate layers in a glass dish. Make a syrup of the sugar and water by boiling them together, without stirring, for ten minutes; then add the wine, and remove at once from the fire; cool it, and pour it over the fruit. In half an hour it will be ready to serve.

It will not do to keep this dish long, as the fruit shrinks and loses its freshness. One fourth of an inch is the proper thickness for the slices of orange, and one sixth or one eighth for the bananas.

ORANGE BASKETS

From the end opposite the stem end of an orange cut out sections in such a way as to form a basket with a handle.

The body of the basket should be *more* than *half* the orange. With a knife and spoon cut and scrape out all the pulp from the inside. Fill the baskets with blocks of orange jelly, or with raspberries, strawberries, or other fruits. They are pleasing to children, and are pretty for luncheon or tea. The edges may be scalloped, and diamonds or rounds cut out of the sides, if one has time.

IRISH MOSS BLANC-MANGE

Irish moss, or carrageen, is a sea moss which grows abundantly along the shores of Europe and America. After gathering, it is dried and bleached in the sun, and then packed for market. It is exceedingly rich in an easily digested vegetable jelly, and is also valuable for food because of its mineral constituents.

To Prepare.

⅓ Cup of dry moss.
1 Quart of milk.
¼ Cup of sugar.

Soak the moss for half an hour in warm water, to soften it and to loosen the sand which is dried and entangled in it. Wash each piece separately under a stream of cold water. Its weight (that of the water) will carry down the sand. Then put the moss in a pudding-bag, and cook it in a double boiler in the quart of milk for one hour. At the end of that time lift out the bag, squeeze it a little, throw away the moss, and put the bag to soak in cold water. Add the sugar to the mixture, strain it into molds, and set in a cool place to harden. It will form a tender jelly-like pudding, which has an agreeable taste, resembling the odor of the sea, which many like. Serve it with cream, and with or without pink sugar.[1]

This blanc-mange may also be made without sugar if it is desirable to have an unsweetened dessert.

---

[1] Pink sugar may be made by putting a few drops of carmine into a cup of powdered sugar, and sifting it several times until the carmine is entirely distributed through it.

PINK BLANC-MANGE

Make a pudding according to the above rule. Color it, just before straining, with three or four drops of carmine, barely enough to give a delicate shell pink, for if it is very dark it is not attractive.

Carmine for use in cooking is made by mixing one ounce of No. 40 carmine (which may be obtained of a druggist) with three ounces of boiling water and one ounce of ammonia. It should be bottled, and will keep indefinitely. It is useful for coloring ice-cream, cake, and puddings.

SALADS

Salads are of two classes: the plain salads, consisting of green herbs or vegetables, such as lettuce, endive, water-cress, cucumber, etc., dressed or seasoned with salt, pepper, oil and vinegar, or oil and lemon-juice; and the so-called meat salads, which consist of one or more green vegetables, with an admixture of fish, lobster, crab, fowl, or game. A salad of whichever kind should be cool, delicate, and prepared by a gentle hand. Ordinary servants do not enough appreciate the "niceties" to make acceptable salads. The lettuce, cress, or whatever green is used, should be thoroughly washed, but not crushed, broken, or roughly handled, drained in a wire basket, dried in a napkin, and then torn with the fingers, *not cut*. Of course, cucumbers, beet-root, olives, etc., are exceptions.

The dressing for salads, whether simply oil and vinegar, or a mayonnaise, should be mixed with a wooden spoon, and an intelligent mind. As for the seasonings, the Spanish maxim which reads as follows is a good guide: "Be a miser with vinegar, a counselor with salt, and a spendthrift with oil." Let the oil be of the first quality of genuine olive-oil. In nearly all the large cities one may get fine oil by searching for it. Once found, there is no longer any difficulty, so long as the brand does not deteriorate.

To vary and flavor the salads of vegetables *only*, use the fine herbs when in season, for instance balm, mint, parsley, cress, and sorrel, chopped or minced, and scattered through the salad. Unless the vinegar is known to be pure cider or wine vinegar, use lemon-juice. Theodore Child says: "Lemon-juice is the most delicate and deliciously perfumed acid that nature has given the cook."

FRENCH DRESSING

French dressing is a mixture of fine olive-oil, vinegar or lemon-juice, or both, salt, Cayenne pepper, and onion-juice. The following proportions will make enough for one head of lettuce:

> 1 Tablespoon of oil.
> A bit of cayenne.
> ½ Saltspoon of salt.
> 4 Drops of onion-juice.
> 1 Teaspoon of lemon-juice.
> 1 Teaspoon of vinegar.

Mix all together well. This dressing may be used with lettuce, tomatoes, cold meat, potato salad, and to marinate chicken, lobster, and crab when they are to be used for salads.

MAYONNAISE DRESSING

> ½ Saltspoon of salt.
> 2 Saltspoons of mustard.
> 2 Saltspoons of sugar.
> ¼ Saltspoon of cayenne.
> Yolk of one egg.
> ½ Cup of olive-oil.
> 2 Tablespoons of lemon-juice.
> 1 Tablespoon of vinegar.
> 1 Tablespoon of thick sweet cream.

These proportions may be multiplied or divided to make larger or smaller quantities. Put the first five ingredients together in a bowl, and mix them well; then add the oil one drop at a time, stirring constantly with a wooden paddle or spoon "round and round," not back and forth. After dropping and stirring for ten minutes, the mixture will become stiff and difficult to turn. At this point stir in a little of the vinegar or lemon-juice. Then drop in more oil, and stir until it again becomes stiff. Continue putting in oil and the acids until all are used, when you should have a thick, smooth cream which, when taken up on the end of the spoon, will keep its shape and not "run." It will take from twenty minutes to half an hour to make it. Last stir in the cream.

Should the dressing "break," or appear as if curdled, it may sometimes be restored to smoothness by beating with a Dover egg-beater, or by adding more egg and stirring for a while without adding oil. If these expedients fail, begin all over again, adding the spoiled dressing to a new one. However, a mayonnaise dressing will not go wrong except in the hands of a careless worker. The only points to be observed are to put the oil in *slowly*, and to stir *constantly* and *rapidly*. The sweet cream is a valuable addition, giving the mayonnaise a delicate, satisfying flavor.

LETTUCE SALAD

Prepare a head of lettuce by washing each leaf separately in a stream of water, tearing off any portion that is bruised or brown, and looking carefully for little green creatures that may be lodged in the creases; they are not easily seen. Then drain the lettuce on a fresh towel or napkin, for if the leaves are very wet the dressing will not cling to them. Next tear it to pieces with the fingers, rejecting the large part of the midrib, put it into a deep bowl, pour on a French dressing, and toss it with a wooden salad-spoon and fork until all the lettuce seems oiled. Serve immediately.

Mayonnaise dressing may be used instead of the French dressing in this salad.

TOMATO SALAD

Wash in cold water and wipe some fair, ripe tomatoes. Cut them in slices one third of an inch thick. Do not peel them. Arrange some clean white lettuce leaves on a silver or china platter, with two large leaves at either end, their stems toward the middle, and two small ones at the sides. Lay on them the slices of tomato, with their edges overlapping each other. Serve with this salad French dressing.

CHICKEN SALAD

Prepare a nice chicken (one not too young) by boiling it until tender. Then set it away in its own broth to cool. (It is a good plan to boil the chicken the day before it is intended for use.) Meanwhile make a mayonnaise dressing. When the chicken has become cold, take it from the broth, and cut it as nearly as possible into half-inch cubes, rejecting all skin, tendons, cords, and bones. Season it with salt and pepper. Tear into small pieces with the fingers some tender, well-cleaned lettuce, and then mix equal quantities of chicken and lettuce with a part of the dressing; arrange it in a shallow salad-bowl, and spread the remainder of the mayonnaise over the top. The yolk of egg hard-boiled and pressed through a wire strainer with the back of a spoon, so that it falls in little crinkled pieces all over the top, makes a pretty garnish. Celery tops, the tiny inside leaves of lettuce, and parsley may be used singly or together for a border.

Chicken salad is usually made with celery instead of lettuce, but the latter is better for an invalid, although tender, delicate celery may be used. Serve a very small quantity, for chicken salad is a concentrated food, and should not be eaten in large amounts by either the convalescent or the well. The chicken, lettuce, and dressing may all be prepared beforehand, but on no account should they be mixed together until just before serving.

POTATO SALAD

For this salad fresh boiled potatoes, red sugar-beets, and French dressing are needed. The potatoes and beets should be cooked in salted water purposely for the salad, and allowed to become just cool. Cold potatoes left over from the last meal may be used, but they are not nice. When the potatoes are cool, cut them into thin slices, season with a little more salt and a bit of white pepper; cut the beets also in thin slices, and mix the two in the proportions of one third beets to two thirds potatoes, with the dressing, or arrange them in alternate layers in a salad-bowl, with the dressing poured over each layer as it is made.

A more dainty way, and one which a person of cultivated taste will appreciate (as it really makes a perceptible difference in the flavor of the salad), is to mix the lemon-juice, vinegar, salt, and pepper together without the oil, and pour it over the different layers as they are laid, and then add the oil by itself. The acids penetrate and season the vegetables, and the oil is left on the outside of each piece.

POTATO SALAD WITH OLIVES

Make a potato salad according to the foregoing rule, except substitute chopped olives for the beets, in the proportion of one eighth olives by measure to seven eighths potato.

CELERY SALAD

"One of the finest salads to be eaten, either alone or with game, especially partridges or wild duck, is a mixture of celery, beet-root, and corn-salad. Watercresses will make a poor substitute when broken into small tufts.

"The beets are cut into slices one sixteenth of an inch thick; the celery, which must be young and tender and thoroughly white, should be cut into pieces an inch long, and then sliced lengthwise into two or three pieces. (N. B.—Select only the tender inside branches of celery.) This salad will require plenty of oil, and more acid than a lettuce salad, because of the sweetness and absorbent nature of the beet-root. The general seasoning, too, must be rather high, because the flavors of the celery and the beet are pronounced." ("Delicate Feasting," by Theodore Child.)

There are many kinds of salads, but they are all based upon the principles stated in these rules. Green herbs or vegetables treated with French or mayonnaise dressing, either by themselves or with meats, form the foundations of all salads.

ICE-CREAM, SHERBETS, AND ICES

For patients suffering with fevers, and for use in very warm weather, good ice-cream and sherbet are most acceptable. They should, however, be used with great care, particularly if the illness be due to disturbance of digestion, for they lower the temperature of the stomach and often cause such disorders as lead to severe illness. Even if this does not happen, they, in order to be raised to a temperature at which digestion will take place, absorb heat from the body, and a person reduced by illness cannot afford to needlessly part with any form of energy.

Sherbet in its literal sense means a *cool drink*. It is of oriental origin, but in this country it has come to mean a frozen mixture of fruit, or fruit-juice, water and sugar. There is a distinction made, however, between water-ice and sherbet. Sherbet has, in addition to the fruit-juice and water, either sugar-syrup, white of egg, or gelatine, to give it sufficient viscousness to entangle and hold air when beaten in a freezer, so that sherbets (unless colored by the fruit used) will be white and opaque like snow. Water-ices, on the contrary, are made without the white of egg, syrup, or gelatine, do not entangle air, and are translucent and what might be called "watery." Both are delicious when made with fresh, ripe fruit, and both may be enriched by the addition of sweet cream if desired.

Freezers. Of the various kinds of freezers perhaps the "Improved White Mountain Freezer" is, everything considered, as good as any. It is strong and freezes quickly when the salt and ice are properly proportioned.

It is well to study the gearing before attempting to use a freezer. The different parts should be taken apart and put together until it is understood how the machine works. See that the paddles in the can do not interfere with each other, and that the crank turns easily. Then put all together again, fasten down the crank-bar across the top of the can, and have everything in readiness before packing the freezer with salt and ice. The object in using the salt is to get a greater degree of cold than could be obtained with the ice alone. The affinity of salt for water is very great—so great, that it will break down the structure of ice in its eagerness for it. Heat is involved in this process of melting, and will be drawn from surrounding objects, from the can, the bucket, the cream, and even the ice itself. The more rapid the union of salt and ice, the more heat is absorbed, consequently the greater is the degree of cold and the quicker the mixture to be frozen will become solid.

Water is converted into steam by a certain amount of heat. *Ice* is transformed into *water* by the same agency, and in the case of the ice-cream freezer heat is drawn from whatever comes in contact with the ice that is warmer than itself. If the melting of the ice can be hastened in any way, the abstraction of heat will be correspondingly greater; hence the use of salt, which is so eager for water that it takes it even in the form of ice. Now it will be easily seen that if the ice is in small pieces, and there is the proper amount of salt for each piece, union between the two will be immediate, the amount of heat used will be very great, consequently the degree of cold will be great. Cold is only a less degree of heat.

Ordinary liquid mixtures that contain a large percentage of water become solid when reduced to a temperature of 32° Fahr.

To Pack an Ice-Cream Freezer. Break a quantity of ice into small pieces by pounding it in an ice-bag (a bag made of canvas or very strong cloth) with a wooden mallet. The ice should be about as fine as small rock-salt. Put into the bucket, around the tin can which is to hold the cream, alternate layers of the pounded ice and salt in the proportions of two thirds ice to one third salt (a quart cup may be used for measuring). Should it happen that you have "coarse-fine" salt, put all the ice into the freezer first, and then the salt on top of it, as it will quickly work down to the bottom. When the packing is complete unfasten the cross-bar and lift off the cover of the can carefully, so that no salt shall get inside; then put in the mixture to be frozen, replace the cover, and fasten the bar. Let it stand till the mixture is thoroughly chilled, then turn *steadily* but not *very fast* for about ten minutes, or until the turning becomes difficult; that is an indication that the contents of the can are freezing. Continue turning for a few minutes longer, to give the cream a fine and even consistency; then take out the paddle, drain off the water through the hole in the side of the bucket, fill in all about the can with coarse ice, and cover it with a thick wet cloth or towel. Let it stand for half an hour to become firm, when it is ready to serve. If it is desirable to keep the ice-cream for a length of time, it may be done by packing the freezer closely with ice and salt, and covering it with wet cloths. Or, the ice-cream may be taken from the can, packed in molds of fanciful shapes, sealed at the edges with melted tallow, and repacked in ice and salt.

PHILADELPHIA ICE-CREAM

The so-called Philadelphia ice-cream is pure, sweet cream, sweetened with sugar, and flavored. For a small quantity use the following:

> ¾ Cup of sugar.
> 1 Teaspoon of vanilla.
> 1 Tablespoon of brandy.
> 1 pint of scalded sweet cream.

Mix and freeze. The whites of two eggs beaten stiff is a valuable addition to this cream.

ROYAL ICE-CREAM

> 1 Tablespoon of flour.
> 1½ Cups of sugar.
> 1 Saltspoon of salt.
> 1 Pint of milk.
> 2 Eggs.
> 1 Pint of sweet cream.
> 1 Tablespoon of vanilla.
> ½ Teaspoon of almond.
> ½ Cup of sherry wine, or
> ¼ Cup of brandy.

Heat the milk until it boils; meanwhile mix the flour, sugar, and salt in a little cold water, and when the milk reaches the boiling-point pour it in; stir it for a minute over the fire in a saucepan, and then turn it into a double boiler and cook it for twenty minutes. At the end of this time beat the eggs very light, and pour them into the boiling mixture slowly, stirring it rapidly; continue stirring, after all the egg is in, for from one to two minutes; then strain the mixture into a dish and set it aside to cool. Last, add the cream and flavorings, and freeze. This makes a rich and delicious cream. It may be colored with carmine a pretty pink, or with spinach a delicate green.

ICE-CREAM WITH AN IMPROVISED FREEZER

Make the Philadelphia ice-cream mixture, or half of it, dividing each ingredient exactly. Put it into a small tin can (the Dutch cocoa-cans are convenient) with a closely fitting cover. Place it in the middle of a deep dish, and surround it with alternate layers of ice and salt, in the same manner as for ordinary freezing, and cover it closely; then lay wet cloths on the top and set it in a cool place. It will become solid in from one to two hours, according to the amount of mixture to be frozen. It is well to cut in the thick layer on the sides of the can once or twice during the freezing. If the cream which you have to use is thick enough to whip, do so; the result, when frozen, will be a very dainty dish.

This is a convenient way of making a little ice-cream for one person.

FROZEN CUSTARD

1 Pint of milk.
1 Saltspoon of salt.
1¼ Cups of sugar.
Yolks of three eggs.
1 Pint of milk or cream.
1 Teaspoon of rose-water.
2 Tablespoons of wine or brandy.

Make a soft custard with the first four ingredients, according to the rule on page 195. When done, strain it into a granite-ware pan and let it cool. Then add the flavoring and the remaining pint of milk or cream, and freeze.

LEMON SHERBET WITH GELATINE

1 Tablespoon of gelatine.
1 Pint of boiling water.
1 Cup of sugar.
$\frac{1}{3}$ Cup of lemon-juice.
1 Tablespoon of brandy.

Soak the gelatine (Plymouth Rock or Nelson's) in a little cold water for *half an hour*. Then pour over it the boiling water, stirring until the gelatine is dissolved; add the sugar, lemon-juice, and brandy, and strain all through a fine wire strainer. Freeze.

Nelson's gelatine and the Plymouth Rock or phosphated gelatine are the best to use for sherbets and water-ices, because they have a delicate flavor, and lack the strong, fishy taste which characterizes some kinds. The phosphated gelatine should, however, never be used except when a slight acidity will do no harm. Avoid it for all dishes made with cream or milk, as it will curdle them. The directions on the packages advise neutralizing the acid with soda; but, as there is no means of determining the amount of acid in a given quantity, it is not a process that recommends itself to an intelligent person.

Phosphated gelatine may, however, be used in sherbets even when milk or cream forms a part of them, for when it is added to a slightly acid mixture which has a low temperature, or is partially frozen, curdling does not take place.

LEMON SHERBET WITH SUGAR SYRUP

1 Pint of boiling water.
1 Cup of sugar.
⅓ Cup of lemon-juice.

Boil the water and sugar together without stirring for twenty minutes. You will thus obtain a thin sugar syrup, which, however, has enough viscousness to entangle and hold air when beaten. As soon as it is cool, add the lemon-juice, strain, and freeze it. This makes a snow-white sherbet of very delicate flavor. Lemon sherbet may also be made with water, sugar, lemon-juice, and the whites of eggs well beaten, instead of with gelatine or syrup.

ORANGE SHERBET

1 Tablespoon of gelatine.
1 Cup of boiling water.
1 Cup of sugar.
1 Cup of orange-juice.
Juice of one lemon.
2 Tablespoons of brandy.

Soak the gelatine in just enough cold water to moisten it, for half an hour. Then pour over it the cup of boiling water, and put in the other ingredients in the order in which they are written; when the sugar is dissolved, strain all through a fine wire strainer, and freeze it.

To get Orange-juice. Peel the oranges, cut them in small pieces, quarters or eighths, put them into a jelly-bag or napkin, and press out the juice with the hand. By this means the oil of the rind, which has a disagreeable flavor, is excluded.

APRICOT ICE

1 Quart of apricots.
1 Quart of water.
½ Quart of sugar.
3 Tablespoons of brandy.

Either fresh or canned apricots may be used for this ice. If fresh ones are chosen, wash and wipe them carefully, cut them into small pieces, mash them with a potato-masher until broken and soft, and add the water, sugar, and brandy; then freeze. The treatment is the same if canned fruit be used. This ice may be made without the brandy, but it is a valuable addition, especially for the sick.

Peaches, strawberries, raspberries, pineapple, and in fact any soft, well-flavored fruit may be made into water-ice by following exactly the above rule, except, of course, substituting the different kinds of fruits for the apricots, and possibly varying the sugar. If pineapple is selected, it should be chopped quite fine, and quickly, so that the knife will not discolor it. Peaches should be pared, and strawberries and raspberries carefully washed. All of these ices are delicious, and most wholesome and grateful in very warm weather, or for feverish conditions when fruit is allowed. If there is a question about seeds, as might be the case in using strawberries, strain the fruit through a coarse wire strainer after it is mashed; it is advisable to do this always in making strawberry, raspberry, or pineapple ice.

COOKED FRUITS

BAKED TART APPLES

Select fair, sound, tart apples. Wash and wipe them, and cut out the cores with an apple-corer, being careful to remove everything that is not clear pulp. Sometimes the tough husk which surrounds the seeds extends farther than the instrument will reach with once cutting; this can be detected by looking into the apple, and removing with the point of the corer anything that remains. If there are dark blotches or battered places on the outside of the apple, cut them off. Everything of that kind is valueless as food, and injures the flavor of that which is good.

When they are prepared place the apples in an earthen baking dish (granite-ware will do), put a teaspoon of sugar and half an inch of dried lemon-peel, or fresh peel cut very thin, into each hole, pour boiling water into the dish until it is an inch deep, and bake in a moderately hot oven; when the skins begin to shrink and the apples are perfectly soft all the way through, they are done; then take them from the oven, arrange them in a glass dish, and pour around them the syrupy juice that is left.

The time for baking varies, according to the species of apple, from half an hour to two hours. They should be basted once or twice during the time with the water which is around them. It will nearly all evaporate while they are baking. If the apples are Baldwins, or Greenings, or any others of fine flavor, the lemon-peel may be omitted. Stick cinnamon may be used instead of lemon-peel for apples which are not quite sour.

BAKED SWEET APPLES

Prepare sweet apples according to the foregoing rule, except use a fourth of a square inch of cinnamon instead of the lemon-peel, and half a teaspoon of sugar for each apple. Sweet apples require two or three hours' baking. They should be cooked until perfectly soft, and until the juice which oozes out becomes gelatinous. Serve cold with sweet cream. Cooked apples are an excellent addition to a diet. They contain acids and salts of great value.

STEWED APPLES

Pare and quarter three slightly sour apples. Put them into a saucepan with a cup of water and two tablespoons of sugar, and stew gently until they are soft, but not broken. Each piece should be whole, but soft and tender. A tablespoon of lemon-juice put in just before they are taken from the fire is a good addition to make if the apples are poor in flavor; or, lemon-peel may be used, and also cinnamon and cloves.

APPLE COMPOTE

Wash and wipe some fair, well-flavored apples (not sweet). Core them with an apple-corer (not a knife), being careful not to leave in any of the hulls, which sometimes penetrate far into the fruit; pare them evenly, so that they will be smooth and of good shape. Then boil them gently, in water enough to just reach their tops, with a square inch or two of thin lemon-peel, and a teaspoon of sugar for each apple, until they are soft, but not broken, watching them carefully toward the last part of the cooking, lest they go to pieces. When done lift them out into a glass dish, reduce the water by further boiling until it is somewhat syrupy, and set it aside to cool. Fill the holes with apple, grape, or any bright-colored jelly, and when the syrup is cold pour it over and around the apples.

STEWED PRUNES

1 Pint of prunes.
1½ Pints of water.
¼ Cup of sugar.
2 Tablespoons of lemon-juice.

Soak the prunes in warm water for fifteen minutes, to soften the dust and dirt on the outside. Then wash them carefully with the fingers, rejecting those that feel granular (they are worm-eaten); stew them gently in the sugar and water in a covered saucepan for two hours. Just before taking them from the fire put in the lemon-juice. They should be plump, soft, and tender to the stone. As the water evaporates the amount should be restored, so that there will be as much at the end as at the beginning of the cooking. French prunes may not require quite so long time for cooking as most ordinary kinds.

CRANBERRY SAUCE AND JELLY

Pick out the soft and decayed ones from a quantity of Cape cranberries; measure a pint, and put with it *half* the bulk of sugar, and *one fourth* the bulk of water. Stew the berries ten minutes without stirring, counting the time from the moment when they are actually bubbling. Done in this way, the skins will be tender, and the juice on cooling will form a delicate jelly. Or, the fruit may be pressed through a soup-strainer and the whole made into jelly.

GRAPE SAUCE

Take any small quantity of grapes. Wash them by dipping each bunch several times in water, unless you know that they have been gathered and handled by clean hands. Separate the skins from the pulps by squeezing each grape between the fingers and thumb. Cook the pulps about five minutes, or until soft and broken. Cook the skins for the same length of time in a separate saucepan, then press the pulps through a strainer into them, until there is nothing left but the seeds. Measure the mixture, and for each measure, pint or cup, as the case may be, add half a measure of sugar, and simmer for five minutes. Many invalids who cannot eat grapes uncooked, on account of the seeds, may take them stewed in this way. More or less than the above amount of sugar may be used, according to the requirements of the individual.

GRAPE JELLY

Separate the pulps from the skins of a quantity of washed grapes. Cook each separately for a few minutes, and slowly, so as not to evaporate the juice. Press the pulps through a soup-strainer, mashing them if they are not broken, until there is nothing left but the seeds; strain into this the juice from the skins, mashing and squeezing out all that is possible. Measure the mixture, and for every cup add a cup of sugar. Put all into a granite-ware saucepan and boil slowly for ten or twelve minutes.

The time required for cooking depends upon the condition of the grapes. If they are very ripe, and it is late in the season, ten minutes is sufficient time to obtain a fine, delicate jelly; but if it is early in the autumn, and the fruit has not been as thoroughly changed by nature as late in the season, twelve or fifteen minutes will be required to obtain the same result. Even less than ten minutes' cooking will sometimes cause the pectin of the fruit to dissolve, which, on cooling, forms the jelly. The time required will always be variable, according to the condition of the fruit, so it is well to ascertain by experiment what number of minutes gives the desired result.

Another and important point to notice in making fruit jellies is, that if the fruit be cooked longer than is necessary to dissolve the jelly-forming substance, that is the pectin, the natural flavor of the fruit is more or less injured; consequently, if grapes which require only ten minutes' boiling are boiled for fifteen, the flavor is inferior to what it would be if they were exposed for the lesser time.

It is impossible to give a rule which shall at all times apply to the making of fruit jellies, on account of the always variable condition of the fruit. But in general, grapes, cranberries, currants, and similar fruits require a short time, while apples, crab-apples, lemons, and oranges will take from one and a half to three hours. One is therefore obliged to test the jelly at intervals by taking out a little on a saucer to cool. If it becomes firm quickly, the mixture is cooked enough; if not, one may get an idea, from the consistency which it has, what further cooking will be necessary.

APPLE JELLY

Wash and wipe good tart apples. Cut them in quarters or, better, eighths, but do not pare them. Stew them in half their bulk of water,— that is, if you have four quarts of cut apples, put in two quarts of water,— until the skins as well as the pulp are perfectly soft. No definite time can be given, because that depends upon the kind and ripeness of the fruit. When done, turn them into a jelly-bag and drain until the juice is all out. Measure it, and for each cup add a cup of sugar, one clove, and one square inch of thin lemon-peel. Simmer gently for half an hour, then test it, to see how near the jellying-point it is, by taking out a little into a cool saucer. With some kinds of apples it will be done in that time, with others it will take an hour or more longer. When a little becomes firm on cooling, remove the whole immediately from the fire, skim it, and strain it into jars or tumblers which have been thoroughly washed in soap and water, and have been standing in boiling water for some minutes.

When the jelly is cool, pour over the surface a thin coating of melted paraffin, let it harden, then pour in another; for, as the first hardens, it may crack or shrink from the sides and leave spaces where ferments may enter; in other words, the jars need to be made air-tight— not that the air does mischief, but because it contains the organisms which, on entering the jelly, cause by their growth the various fermentative changes known to occur in fruits. The object then will be to exclude all micro-organisms.

There are other ways of sealing jelly than by the

use of paraffin, as, for instance, with paper soaked in alcohol, or coated with oil; but paraffin, if properly used, is a sure, easy, and economical means.

A wad of sterilized cotton batting, packed into the mouth of the jar or tumbler, like a stopper, is sometimes employed, but it is not as effectual as the paraffin; for that, being poured in hot, sterilizes the surface of the jelly, thus killing any organisms that may have lodged upon it during the cooling. Organisms cannot go through batting; but, though it may be properly sterilized, it cannot be packed over the jelly until it has become firm, and during the time ferments may have settled upon it. Paraffin is a most satisfactory means of preserving jelly, and the only precaution necessary in using it is to put on two layers, the second one two or three hours after the first, or when all contraction has ceased.

BREAD

The two most practicable methods of making bread are with yeast, and with cream of tartar and bicarbonate of soda.

Yeast is a micro-organism—an exceedingly minute form of plant life—which by its growth produces carbonic acid and alcohol. When this growth takes place in a mass of flour dough, the carbonic acid generated, in its effort to escape, puffs it up, but, owing to the viscous nature of the gluten, it is entangled and held within. Each little bubble of gas occupies a certain space. When the bread is baked, the walls around these spaces harden in the heat, and thus we get the porous loaf.

Barley, rye, and some other grains would be very useful for bread if it were not that they lack sufficient gluten to entangle enough carbonic acid to render bread made from them light.

Good bread cannot be made without good flour. There are two kinds usually to be found in market, namely *bread* flour, and *pastry* flour. The former is prepared in such a way that it contains more gluten than the latter. In making Pastry, or St. Louis flour, as it is sometimes called, the grain is crushed in such a manner that the starch, being most easily broken, becomes finer than the gluten, and in the process of bolting some of the latter is lost. For pastry and cake this kind is best. Lacking gluten, bread made from it is more tender, whiter, but less nutritious than that made from so-called *bread* flour.

New Process, or bread flour may be distinguished by the "feel," which is slightly granular rather than powdery, by its yellow color, and by the fact that it does not "cake" when squeezed in the hand; while St. Louis is white, powdery, and will "cake."

The best method to pursue in buying flour is, first, to find a good dealer, upon whose advice you may rely. Next, take a sample of the flour recommended and, with a recipe which you have *proved* to be correct, try some; if the first loaf of bread is not satisfactory, try another, and then another, until you are confident that the fault lies in the flour, and not in the method of making. Finally, having found a brand of flour from which you can make yellow-white instead of snow-white bread, which has a nutty, sweet flavor, which in mixing absorbs much liquid, and does not "run" after you think you have got it stiff enough, and which feels puffy and elastic to the hand after molding, keep it; it is probably good.

Often the same flour is sold in different sections of the country under different names, so that it is impossible to recommend any special brand. Each buyer must ascertain for herself which brands in her locality are best. It is just as easy to have good bread as poor. It only requires a *little* care and a *little* intelligence on the part of the housekeeper.

Having found a brand of good flour, next give your attention to yeast. In these days, when excellent compressed yeasts may be found in all markets, it is well to use them, bearing in mind that they *are* compressed, and that a very small quantity contains a great many yeast cells, and will raise bread as well, if not better, than a large amount.

Home-made liquid yeast is exceedingly easy to prepare. It simply requires a mixture of water and some material in which the plant cells will rapidly grow. Grated raw potato, cooked by pouring on boiling water, flour, and sugar form an excellent food for their propagation. A recipe for yeast will be given later.

Now we have come to the consideration of what will take place when the two, flour and yeast, are made into dough. According to some accounts of the subject, the yeast begins to act first upon the starch, converting it into sugar (glucose $C_6H_{12}O_6$). While this is taking place there is no *apparent* change, for nothing else is formed except the glucose, or sugar. Then this sugar is changed into alcohol and carbonic acid; the latter, owing to its diffusive nature, endeavors to escape, but becomes entangled in the viscous mass and swells it to several times its original bulk.

This has been the accepted explanation; it is now, however, believed not to be correct. It is thought, and I believe demonstrated, that the yeast plant lives upon sugar; that it has not the power to act directly upon starch, but that it is capable of *producing* a substance which acts upon starch to convert it into sugar.

The production of the carbonic acid is the end of desirable chemical change, and when it has been carried to a sufficient degree to fill the dough with bubbles, it should be stopped.

Kneading bread is for the purpose of distributing the gas and breaking up the large bubbles into small ones, to give the loaf a fine grain. One will immediately see that kneading before the bread is raised is a more or less useless task. Kneading is a process which should be done gently, by handling the dough with great tenderness; for if it is pressed hard against the molding-board, the bubbles will be worked out through the surface, and the loaf consequently less porous than if all the gas is kept in it.

The best temperature for the raising of bread (in other words, for the growing of yeast) during the first part of the process is from 70° to 75° Fahr. It may touch 80° without harm, but 90° is the limit. Above that acetic fermentation is liable to occur, and the bread becomes sour. When the bread is made into loaves, it may be placed in a very warm temperature, to rise quickly if it is intended for immediate baking. Besides killing the yeast, the object sought in baking is to form a sheath of cooked dough all over the outside, for a skeleton or support for the inside mass while it is cooking. Baking also expands the carbonic acid, and volatilizes the alcohol. The latter is lost.

A good temperature in which to begin the baking of bread is 400° Fahr. This may gradually decrease to not lower than 250°, and the time, for a good-sized brick loaf, is one hour. If it is a large loaf, increase the time by a quarter or a half hour.

"The expansion of water or ice into 1700 times its volume of steam, is sometimes taken advantage of in making snow bread, water gems, etc. It plays a part in the lightening of pastry and crackers. Air at 70° Fahr. expands to about twice its volume at the temperature of a hot oven, so that if air is entangled in a mass of dough it gives a certain lightness when the whole is baked. This is the cause of the sponginess of cakes made with eggs. The viscous albumen catches the air and holds it."[1]

There are other means of obtaining carbonic acid to lighten bread, besides by the growing of yeast. The most convenient, perhaps the most valuable, method is by causing cream of tartar and bicarbon-

[1] Mrs. Richards.

ate of soda to unite chemically. (The products of the union are carbonic acid and Rochelle salts.) The advantage of using these over everything else yet tried is, that they do not unite when brought in contact except in the presence of water and a certain degree of heat. Rochelle salts, taken in such minute quantities as it occurs in bread made in this way, is not harmful.

Cream of tartar bread, if *perfectly* made, is more nutritious than fermented bread, for none of the constituents of the flour are lost, as when yeast is used.[1]

The difficulty of obtaining good cream of tartar is very great. It is said to be more extensively adulterated than any other substance used for food. Moreover, in the practice of bread-making the cream of tartar and soda are generally mixed in the proportion of two to one—that is, two teaspoons of cream of tartar to every teaspoon of soda; but this is not the *exact* proportion in which they neutralize each other, so that under ordinary circumstances there is an excess of soda in the bread.

To be exact they should always be combined by weight, as is done in making baking-powders, the proportion being 84 parts of soda to 188 of cream of tartar, or, reducing to lower terms, as 21 to 47—a little less than half as much soda as cream of tartar. For practical use in cooking there are no scales known to the author for the purpose of weighing these materials, so the proportion will have to be approximated with teaspoons, and a fairly accurate result for bread-making may be obtained most easily by measuring a teaspoon of each in exactly the same manner, and then taking off a little from the soda.

[1] A portion of the starch and sugar is consumed to feed the growing yeast. It has been estimated that about ¼ of a barrel of flour is lost in raising bread—that is, that amount is consumed by the yeast used.

With good materials, care in measuring them, and a hot oven to set the bread before the gas escapes, cream of tartar biscuits are both wholesome and palatable.

LIQUID YEAST
(HOME-MADE WITH GRATED POTATO)

1 Medium-sized potato.
1 Tablespoon of sugar.
1 Tablespoon of flour.
1 Teaspoon of salt.
1½ Pints of boiling water.
⅛ of a two-cent cake of Fleischmann's yeast.

First see that there is a supply of boiling water. Then put the salt, sugar, and flour together in a mixing-bowl. Wash and peel the potato, and grate it quickly into the bowl, covering it now and then with the flour to prevent discoloring. As soon as the potato is all grated, pour in the boiling water and stir. It will form into a somewhat thick paste at once. Set it aside to cool. Then dissolve the yeast in a little cold water, add it, and set the mixture to rise in a temperature of 70° to 80° Fahr.

In a short time bubbles will begin to appear; these are carbonic acid, showing that the alcoholic stage of the fermentation has begun. In six or eight hours the whole will be a mass of yeast cells, which have grown in the nutrient liquid. It is then ready for use. It should be bottled in wide-mouthed glass or earthen jars, and kept in a cool place. It will remain good for two weeks. At the end of that time make a fresh supply.

Yeast is an organism—a microscopic form of plant life—which grows by a species of budding with great rapidity when it finds lodgment in material suitable for its food. The dissolved compressed yeast is like seed, which, when put into a fruitful soil, grows so long as sustenance lasts.

WATER BREAD

    1 Pint of boiling water.
    1 Tablespoon of sugar.
    1 Teaspoon of salt.
    1 Tablespoon of butter.
    $\frac{1}{8}$ Cup of liquid yeast, or
    $\frac{1}{5}$ of a two-cent cake of Fleischmann's yeast.
    Enough sifted flour to make a stiff dough.

Put the sugar, salt, and butter with the boiling water into a mixing-bowl or bread-pan. Stir until the sugar is dissolved and the water lukewarm, then add the yeast (if compressed, it should be dissolved in a little water). Last, stir in the flour until a dough stiff enough to mold easily is made. Mold it for a minute or two to give it shape and to more thoroughly mix the ingredients, and then set it to rise in a room warm enough to be comfortable to live in — that is, having a temperature of 70° Fahr. It should remain in this temperature for eight hours. Cover it closely, that the top may not dry.

It is often convenient to let bread rise over night. There is no objection to this, provided the bread is mixed late in the evening, and baked early the next morning. Care must be taken, however, that the room in which it is left is warm enough to insure rising in the time given. On the other hand, if allowed to rise too long, or at too high a temperature, the fermentation is carried so far that an acid is produced, and the dough becomes sour.

Eight hours at 70° Fahr. is a good rule to keep in mind. During the time of raising the dough should double itself in bulk. If this does not happen, or it does not appear to have risen at all, either the yeast was not good, or the temperature was too low.

When the bread has risen sufficiently, cut it down, and knead it for five minutes on a bread-board, to distribute the gas and break the large bubbles, so that the bread may have an even grain; then shape it into a loaf, put it into an oiled baking-pan, and let it rise quickly in a warm place, until it again doubles itself. The amount of dough indicated in the rule will make one large loaf, or a medium-sized loaf and some biscuit. Multiply the rule by two if you want two loaves. Bake the bread in an oven which is hot at first, but gradually decreases in temperature, for an hour and a quarter. If you have an oven thermometer use it.[1]

MILK BREAD

1 Pint of *scalded* milk.
1 Tablespoon of sugar.
1 Teaspoon of salt.
⅓ Cup of liquid yeast, or
⅙ Cake of Fleischmann's yeast.

Measure the milk after scalding, but otherwise proceed exactly as in the making of water bread.

---

[1] Oven thermometers may be obtained of Joseph Davis & Co., Fitzroy Works, London, S. E., England. 400° Fahr. is a good temperature for the first fifteen minutes. Some writers give 380°, but the higher temperature is better, provided it can be gradually decreased; it should not fall below 250° until the loaf is done.

STICKS

1 Cup of *scalded* milk.
½ Teaspoon of salt.
1 Tablespoon of sugar.
2 Tablespoons of butter.
⅛ Cake of yeast, or
¼ Cup of liquid yeast.
White of one egg.
Flour enough to make a slightly soft dough.

Dissolve the salt and sugar, and soften the butter in the hot milk, which must be measured *after* heating. When it is cooled to lukewarmness, put in the yeast (which, if compressed, should be dissolved in a little cold water), the beaten white of the egg, and flour enough to make a dough *slightly* softer than that for ordinary bread. Let it rise overnight, or until light. Then cut it into small pieces, shape the pieces into balls, and roll and stretch them into tiny slender sticks, from ten to twelve inches long, about half an inch thick in the middle, and tapering toward each end. Place them, two inches apart, in shallow, buttered pans, and put them in a warm place for an hour to rise; then bake them in a moderate oven fifteen or twenty minutes, or until they are a golden brown. Sticks are good at any time; they are especially nice served with soup, or for lunch, with cocoa or tea.

This dough may also be made into tiny loaves for tea-rolls.

RUSK

1 Tablespoon of sugar.
½ Teaspoon of salt.

1 Cup of *scalded* milk.
¼ Cup of liquid yeast, or
⅕ Cake of compressed yeast.
Flour enough to make a soft dough.

Mix the above ingredients together, and let the dough rise overnight in the usual time given to bread. Then beat one-fourth of a cup of butter, one-fourth of a cup of sugar, and one egg together, and work the mixture into the dough, adding a little more flour to make it stiff enough to mold. Set it to rise a second time; then shape it into rolls or tiny loaves, allow them to rise again until quite light, or for an hour in a warm place, and bake like bread.

DRIED RUSK

Cut the rusk when cold into thin slices, dry them slowly in the oven, and then brown them a delicate golden color.

Dried rusk is exceedingly easy of digestion, and makes a delicious lunch with a glass of warm milk or a cup of tea.

GRAHAM BREAD

1 Pint of milk.
2 Tablespoons of sugar.
1 Teaspoon of salt.
⅕ Cake of compressed yeast.
2 Cups of white flour.
Enough Graham flour to make a dough.

Scald some milk, and from it measure a pint; to this add the sugar and salt. While it is cooling sift some Graham flour, being careful to exclude the chaff or outside silicious covering of the grain, but *nothing else*. When the milk has become lukewarm, put in the yeast, which has previously been dissolved in a little cold water, and the white flour (sifted), with enough of the Graham to make a dough which shall be stiff, but yet not stiff enough to mold. Mix thoroughly, and shape it with a spoon into a round mass in the dish. After this follow the same directions as for water bread, letting it rise the same time, and baking it in the same manner.

After the dough has risen, although it is soft, it can be *shaped into a loaf* on the bread-board, but not molded.

CREAM-OF-TARTAR BISCUIT

First, attend to the fire; see that you have a clear, steady one, such as will give a hot oven by the time the biscuits are ready for baking. Then sift some flour, and measure a quart. Into it put two teaspoons of cream of tartar, and one of soda, the latter to be measured exactly like the teaspoons of cream of tartar, and then a very little taken off. This is a more accurate way of getting a scanted teaspoon than by taking some on the spoon and guessing at it. Add one teaspoon of salt, and sift all together four times, then with the fingers rub into the flour one spoon of butter.

At this point, if it has not been already done, get the baking-pans, rolling-pin, board, dredging-box, and cutter ready for use. Then with a knife stir into the flour enough milk to make a soft dough. Do this as quickly as convenient, and without any delay mold the dough just enough to shape it; roll it out, cut it into biscuits, and put them immediately into the oven, where they should bake for thirty minutes.

Pocket-Books. Work or knead together the pieces that are left after making cream-of-tartar biscuit (or make a dough on purpose), roll it out very thin, cut it into rounds, brush them over with milk or melted butter, fold once so as to make a half-moon shape, and you will have "pocket-books."

Twin Biscuit. Roll out some dough very thin, cut it into very small rounds, and place one on top of another, with butter between.

Iced water may be substituted for milk in the above rule. In baking, however, the oven should be unusually hot, so as to take advantage of the expansion of the water. Also, baking-powder may be substituted for the cream of tartar and soda, using a fourth more of the baking-powder than of the two together.

SNOW-CAKES

½ Tablespoon of butter.
1 Tablespoon of sugar.
Whites of two eggs.
1½ Cups of flour.
1 Saltspoon of salt.
1½ Teaspoons of baking-powder.
1 Cup of milk.

Measure each of the ingredients carefully, then sift the flour, salt, and baking-powder together four times. Cream the butter and sugar with a little of the milk, then add the whites of the eggs well beaten, the rest of the milk, and last the flour. Bake this batter in hot buttered gem-pans from twenty minutes to half an hour. These cakes are delicious eaten hot for lunch or tea. This mixture may also be baked in small, round earthen cups.

GRAHAM GEMS

1 Cup of milk.
½ Teaspoon of salt.
½ Cup of white flour.
1 Cup of Graham flour.
2 Tablespoons of sugar.
1 Teaspoon of cream of tartar.
½ Teaspoon of soda (*slightly* scanted).
1 Tablespoon of melted butter.

Sift and measure the Graham flour, add the cream of tartar, soda, and white flour, and sift again. Mix the milk, salt, and sugar together, and stir it into the flour; last, put in the melted butter, beat for a minute, and then drop a spoonful in each division of a roll gem-pan, which should be well buttered, and made very hot on the top of the stove. Bake in a hot oven from twenty-five minutes to half an hour. Serve hot.

OATMEAL MUFFINS

2¼ Cups of flour.
2 Teaspoons of baking-powder.
1 Teaspoon of salt.
2 Tablespoons of sugar.
1 Egg.
1 Cup of milk.
1 Cup of cooked oatmeal.
1 Tablespoon of butter melted.

Sift the flour and baking-powder together twice. Beat the egg very light, stir into it the salt, sugar, and milk, then add the flour, and last the oatmeal and butter; beat for half a minute, and bake immediately in gem-pans or muffin-rings in a hot oven for half an hour.

N. B.—The oatmeal should not be cooked to a soft, thin mush, but should be rather dry; so, in preparing it, use less water than for porridge. These cakes are to be eaten hot.

GLUTEN BREAD

Gluten flour is prepared in such a way that much of the starch of the grain is excluded. It is frequently required for persons suffering with diabetes, who cannot digest either sugar or starch. It should be made with flour, water, yeast, and salt only. Do not use milk for mixing, as it contains sugar.

One pint of water, one half teaspoon of salt, one fifth of a cake of yeast, one tablespoon of butter, and enough flour to make the usual bread dough will be required. Otherwise the process is exactly the same as for ordinary bread.

BAKING-POWDER

Baking-powder is a mixture of cream of tartar, bicarbonate of soda, and arrowroot. The latter is used to keep the two chemicals dry, and thus prevent the slow union which would otherwise take place. Sometimes tartaric acid is used instead of cream of tartar. The following rule may be relied upon:

Tartaric acid	2 oz. by weight.
Bicarbonate of soda	3 " " "
Arrowroot	3 " " "

Mix and sift together thoroughly. Keep in a dry place, in a wide-mouthed bottle.

CAKE

Cake of the simpler kinds, especially sponge cake, is frequently given to the sick. Good sponge cake, served with sweet cream or a glass of milk, is an excellent lunch for an invalid. Some of the plain kinds of butter cakes — those made with a little butter — such as white, feather, and similar varieties, are excellent food.

Consider for a moment what they contain: eggs, milk, butter, sugar, and flour — five of the most valuable of all our food products. Yet there are those who pride themselves upon not eating cake, which idiosyncrasy can only be explained in one of two ways: either the cake which they have had has not been properly made, or else it has been so good that, during a lapse of judgment, they have eaten too much.

The dark fruit cakes should be avoided by both sick and well, on account of the indigestible nature of the dried fruits used in them, and also because they are often compact and close-grained, not light.

There is a custom prevalent in many kitchens of using what is called "cooking" butter — that is, butter which is off taste or rancid — for cake. It is but poor economy, even if it can merit that name at all. If you have no other butter for cake, don't make any. Sweet butter and fresh — not "store" — eggs are *absolutely necessary*. Also, a dainty worker to mix the ingredients with accuracy and care, and to oil the pan in which the cake is to be baked, so that the outside shall not taste of fat. Many an otherwise nice cake has been spoiled by oiling the pan in which it was baked with dirty or rancid grease. Use a very little sweet butter or olive-oil.

THE PROCESS OF CAKE MAKING

All ordinary cakes are made in much the same way as to the order in which their ingredients are mixed. First the butter and sugar are creamed together, then the yolks of the eggs are beaten and added, with the milk, to the butter and sugar; then the flour, into which the cream of tartar and soda have been well mixed by sifting them together several times, is put in; and last, the beaten whites of the eggs.

Care in Baking. For sponge cake made with baking-powder, or soda and cream of tartar, an oven moderately heated will be required—that is, one of 300° Fahr., or one which will *slightly* brown a loaf in twenty minutes.

For sponge cake made without raising material, such as the old-fashioned kind, in which only eggs, sugar, and flour are used, a slow oven is necessary.

For butter cakes a temperature somewhere between 350° and 380° will not fail.

The baking of cake is the most difficult part of the process, on account of the constantly variable condition of ovens in common iron stoves, and because it is more easily spoiled than bread and other foods usually cooked in an oven. One is obliged to exercise a new judgment every time cake is made. Even thermometers are only a partial help, for if an oven has a temperature of 300° Fahr. at a certain time, there is no means of being sure what the temperature will be half an hour from then. However, by giving attention and some practice to it, one may gain considerable skill in managing fires. Should the cake be cooking too fast, and arranging the stove dampers does not lessen the heat, a piece of buttered paper laid over the top will protect it, and will not stick. Layer, or thin cakes, require a hotter oven than loaves.

Pans for baking cake should be lined with buttered paper (the buttered side up), letting it overlap the sides for about an inch to assist in lifting out the cake. An earthenware bowl and a wooden spoon should be used for mixing.

Get everything ready before beginning to mix cake, the oven first of all. Bake as soon as possible after the flour is in, for carbonic acid begins to be formed as soon as the soda and cream of tartar come in contact with the liquid, and some of it will escape unless the mixture is baked at once. Do not stop to scrape every bit from the bowl; that can be attended to afterward, and a little patty-cake made of what is left.

INVALID'S SPONGE CAKE

2 Cups of pastry flour measured after sifting.
1 Teaspoon of cream of tartar.
½ Teaspoon of soda (slightly scanted).
4 Eggs.
1½ Cups of powdered sugar.
½ Cup of water.
2 Tablespoons of lemon-juice.

Get everything ready before beginning to make the cake; oil the pan, or oil paper and line the pan with it; measure the flour, cream of tartar, and soda, and sift them together four times; measure the sugar, water, and lemon-juice, and separate the yolks from the whites of the eggs. Beat the whites of the eggs with half the sugar until they are very light. Then beat the yolks very light, or until they become lemon-colored, add the remaining half of the sugar and beat again, and then a little of the water if it is difficult to turn the egg-beater. When the sugar is well mixed, add the remainder of the water, the lemon-juice, and the flour. Beat for a few seconds, but not long, as all mixtures that have cream of tartar and soda should be baked as quickly as possible. Last of all *fold* in (not beat) the whites of the eggs lightly, so as not to break out the air which has been entangled by the beating, as it helps to make the cake light.

Bake in a moderate oven from forty-five to fifty minutes, or until the cake shrinks a little from the pan.

FEATHER CAKE

$\frac{1}{4}$ Cup of butter.
1 Cup of sugar.
2 Eggs.
1$\frac{1}{2}$ Cups of pastry flour.
$\frac{1}{2}$ Teaspoon of soda (slightly scanted).
1 Teaspoon of cream of tartar.
A little grated nutmeg.
1 Teaspoon of vanilla.

See first of all that you have a proper fire. Measure the ingredients, and get everything ready before beginning — mixing-bowl, pans, etc. Use a wooden cake spoon, with slits in the bowl, for mixing. Line the pans with buttered paper. Then cream the butter, adding to it half the sugar and half the milk, the latter very slowly; separate the yolks of the eggs from the whites, and beat them with the remaining sugar; when they are very light add the rest of the milk. Beat the whites until stiff. Now mix the creamed butter and yolks together with the flavoring, then stir in the flour, and last the whites, which are to be cut and folded in, *not beaten*. Bake it in shallow pans in a moderate oven forty minutes, or about that time. When the cake begins to shrink a little from the sides of the pan, there is no doubt that it is cooked enough. This recipe may be used for a variety of plain cakes.

For Chocolate Cake. Melt and stir into the above mixture two ounces of Baker's chocolate, or two teaspoons of cocoa wet in a little warm water.

For Rose Cake. Color the feather cake mixture with six drops of carmine.

LAYER CAKE

Oil three layer cake pans, or pie-plates. Make the feather cake mixture, and divide it into three portions. Bake one white, color another pink with three or four drops of carmine, and the third brown with an ounce of melted chocolate. Bake in a hot oven for fifteen minutes. When cool, join the layers with White Mountain frosting, and frost the top of the last layer. Any of the fillings given under the head of "Cake Filling" may also be used.

When chocolate is used in cake, it is not necessary to grate it or even to break it into small pieces. It contains a large proportion of fat which liquefies at a low temperature, consequently it is necessary only to heat it slowly to reduce it to the liquid state.

CARMINE FOR COLORING

The following rule for making liquid carmine for coloring cake, ice-cream, blanc-mange, etc., will be found useful:

  1 Ounce of No. 40 carmine.
  3 Ounces of boiling water.
  1 Ounce of ammonia.

Bottle for use. It will keep indefinitely.

WHITE CAKE

  1 Tablespoon of butter.
  1 Cup of sugar (powdered).
  1¼ Cups of pastry flour.
  ½ Teaspoon of soda.
  1 Teaspoon of cream of tartar.
  Whites of four eggs.
  ¼ Teaspoon of almond extract, or
  1 Teaspoon of rose-water.

Proceed, as with all cake mixtures, by getting everything ready before beginning to mix any of the ingredients, not forgetting the fire. Then cream the butter with the sugar, and add the milk to it slowly, so that the cream shall not break. Beat the whites of the eggs very stiff. Then to the butter, sugar, etc., add the flour, with which the cream of tartar and soda have been sifted at least four times, and the flavoring; last, fold in the whites of the eggs, and bake in a round loaf for an hour and a quarter or an hour and a half in a *slow* oven.

DREAM CAKE

Make a white cake mixture. Bake it in shallow layer-cake pans, in a moderate, not slow, oven. Join them with a caramel filling, and frost the top with the same, or use White Mountain frosting instead of the caramel, flavored with rose-water, and left either white, or colored a delicate shell pink with carmine.

CAKE FILLING AND FROSTING

WHITE MOUNTAIN FROSTING

Boil together, *without stirring*, one cup of granulated sugar with one third of a cup of boiling water, for eight or ten minutes. When the sugar has been boiling five minutes, beat the white of one egg until it is very light. Then test the sugar mixture by letting a little run off the side of a spoon. If in falling it forms a delicate thread, it is just at the point to stop the boiling. When it has reached this point, pour it at once into the beaten egg in a small stream, stirring the egg constantly to keep it smooth. Continue stirring for two or three minutes until it begins to thicken, then spread it either between layer cakes for filling, or use it for frosting.

CARAMEL FILLING

1 Cup of brown sugar.
¼ Cup of sweet cream.
1 Teaspoon of butter.

Boil all together until it threads, stirring it slowly as it boils. It will take about eight minutes. Use either for frosting or filling.

CHOCOLATE ICING

½ Cup of sugar.
4 Tablespoons of water.
2 Eggs.
1 Ounce of chocolate, or
1 Tablespoon of **Dutch** cocoa.
1 Teaspoon of vanilla.

Boil the sugar, water, and chocolate together, two minutes, to render the chocolate smooth. Then add the beaten eggs. Cook two minutes more, stirring slowly and gently. Add the vanilla just as it is taken from the fire, and use at once, as it becomes firm quickly. It is good either for icing cakes or for filling.

CREAM FILLING

Make a cream sauce with one cup of milk, a tablespoon of butter, and a tablespoon of flour. Beat one egg with half a cup of sugar, and stir it into the sauce slowly. Cook for two minutes, or until the egg is done. It should look like a thick smooth cream. Flavor it with a piece of cinnamon bark boiled in the milk, or with vanilla or almond. Use this cream for filling, for layer cakes, or split a thin sponge cake in two, and spread it between the halves.

DIET LISTS OR MENUS FOR THE SICK

Diet for the sick may be divided into three kinds: Liquid, Light, and Convalescent's or Invalid's Diet.

Liquid diet consists entirely of liquids, of which milk is the most valuable. The meat broths (those made with beef, chicken, and mutton), oyster and clam broth, albumen water, eggs in the form of eggnog, egg cream, and mulled wine, and tea and coffee are excellent. To this list may be added, as the patient shows signs of recovery, soft custards, and jellies made with wine, lemon, coffee, or orange-juice, which quickly become liquid when eaten.

A patient is given liquid diet during times of severe and dangerous illness. Usually the amount of food and intervals at which it is to be given are prescribed by the physician.

The following table may be of assistance to those who are without such aid:

LIQUID DIET

No. 1

8 A. M.	Hot milk	¾ of a cup
10 A. M.	Hot coffee with cream and a little sugar	½ of a cup
12 M.	Beef-juice	2 tablespoons
2 P. M.	Warm milk	¾ of a cup
4 P. M.	Wine whey	½ of a cup
6 P. M.	Hot milk	¾ of a cup
8 P. M.	Hot cocoa	¾ of a cup

No. 2

8 A. M.	Hot milk	¾ of a cup
10 A. M.	Chicken broth	¾ of a cup
12 M.	Egg-nog	½ tumbler
2 P. M.	Milk	¾ of a cup
4 P. M.	Hot tea with cream and sugar	¾ of a cup
6 P. M.	Chicken broth	¼ of a cup
8 P. M.	Hot milk	¾ of a cup

No. 3

8 A. M.	Hot milk	¾ of a cup
10 A. M.	Beef broth	¾ of a cup
12 M.	Beef-juice	2 tablespoons
2 P. M.	Milk, either warm or cold	¾ of a cup
4 P. M.	Oyster broth with milk	¾ of a cup
6 P. M.	Hot milk	¾ of a cup
8 P. M.	Hot cocoa	¾ of a cup

No. 4

8 A. M.	Hot cocoa	¾ of a cup
10 A. M.	Hot milk	¾ of a cup
12 M.	Beef-juice, warm or cold	¾ of a cup
2 P. M.	Beef broth, hot	¾ of a cup
4 P. M.	Wine jelly	2 tablespoons
6 P. M.	Hot cocoa	¾ of a cup
8 P. M.	Hot milk	¾ of a cup

No. 5

8 A. M.	Hot milk	¾ of a cup
10 A. M.	Coffee with cream and sugar	½ of a cup
12 M.	Hot beef broth	¾ of a cup
2 P. M.	Orange jelly	3 tablespoons
4 P. M.	Mulled wine	¾ of a cup
6 P. M.	Warm or cold soft custard	½ of a cup
8 P. M.	Warm cocoa	¾ of a cup

If nourishment is to be given throughout the night, either hot or warm milk or cocoa is good. They are soothing and sometimes induce sleep. Tea and wine whey should be avoided at night, unless, of course, the patient needs stimulating, in which case use the wine only, for tea often causes wakefulness.

The whites of eggs beaten and strained, and mixed with finely crushed ice, is a valuable form of food for a typhoid fever patient. Toast-water and cracker tea are good in all feverish conditions. Milk may be varied by making it into milk-punch, with a very little sugar (a scanty teaspoon) and a tablespoon of brandy or sherry to each tumbler, or it may be made with a few drops of vanilla, instead of the brandy or sherry.

LIGHT DIET

Light diet consists of everything included in liquid diet, and in addition fruits, such as grapes and oranges; porridge of granum or farina; soft-cooked or poached eggs; dry, water, milk, and cream toast; the *maigre* soups, such as celery and mock-bisque, and chicken; delicate puddings, coffee and velvet cream, and baked custards, with perhaps for dinner a meat ball, a small bit of beefsteak or roast beef, and a baked potato.

Jellies made with gelatine, especially when flavored with wine, are a very valuable form of food with which to make the transition from liquid to light diet. They are palatable, nutritious, and, being in solid form, are satisfying to the minds of those who think they are not getting much to eat when fed on liquids alone.

The change from liquid to light diet should be made gradually, adding one kind of solid food at a time. Perhaps after the jellies a bit of water or milk toast, then an egg, then a little soup or pudding, until, as strength is gained, the person is able to take anything in the list, and finally is able to eat almost any kind of nutritious and well-prepared food.

First Day.

Breakfast.

Poached Egg on Toast. Cocoa.

Lunch.

Milk-punch.

Dinner.

Raw Oysters. Cream-crackers. Port Wine.

Lunch.

1 Cup of Hot Beef Broth.

Supper.

Milk Toast. Wine Jelly. Tea.

Second Day.

Breakfast.

Soft-cooked Egg. Milk Toast.
Coffee with Sugar and Cream.

Lunch.

1 Cup of Soft Custard.

Dinner.

Cream-of-celery Soup. Sippets.
A little Barley Pudding, with Cream. Sherry Wine.

Lunch.

Milk-punch.

Supper.

Water Toast, Buttered. Wine Jelly. Tea.

Third Day.

Breakfast.

Scrambled Egg.   Cream Toast.   Cocoa.

Lunch.

1 Cup of Hot Chicken Broth.

Dinner.

Chicken Panada.   Bread.   Port Wine.
A little Tapioca Cream.

Lunch.

An Egg-nog.

Supper.

Buttered Dry Toast.   Baked Sweet Apples and Cream.
Tea.

Fourth Day.

Breakfast.

An Orange.
Farina Mush, with Cream and Sugar.
Poached Egg on Toast.   Baked Potato.   Cocoa.

Lunch.

1 Cup of Hot Soft Custard.

Dinner.

Potato Soup.   Croutons.
A small Piece of Beefsteak.   Creamed Potatoes.
Baked Custard.   Coffee.

Lunch.

1 Cup of Chicken Broth, with Rice.

Supper.

Raw Oysters. Banquet Crackers.
Graham Bread, Toasted. Wine Jelly. Tea.

FIFTH DAY.

Breakfast.

An Orange.
Coffee. Mush of Wheat Germ, with Cream and Sugar.
Broiled Mutton Chop. Toast.

Lunch.

1 Cup of Mulled Wine.

Dinner.

Chicken Soup. Bread.
Creamed Sweetbreads. Duchess Potato.
Snow Pudding. Cocoa.

Lunch.

Siphon Soda, with Coffee Syrup and Cream.

Supper.

Buttered Dry Toast. Orange Jelly.
Sponge Cake and Cream. Tea.

CONVALESCENT'S DIET

Convalescent's diet includes the liquid and light diets, and, in addition, all easily digested and nutritious food. For meats, game, especially venison and birds, beef, mutton, and chicken may be given, but never either pork or veal. They are difficult of digestion. Eggs in all ways, soft-cooked, scrambled, poached, and as omelets, well-baked potatoes, creamed potatoes, celery, snow pudding, cream of rice pudding, and tapioca cream, jellies, both those made from gelatine and fruits, Graham bread, Graham gems, rusk, and, in fact, any well-made bread, and good cake.

A convalescent may use for drinks plenty of good milk, cocoa, *carefully made* tea and coffee, occasionally good wine, and the different mineral and drinking waters. Some foods to be avoided are pastry, dark or badly made cakes, pork, veal, any highly seasoned meat dish made with gravy, all kinds of fried food, sausages, heavy puddings, badly made bread, lobsters and crabs.

SPRING

No. 1

Breakfast.

An Orange.
Porridge of Wheat Flakes, with Cream and Sugar.
Omelet, with Broiled Ham.
Coffee. Hot Graham Gems and Butter.

Lunch.

1 Cup of Hot Beef Broth. A Cream-cracker.

Dinner.

Chicken Soup. Creamed Fish.
Mashed Potato. Snow Pudding.
White Cake. Tea.

Lunch.

1 Cup of Hot Milk.

Supper.

Broiled Squab on Toast. Creamed Potatoes.
Bread and Butter. Jelly.
Cocoa.

No. 2

Breakfast.

An Orange.
Farina Porridge, with Cream and Sugar.
French Chops (Mutton). Baked Potato.
Cream Toast of Graham Bread.
Cocoa.

Lunch.

1 Cup of Cracker Gruel.

Dinner.

Mock-bisque Soup. Sticks.
Roast Beef. French Peas. Mashed Potato.
Bread and Butter.
Baked Cup Custard. Coffee or Claret.

Lunch.

1 Cup of Hot Bouillon.

Supper.

Scrambled Eggs.   Creamed Potatoes.
Water Toast, with Apple Compote.
Feather Cake.   Tea.

SUMMER

No. 1

Breakfast.

Blackberries.
Farina Porridge, with Cream and Sugar.
Broiled Steak.   Baked Potatoes.
Dry Toast.   Cocoa.

Lunch.

1 Tumbler of Kumiss.

Dinner.

Potato Soup made with New Potatoes.
Baked Fish.   Mashed Potatoes.   Peas.
Chicken Salad.   Lemon Jelly.
Tea.

Lunch.

Soda-water, with Vanilla Syrup and Cream.

Supper.

Cold Broiled Chicken.   Bread and Butter.
Blueberries.   White Cake.
Cocoa.

No. 2

Breakfast.

Blueberries.
Broiled Perch. Baked Potatoes.
Hot Snow Cakes, with Butter.
Coffee.

Lunch.

Milk-punch.

Dinner.

Broiled French Chop. Duchess Potato.
Peas. Tomato Salad.
Tapioca Cream. Wine Jelly.
Lemonade.

Lunch.

Egg-nog.

Supper.

Hot Water Toast, Buttered. Berries.
Omelet, with Parsley.
Tea. Soft Custard in Cups.

AUTUMN

No. 1

Breakfast.

Oatmeal Mush, with Cream and Sugar.
Broiled Steak. Baked Potatoes.
Oatmeal Muffins, Hot, with Butter.
Coffee.

Lunch.

1 Cup of Hot Beef Broth. A Banquet Cracker.

Dinner.

Celery Soup. Sippets. Roast Pheasant, with Jelly.
Potato. Stewed Mushrooms.
Velvet Cream. Cocoa.

Lunch.

A thin Sandwich of Bread and Butter. Tea.

Supper.

Raw Oysters. Cream Toast. Baked Apples.
Rusk. Tea.

No. 2

Breakfast.

Cantaloup.
Farina Porridge, with Cream and Sugar.
Broiled Mutton Chop. Baked Potatoes.
Dry Toast. Coffee.

Lunch.

1 Cup of Hot Chicken Broth.

Dinner.

Oyster Soup. Sticks.
Roast Beef. Creamed Potatoes.
Celery Salad.
Coffee Cream. Tea.

Lunch.

A Cup of Hot Oatmeal Gruel.

Supper.

Poached Egg on Toast. Cocoa.
Graham Bread and Butter. Sponge Cake.

WINTER

No. 1

Breakfast.

An Orange.
Oatmeal Porridge, with Cream and Sugar. Coffee.
Broiled Steak. Baked Potato. Cream Toast.

Lunch.

Egg-nog.

Dinner.

Celery Soup. Croutons.
Roast Chicken. Creamed Onions. Duchess Potato.
Lettuce Salad (plain). Velvet Cream. Coffee.

Lunch.

Cocoa Cordial. Sponge Cake.

Supper.

Fancy Roast of Oysters. Dry Toast.
Chocolate, with Whipped Cream. Orange Jelly.

No. 2

Breakfast.

An Orange.
Wheat Germ, with Cream and Sugar.
Broiled Partridge. Dry Toast. Coffee.

Lunch.

1 Cup of Hot Chicken Broth.

Dinner.

. Consommé.   Bread.
Roast Beef.   Mashed Potatoes.
Tomato Salad.
Cream of Rice Pudding.   Coffee.

Lunch.

1 Cup of Mulled Wine.

Supper.

Venison Steak, with Port Wine Sauce.
Toast.   Sponge Cake, with Sweet Cream.
Cocoa.

SERVING

If cooking be a science, then serving is an art. It perhaps more closely resembles painting than any other, for a well-spread table should be a picture, and each separate dish a choice bit in the landscape. The invalid's tray should be a dainty Dresden water-color of delicate hues and harmonious tints.

It is not easy to give definite directions in regard to serving, for it involves so much of good taste in so many directions, and depends so largely upon the individual and the circumstances. It requires intelligent study, a cultivated habit of thought, and the appreciation of symmetry, and the harmony of colors; to do it well one must ever judge anew and arrange again, for no two meals are exactly alike in all their details.

Of course, the most important thing in serving is the thing to be served. A badly prepared or unwholesome dish, no matter how beautifully it may be presented, is worthless—perhaps even worse, for it may prove a positive source of evil. An indifferently done steak, served on a silver platter, is less acceptable than one perfectly cooked on plain china, or a bit of burned toast on Dresden ware than a daintily browned piece on a common white plate. Put the force, therefore, of your efforts on securing that which is wholesome in itself, adapted to the needs of the patient, and perfectly cooked; then serve it in the most attractive manner at your command.

Good serving is a necessity for the sick. It should never be regarded as simply ornamental. When a person has the hunger of health, colors and dishes are not of great account; but when one is ill, or exhausted with fatigue, sometimes a pretty color, a dainty cup, or beauty of arrangement makes all the difference, and one is tempted to eat when otherwise the food would remain untouched.

Simplicity should rule at all times the arrangement of an invalid's tray. Anything like display is entirely out of place. Japanned trays of oval shape are the ones in general use. When one is fortunate enough to possess a silver tray, the dishes may be placed directly upon it, or on a doily, which covers the center of it. All other trays should be completely covered with a dainty snowy napkin, or tray-cloth.

After the napkin has been neatly spread upon the tray, place a plate in the middle of the side nearest to you, and then arrange the other dishes about it, with the tiny earthen teapot on the right, and the sugar-bowl and cream-pitcher of silver next to it; the knife, fork, and spoons should be on the right and left of the plate, never in front of it. The various dishes to be served should then be arranged symmetrically in other parts of the tray, not scattered about without the appearance of order.

Never crowd a tray. Calculate beforehand how many dishes you will probably have, and select a size accordingly. Serve a single glass or a single cup on a small round or oval tray with a doily, never on a large tray, such as might be selected for a meal.

When practicable use silver dishes for meats, soups, coffee, hot milk, or any hot food; when these cannot be had, use hot china.

Avoid discords in color. Most women have an instinctive appreciation of color, and by giving some thought to the subject of **harmonies,** and observing the methods of others who are known to have good taste in such matters, bad blunders in the arrangement of a tray or a table may be avoided.

Red with *yellow, blue* with *green,* and *yellow* with *pink* are inharmonious combinations of color; but *yellow* with *white, blue* with *white, dull orange* with *brown, violet,* and *pale gold* are exquisite together.

A cup of chocolate in pale pink or dull red, coffee in buttercup yellow, especially when served without cream, and green tea in Nile green, appeal to the eye as well as to the taste, giving double pleasure — gratifying two senses instead of one.

Color plays a very important part in serving food. It produces strong effects in some persons who are deeply moved by harmonies or discords in it, as others are by harmonies or discords in music. Color appeals to the esthetic side of some natures much more forcibly than many of us are aware.

The story is told of a lady, possessed of unusually keen color-perception, who had been living for many months in a house furnished in monotonous hues, and in which the table was always set in plain white cloth and white china. Being invited to lunch with a friend in the neighborhood, she was moved to tears at the sight of a beautiful table, decorated with a scarlet cloth, flowers, and harmoniously contrasting colored china.

The effect of the colors upon the emotions was similar to that which is sometimes produced by an exquisite strain of music. Who can say how much of subtle refining influence may be exerted by such things? Regarded as a general thing only in the light of the ornamental, they are too often looked upon as luxuries, and therefore dispensable; but whatever ministers to the esthetic side of the mind must be elevating, and the influence of neatness, of beautiful surroundings, of harmonious colors, of art in any form, inevitably produces an effect upon character. In time such surroundings become necessities, and when the individual is deprived of them they are missed, and he feels a sense of dissatisfaction with those of meaner kind—perhaps dissatisfaction with a poorer or lower life in any way—and imperceptibly these seeming ornaments of existence may be the means which shall lift many an one into a higher plane of life, so that, aside from their practical value, all the niceties of household affairs may have a lasting effect for good upon character.

To be progressive, one must be constantly in a frame of mind to learn, and ever on the alert for information. Fashions change in serving foods as in other things. However, there are certain fixed principles which always remain unchanged. Perfect neatness, orderly and pleasing arrangement, and harmonious coloring are ever essential.

For the invalid's tray use the prettiest china obtainable. In a private house there are always some choice and precious pieces—teacups, quaint silver pitchers and spoons, pretty plates, and delicate thin tumblers. These will be gladly placed at the disposal of the sick one, especially if the nurse will volunteer to be responsible for them.

To prepare a meal for an invalid after planning the food, the first necessary articles are a tray clean on both sides, a neat napkin to spread over it, and exquisitely clean dishes done by a servant known to be neat, or by one's self. It not infrequently happens, especially in houses in which the mistress leaves everything to the servants, and never goes into the kitchen, that dishes are washed in such surroundings of dirt, and wiped with such unclean towels, as to be dangerous for any one to use. It is therefore necessary for a nurse to understand about such matters, and to see to it that her patient's dishes are above suspicion. In fact, it is a dainty attention on her part to care entirely for the tray-dishes of her charge.

In some forms of disease it is absolutely necessary, in order to prevent contagion, that a nurse should attend altogether to the tray and dishes, for it would almost never occur that any member of a household would understand an effectual method of sterilization.

In a contagious disease everything that goes to the bedside — dishes, knives, forks, spoons, napkin, the tray itself — should be rendered sterile by boiling in water for half an hour, or by treatment with steam for a similar time, before any one, except the nurse, even touches them.

Nothing should be used in the way of linen or dishes that cannot be washed without spoiling; therefore fancy silk doilies and other similar furnishings are to be avoided.

When it is necessary to taste of food before giving it to a patient, take some into a separate dish, and use a separate spoon or fork; or, if it is a liquid, take out a little with a spoon into another spoon, being careful that the one used for tasting does not at any time touch the liquid.

Never touch the bowls of spoons, nor the inside of plates and cups, with the fingers, unless the hands are prepared by thorough cleansing for it. A nurse who understands antiseptic surgery, and knows how easily contagion is carried, will appreciate the necessity of these precautions. The hands should be washed after arranging a bed, using a handkerchief, arranging the hair — in fact, always before handling either food or dishes.

Food and drink should not be allowed to remain

exposed to the air for any length of time. Most kinds of food are excellent media for micro-organisms to flourish in, and consequently the food, if it be such as might be eaten afterward, deteriorates.

Then, from an esthetic point of view, it is the height of untidiness to allow a tray to remain in the sick-room any length of time after the meal has been eaten. It should be immediately removed with all traces of the meal, as should also fruit, glasses for water, lemonade, milk, etc., which may be used at different times during the day.

If the patient objects and wishes to have what is left for future use, assure him that it is near at hand, and being kept cool and clean for him. By punctually fulfilling promises made about such matters, he will very quickly learn to trust a nurse, not only in these, but in other things.

For decoration for a tray nothing should be used besides pretty china and flowers. A slender glass or silver vase with a blossom or two, or a delicate fern with a white or pink flower, are always suitable. It is well to use ferns and other fresh green decorations liberally, especially in winter. Green is always grateful to the sight, and sometimes a single spray will give pleasure to an invalid for hours.

Violets, roses, orchids, and all flowers that are dainty in themselves, are always in good taste, but a very few or a single blossom is all that is allowable. A big bouquet on a tray or an invalid's table is as out of place as a whole roast or a whole pudding. Flowers with strong odors or primary colors should be avoided, such, for instance, as marigolds, fleur de lis, and dahlias. They are handsome in a garden or a hall, but not at the bedside.

Little attentions in the way of ornamentation, and thoughtfulness as to an invalid's meal, are deeply appreciated. They show that an effort has been made to please, and to many sick ones the feeling that they are a constant care to those about them is a very oppressive one. It should be the pleasure of a good nurse to dispel such thoughts. It is the duty of every nurse to do so.

Variety for those who are sick (after they are out of danger, and waiting for strength to return) is just as necessary as for those who are well, and for the same reason — that is, to furnish the body with all those substances required for perfect nutrition. Many think that because a person is ill, or an invalid, he must be denied all things that are good, and fed upon such dishes as well persons generally abhor, like water gruel, thin oyster stews, and half-cooked cornstarch pudding.

It is curious how such an idea should have been lodged in the mind, but it is probably a relic of the old treatment in the days before antiseptic surgery and the modern practice of medicine. Now, as soon as a patient is out of danger, careful feeding with a variety of wholesome, perfectly cooked, nutritious food — of course, wisely administered as to quantity — is an essential part of the treatment, and constitutes nearly the whole cure in some forms of disease of the nervous system.

The body, depleted and exhausted by long-continued sickness, is without resources, and must draw from food (and, of course, air) all those substances needed for repair and the restoration of bodily vigor. To insure this, different kinds of food are required, for no single one, not even milk, contains everything needed.[1] Fruits of various kinds, green salads and

---

[1] There is, of course, an exception in the case of the use of milk for young children, it being a perfect food for them during the first year or year and a half of life.

vegetables, fish, beef, and mutton should be used, as well as milk, eggs, chicken, and toast.

Ease in serving the sick is an accomplishment in a nurse, and a certain amount of *seeming* indifference is an advisable quality to cultivate. It is a good plan to take every *possible care* in preparing a meal for a sick person, and then to appear not to notice whether he eats; for sometimes sensitive people, in their desire not to disappoint, or in their endeavors to please, will eat when they do not care for food.

Endeavor to remember individual tastes, and try to gratify them; always do so when it is in your power, for these individual preferences are often true instincts of the individual nature striving to secure that which is best for it. If a man asks for the second joint of a fowl, don't take to him a cut from the breast, even though *you* may think it the choicest portion.

Food should be given at *regular intervals*. If a patient is very ill, the rule is to administer nourishment in small quantities and often. Sometimes a patient is too feeble to help himself to food, and then he must be fed by the nurse. When such is the case, she should be extremely careful, no matter what the pressure of other work may be, not to hurry him. Give him plenty of time,—first, that the food may remain in the mouth long enough to be mixed with the saliva, for saliva is one of the digestive juices; and second, so that it may be thoroughly masticated and broken; otherwise it will be thrown into the stomach in large masses, and may not digest at all.

The *quantity* of food given will always depend upon the condition of the person, and will consequently vary for each individual. Give rather *too little* than too much, with, of course, the understanding that there is always an abundance to be had. A little is often a challenge, especially to one of delicate appetite; a large quantity is always vulgar. It is much better to carry a second portion to one who needs it than to offer too much at first.

No exact and definite directions can be given for the serving of special dishes, for a nurse's resources in the way of china, etc., are so uncertain; but a few hints in regard to some principles that, no matter what the circumstances are, never change may be found of service.

For instance, water, lemonade, milk, milk-punch, and all other cold drinks are most healthful when *cool*, not ice-cold. Ice-cold water, ice-cold milk, and all chilled drinks are *always forbidden* for both sick and well, except in fevers, in extremely hot weather, and in unusual cases, when only a few spoons of liquid are taken. Even in these cases it is a question whether *cool* liquids would not do as well. We all know the danger of taking a large quantity of ice-cold drink when overheated. Even death has frequently resulted from it.

Serve tea, coffee, cocoa, bouillon, broth, gruel, and all hot drinks in cups which are *hot*, not lukewarm. Soup as a part of a meal should be served in a covered silver dish when practicable, for silver may be made very hot, and no other is so pretty. In lieu of silver use a covered china dish, or a bouillon-cup made hot in an oven beforehand. Remember that the *warmth* of all these foods is one of their valuable qualities.

Beef-juice and beef-tea may be offered in a red wine-glass, to conceal the color, which is sometimes at first unpleasant to those unaccustomed to the use of rare beef; but the taste of these is so acceptable and savory that, after taking a few spoons, the objection vanishes.

Cups and tumblers ought not to be filled to more than within a half inch of the top. The best argument for this custom is, that it is considered good form; but there is a good reason back of it, as is the case in most other established customs. If a cup be filled to the brim it cannot be moved without spilling the liquid over the outside; this occasions wiping, which it is especially difficult to do, and waste of a certain portion of the contents; then it is not easy to drink from a cup so filled.

Fruits, such as oranges, grapes, peaches, and tomatoes, should be served cool, but not cold or chilled. The ideal way to eat fruits is without artificial cooling. A peach is never so delicious as at the moment it is gathered from the tree, just ripe, and tomatoes have the finest flavor eaten directly off the vines; but it is seldom that these fruits or others can be so obtained, and we, knowing that fruits do not keep well except in cool places, are apt to associate a certain degree of coolness with them. The objection to serving fruits very cold is that, besides the fact that they are not as readily digested so, their delicate flavor is lost, for the cold contracts the sensitive papillæ of the tongue, and thus the power of tasting is temporarily deadened.

Oranges, peaches, and plums may be used uncooked, as they are extremely easy of digestion so, and also grapes, unless there is objection to the seeds, in which case they should be cooked, and the seeds strained out. Apples and pears are safer cooked; tomatoes may be eaten either way.

Transparent jellies are pretty served in glass dishes, and ice-cream, sherbets, and ices in china saucers, or ice-cream dishes of pink, or other delicately warm colors. Ice-cream, uncolored, in shell pink, is much more attractive than it is in cold mauve or green. Water-ices, which usually have color of their own, may be served in dishes to match it. Raspberry or strawberry ice is lovely in dull rich red; apricot ice in yellow — that is, a certain shade of écru which harmonizes with the color of the fruit — and pineapple and lemon ice in Dresden ware are very pretty.

Eggs should be opened into a hot, though not very hot, egg-glass. It is the proper thing to do so even when a patient is well enough to open them for himself, for, although the supply may have been obtained from the very best sources, there is always the risk that some of the eggs may be old, too old to be good.[1]

Oysters in the half-shell are served simply with salt, pepper, and lemon-juice, or horse-radish. A quarter or a half of a lemon is placed on the oyster-plate with the oysters, and after the salt and pepper are sprinkled on a few drops of lemon-juice are squeezed over each oyster, or a bit of horse-radish is placed on each.

Broiled oysters may be served with a sauce of melted butter, seasoned with salt, pepper, and lemon-juice or vinegar.

Toast is particularly acceptable with nearly all kinds of cooked oysters, and fancy shapes, such as tiny rounds, squares, and points, are excellent with stews, soups, and roasts, instead of crackers.

Dry toast ought to be eaten directly off the toaster, and, except in serious illness, butter may be given with it. Orange, gooseberry, raspberry, and other marmalades, currant, apple, and grape jellies, and baked sweet apples or apple-sauce, are excellent with either dry or water toast. Cooked apples in any form are delicious with milk and cream toasts.

[1] In England it is the custom to serve eggs in the shell, and it is considered bad form to open them, but in America the latter way is general; for an invalid there is no question but that it is the most convenient way to do.

It is the fashion just now to serve junket, slip, soft custard, lemon cream, tapioca cream, and similar delicate desserts in cups and saucers, not glasses. The quainter the pattern of the china, the prettier the effect.

A plan for a breakfast, to consist of a peach, rolled wheat porridge, beefsteak, baked potato, coffee, and toast:

(1) Put the porridge, which should have been cooked the day before, on the fire to heat, and the potato into the oven to bake.

(2) Set some water to boil for the coffee, and the milk to heat to serve with it.

(3) Trim the steak, which should be a small piece an inch thick, an inch and a half wide, and three or four inches long; cut the bread, and make a butter-ball by rolling a bit of butter between two spatters made for the purpose.[1]

(4) Set a plate, cup and saucer, and dishes for serving the food, in the warming-oven to heat.

(5) Arrange the tray with a fresh napkin, knife, fork, spoons, salt and pepper, fine granulated sugar and cold cream for the porridge, and some lumps of loaf sugar for the coffee.

(6) Fifteen minutes before the potato is done make the coffee, and ten minutes later broil the steak; in the interim pare the peach, laying it open from the stone, and toast the bread.

Now, if calculation as to the time has been well made, everything will be ready — the potato baked, the porridge steaming, the coffee cooked, and the steak and toast waiting in the oven.

(7) Serve the fruit on a tiny fruit-plate, the por-

---

[1] The spatters should be soaked in boiling water for a few minutes, and then in cold water, to prevent the sticking of the butter.

ridge in a hot saucer, and the coffee, together. When the fruit and porridge are finished, offer the potato, wrapped in a doily to keep it warm, the steak in a hot covered silver dish, and the toast on an individual bread-plate. Or all may be served together when for any reason it seems best to do so: for instance, if the tray has to be carried a long distance, or up many flights of stairs.

The above arrangement is simply beginning with the things which require the longest time, and then taking each in such order that all shall be finished at the same moment.

By understanding the length of time required for each dish, there need be no hurrying, nor will anything be cooked too soon.

Dinner should be planned in the same way, and also supper. Even when there is not much cooking to be done the same idea prevails — that is, to begin with whatever requires the longest time, and to do last those dishes which spoil by standing; in other words, to be systematic, (1) because your meal is in better condition when so done, and (2) because it is easier for yourself. There then will be neither hurry nor worry, and work which ends with a satisfactory result is always a pleasure.

THE FEEDING OF CHILDREN

There are three ways in which a child may be supplied with food during its infancy: by its mother; by a substitute for its mother—a wet nurse; and by artificial feeding. This chapter will treat only of the latter method.

The child is fortunate whose mother can supply it with a sufficient quantity of wholesome milk. There is nothing more to be desired for it during the first ten or twelve months of its life. But often a mother, for one reason or another, is not able to nurse her child, and other means of feeding must be sought. In such cases, among the wealthier classes, a wet nurse is sometimes employed; but with the majority of people there is no alternative except artificial feeding. When this has been decided upon, the question naturally arises as to what shall be the best substitute for the natural nourishment of the child—mother's milk, which must always be taken as the perfect type of infants' food.[1] To this subject doctors and hygienists have given much attention for a long time.

---

[1] It should not be inferred from this that mother's milk is the best under *all* circumstances. It not infrequently happens that a mother, disregarding all indications to the contrary, will continue to nurse her baby after it has become disastrous both to herself and the infant to do so. If a baby remains puny, and the mother is exhausted and languid without any known cause, it is the part of wisdom to call in the aid of a physician, and have the milk analyzed. Good and careful feeding is infinitely better than nursing a baby upon impoverished milk, even if the quantity seems sufficient. A mother, in nursing her child, should do so at stated regular intervals. If it is injurious for a grown person to eat at odd times all day long, it is far more injurious for an infant. It will not hurt a child to be occasionally hungry, or even to cry,

Many kinds of food preparations have been made and tested. The result has been that, almost without exception, authorities agree that milk from healthy, well-fed cows, properly prepared, is the most valuable substitute for human milk that is at present known.[1]

The following analyses give the comparison between cow's milk and human milk:

	Human Milk.	Cow's Milk.
Nitrogenous substances	2.35%	4.30%
Fat	3.40%	3.80%
Sugar	4.85%	3.70%
Salts	.20%	.60%
Water	89.20%	87.60% [2]

Cow's milk varies considerably in nutritive properties, and for the growing infant who receives no other food it is extremely important that it be of the first quality. It should be tested in every possible way to enable one to form a correct estimate of its value, and unless unquestionably good should be rejected.[3] When fresh from the cow, not more than two hours old, and of superior quality, it need not be sterilized, but should be put into perfectly cleansed and sterile vessels,[4] and kept in an ice-box, or refrigerator, at a temperature of 50° to 60° Fahr.[5]

When obliged to buy the ordinary milk of commerce, select if possible that which is put up in glass

whereas it *will* hurt it seriously and perhaps induce life-long dyspepsia if food is introduced into the stomach while there yet remains in it that previously taken in an undigested, or partly digested, condition. The cry which a young mother thinks indicates hunger, and hopes to allay by feeding, is often only a dyspeptic pain, which is increased by the very means she takes to lessen it.

[1] The milk of goats and asses is said to be more easily digested than cow's milk, but is procurable only in exceptional cases.
[2] From Uffelmann's "Hygiene of the Child."
[3] See chapter on Milk.
[4] Vessels for holding milk may be made sterile by boiling them in water for fifteen minutes. Glass is best.
[5] A low temperature retards the growth of micro-organisms.

jars. There are farmers who do this. Each jar is sealed, marked with the owner's name and address, and the date of sending. Such milk does not become contaminated with bad air in transit, cannot be tampered with by middlemen, and must be free from dirt, as it would show through the glass; each customer gets exactly a quart, with all the cream that belongs to it; moreover, the owner, having attached his name, has thus put his reputation at stake, and is not likely to sell inferior milk. When this is not practicable, search for the best and cleanest dairy, and see that the milk is delivered as soon as possible after being received at the dairy. Milk should not be bought from small stores.

The best milk comes from cows that have good pasturage, with clean running water, and that are fed in winter on dry fodder and grain, and not on ensilage and brewery waste.

According to the reports of the American Public Health Association, *one fifth* of all the deaths among infants may be traced to the milk supply, and there is no doubt that most of the sickness of bottle-fed children, during the summer months, is directly due to the unhealthy condition of their food.

It then becomes the imperative duty of every mother, nurse, or other person who has the care of children, to learn, if she does not already know, the simpler tests for milk, and something of the philosophy of the feeding of her charge.[1] When such knowledge is more general, and women are able to determine intelligently the quality of the milk which is offered them, then will milk-dealers be forced to cease mixing, adulterating, and otherwise tampering with the milk, which, as a general thing, is sold at the farms in excellent condition.

[1] Test for reaction, fat, and specific gravity. See article on Milk.

The first object is to secure a good quality of milk; then comes the consideration of how it shall be prepared: this must be in such manner as shall render it as nearly like human milk, in composition and digestibility, as possible.

Comparison of the tables just given shows that cow's milk contains more nitrogenous matter and salts, and less sugar, than human milk.[1] By diluting with water to reduce the protein and salts, and adding sugar and a little cream, the proportions of these different substances may be made to approximate those in mother's milk. In both the sugar is the same—lactose, or milk-sugar; the fats are also much alike in each; but the albuminous matter of cow's milk differs somewhat from that of human milk, particularly in the way in which it coagulates in the presence of acids. Human milk forms into small, light, feathery curds; cow's milk into large, compact, not so easily digested masses. It is necessary, therefore, to seek the means for preventing the coagulation of milk in large curds in the stomach of the child—in other words, to so treat cow's milk that it shall coagulate more like human milk. This may be done in two ways:

(1) By mixing into the milk some substance which shall separate the particles of albumen from each other, and so cause it to form into smaller masses.

(2) By partial predigestion.

To accomplish the first, it is necessary to use some diluting substance of a harmless nature; if it be nutritious, so much the better. For this, Mellin's food, barley-water, veal broth, lime-water, and gelatin are recommended.

Mellin's food is a partially predigested grain, in such

---

[1] The following mineral substances occur in both cow's and woman's milk: potassa, soda, lime, magnesia, iron, phosphoric acid, sulphuric acid, and chlorin.

a condition that it can be assimilated by the infant; barley-water is valuable for its potash salts, in which cow's milk is deficient, and which the growing babe needs; veal broth is rich in lime; and lime-water neutralizes the acid of the gastric juice, so that milk is not acted upon so strongly, and consequently forms into a lighter curd.

The second method is that of partial predigestion, and is accomplished by the use of peptonizing agents, among which Fairchild's peptogenic milk-powder is good (directions for its use will be given later). On account of the expense of these preparations it is not probable that they will come into general use, except in cases of sickness.

It is therefore evident that dependence must be placed almost entirely upon attenuants to render the casein of cow's milk more easily digestible. Probably for this Mellin's food is as good, if not better, than any other of the recommended preparations. It is not injurious, is nutritious in itself, and is a good diluting agent, causing milk to form into looser curds than it would otherwise do, and it contains sufficient sugar to require no further addition of this substance.

Now arises the question whether milk shall be sterilized for infants' feeding. The weight of evidence seems to be as follows: if it is possible to see the conditions under which the cows live, and to *know* that they are unquestionably good, that the animals are in perfect health, that the milk is drawn from cleansed udders into cleansed vessels by clean hands, kept in a cool place, and used fresh, then it is probably wise not to sterilize it. All milk otherwise obtained should be made sterile before using, and as soon as possible after milking. Looking to the standard—human milk—there are no organisms in it. That alone is sufficient reason why cow's milk should be freed from them.[1]

Again, most bottle-fed children do well during the cold weather of autumn and winter; in summer the mortality is very great among them, especially in the poorer districts of large cities. It is well known that the chances for life with children nourished by mother's milk are greater than with those artificially fed. Why should this be? There is no doubt that it is owing to the presence in cow's milk of extraneous substances, the products of bacterial growth — products which are often absolute poisons; and it is highly probable that cholera infantum, in a vast majority of cases, may be traced to the action of such poisons.

Under favorable conditions of temperature, such as prevail in the warm months of summer and early autumn, micro-organisms grow with almost incomprehensible rapidity in any substance which is suitable food for them. Milk is such a substance; and, as bacteria multiply with wonderful rapidity, millions forming in a few hours in every thimbleful,[2] it is perfectly evident that they must produce something. This something may or may not be of a harmful nature, depending upon what species of organism produces it. I have no evidence at hand to show what is the nature of the product of any one organism which finds a home in milk; but there are instances on record where the nature of the product of certain bacteria is known: for example, the diphtheria bacillus. This little rod, growing upon the outside of the ton-

---

[1] It is worthy of notice, in this connection, that children have been known to be made ill by drinking water which has stood for a length of time — such water containing great numbers of bacteria, but none of the so-called *disease-producing* organisms. The same water, when boiled, produced no ill effects.

[2] Stated by Sedgwick.

sils in the human throat, produces a most virulent poison, which, taken up by the circulation, pervades the whole body, and often so enfeebles its functions as to destroy it.[1]

Reasoning from analogy, it is not impossible to suppose that other organisms may produce substances of a similar character, poisonous in their effects, and which, when taken into the alimentary canal, may produce very grave digestive disorders.[2]

Further, bacteria, by their multiplication, use some of the constituents of milk for their food, thus changing its composition. It is very important to prevent this growth, or, in case it has begun, to check it before it has rendered the milk unwholesome food. Hence the necessity of sterilizing *immediately* all milk which is not received directly from the cow. Besides, cows are often infected with tuberculosis, foot-and-mouth disease, splenic fever, pneumonia, and other dangerous disorders. Their milk may be a direct cause of infection. When it is sterilized there is less danger from it; but even then it is not, of course, a wholesome food, because of the poisons which may be produced in the animal during the progress of the disease, and because a sick and weakened cow cannot give wholesome milk.[3]

In many cities, through the influence of children's hospitals and sanitariums, the knowledge and methods

---

[1] Welsh.

[2] Since writing the above I have learned that Prof. Vaughan has isolated a poisonous matter — the product of the growth of certain organisms which multiply readily in milk — which caused active vomiting, purging, collapse, and death when injected into the lower animals.

[3] In England and America many cases of scarlatina, typhoid fever, and diphtheria have been traced to the milk supply. But there is no satisfactory evidence that those diseases were transmitted from the cow; more probably the milk, which is an especially good nutritive medium for bacteria, became infected after leaving the cow. In October, 1891, an epidemic of diphtheria prevailed in Melrose, Mass. Thirty-three cases were reported. On investigation it was found that every case

of sterilizing milk for infants' food are gradually spreading.

Circular wire frames, made something like casters, and fitted with eight bottles, each holding enough milk for one feeding, may be bought for the purpose of sterilizing at almost any pharmacy. The frame is to be set in a kettle with water in the bottom, which on boiling produces steam, the heat of which does the sterilizing.[1] This is an easy method. Another good way is to sterilize at a lower temperature for a longer time, as less change is produced in the constituents of the milk by the lower degree of heat. This may be easily done by immersing the bottles in water at 190° Fahr., and maintaining that temperature for an hour.[2]

Care of Feeding-bottles. Great care must be taken in cleansing feeding-bottles. When they can be

---

could be traced to the milk supply. The farm from which it came was situated in an adjoining town, and the family of the dealer had been afflicted with diphtheria, two of the children having died. The use of the milk was, of course, promptly stopped.

[1] A simple and inexpensive apparatus for sterilizing milk consists of a covered tin kettle ten inches in height by eight inches in diameter, a wire basket, which fits easily into the kettle, supplied with supports or legs projecting one and a half inches from the bottom, one dozen eight-ounce nursing-bottles, and a bundle of fresh cotton wadding. The whole apparatus, costing about $1.25, is kept in most drug stores.

Milk for twenty-four hours' use is properly sweetened and diluted with water in a clean pitcher, and as much of this as the child will take at one feeding is poured into each bottle, and the bottle stopped with cotton wadding, which should fit only moderately tight in the neck of the bottle. The kettle is filled to the depth of one half to one inch with water, the basket containing the bottles placed in it, the kettle covered and placed over a fire until the steam comes out from the sides of the top for half an hour, when the basket containing the bottles should be removed and put in a cool place. When the milk is to be used, it should be heated by placing a bottle in warm water for a few minutes. The cotton is then removed, and a sterilized nipple attached. After the feeding the bottle is cleansed and kept in an inverted position until used again. The above directions are those of Dr. Booker, specialist of children's diseases, Johns Hopkins Hospital.

[2] In the Walker-Gordon Milk Laboratory, in Boston, milk is sterilized at 175° to 180° Fahr. for fifteen minutes, and it is claimed that this tem-

washed immediately after using, it is easy to make them perfectly clean; but when this is impracticable they should be put to soak in *cold* water, then washed with hot soap-suds, and last boiled for ten minutes in clear water. If flecks dry on the inside, put a teaspoon of rice, or coarse salt, into the bottle with a little water, and shake well until all is removed. Never use shot: it might cause lead poisoning.

Plain rubber nipples alone should be used, never the tube attachment. The nipples should be washed clean and dried after each nursing. Before again using the nipple it should be put into boiling water for ten minutes, and only the rim of it should be touched in handling. The nipple should never be put into the mouth of another person to test the milk.

Condensed Milk. When a large percentage of the water of milk is evaporated, and sugar added, a thick syrup is formed, known as condensed milk.

It is made extensively in Switzerland and America. When sealed air-tight in cans it will keep indefinitely.

Its average composition—a mean of 41 analyses by Prof. Leeds—is as follows:

Water	30.34%
Fat	12.10%
Milk-sugar	16.62%
Cane-sugar	22.26%
Albuminoids	16.07%
Ash	2.61%
Total,	100.00

perature gives the best results for milk to be used within twenty-four hours. If the milk has to be kept a longer time, a higher temperature is necessary, as only the bacteria and not the spores are destroyed by 175° Fahr.

Machines are in use in France which will heat great quantities of milk to about 155° Fahr. and then rapidly cool it. Not all, but nearly all, forms of bacteria likely to be found in milk are destroyed at the temperature of 155°, and the good flavor of the milk is not injured. Such milk is known as *Pasteurized milk*.

Owing to the additional sugar it is impossible to dilute it so that the protein and sugar shall approach the standard of human milk.

Children fed with it are plump, but have soft flesh; they are large, but not strong, and lack the power of endurance and resistance to disease. Their teeth come late, and they are very likely to have rickets.[1] This is enough to indicate that it is not a proper food upon which to feed a child exclusively.

Condensed milk is valuable in emergencies or in traveling, and may also be used occasionally when for any reason the milk supply fails. It has the advantage of being free from ferments and easily kept.

There are physicians who recommend the use of condensed milk, and no doubt, compared with the germ-laden, watery fluid called milk, obtainable in the poorer sections of large cities, it is infinitely better. It should always be diluted with at least ten times its bulk of water.

Preserved Milk. Preserved milk is milk which has been condensed and canned without the addition of sugar. It would be a valuable food for children were it not that it is expensive, and will keep but a few hours after the can is opened. By sterilizing it in flasks with narrow necks, plugged with cotton, it may be kept as other milk is for an indefinite time. As soon as the can is opened, the contents should be poured into a glass or earthen vessel, for, on exposure of the milk to the air, chemical action takes place with the tin.[2]

Farinaceous Foods. There are many farinaceous forms of food prepared for the use of infants and children. Probably the most valuable of them are

---

[1] See the works of Drs. Louis Starr, Uffelmann, and Jacobi.

[2] The amount of condensation in preserved milk may be easily ascertained by noting the amount of water which is necessary to add in order to make its specific gravity equal to that of ordinary milk.

those made according to the Liebig process. The starch of the grain from which such foods are prepared is, in the process of manufacture, changed into soluble dextrine, or sugar (glucose), by the action of the diastase of malt: the very thing which an infant cannot do.

When we consider that the digestion of starch in the alimentary canal consists of this change into glucose, and that it is effected principally by the saliva and the pancreatic juice, the significance of the value of such foods will be seen.

It is also well to bear in mind that neither of these functions (the secretion of saliva and pancreatic juice) is developed in an infant until it enters the third month of its life, and then but very imperfectly. That alone shows the necessity of *excluding all starch* from its food up to that age.

Mellin's food and malted milk are prepared according to the Liebig process. In them the starch has been converted into soluble matter by the action of the ferment of malt. It is really a partial predigestion. Mellin's food does not contain milk.

The following analysis of Mellin's food is one made by Professor Fresenius, of Wiesbaden, Germany:

Non-nitrogenous substances soluble in water 69.38%
Non-nitrogenous substances insoluble in water 3.18%

Total carbohydrates 72.56%

Nitrogenous substances soluble in water............ 4.69%
Nitrogenous substances insoluble in water.......... 5.06%

Total albuminoids. 9.75%

Total salts, mostly phosphoric acid, carbonic acid, and potassa 4.37%

Total moisture 13.32%

Cane sugar, none. Reaction, alkaline.

THE FEEDING OF CHILDREN

Comparative analysis of Mellin's food, prepared for use, with that of **woman's** milk and cow's milk.

Constituents.	Mellin's Food.	Woman's Milk.	Cow's Milk.
Fat	2.36%	4.00%	3.30%
Albuminoids	2.83%	2.50%	3.50%
Carbohydrates	6.81%	6.50%	5.00%
Salts and inorganic matter	.74%	.50%	.70%
Water	87.26%	86.50%	87.50%
Cellulose	A trace.	......	......
Cane-sugar	None.	......	......
Starch	None.	......	......

Dr. A. Stutzer, Bonn, Germany.

This analysis shows that Mellin's food bears comparison with milk. It is easily digested, and as an *attenuant* for milk may be used without harm during the early months of life, but it should not be used to the exclusion of milk for more than a few days at a time, and then only when milk is not retained by the stomach.

Later it is doubtless a valuable addition to the regular daily food of the child.

Malted milk is made from selected grain and desiccated or dried milk. To prepare it for the infant it needs only the addition of water. It is probably one of the best substitutes for milk, but should not be used for any length of time when it is possible to get good milk.

The starch of grains may be converted into dextrine and glucose by the action of heat as well as by the action of diastase, so that when flour is subjected to a certain temperature, and for a certain time, this change is produced.

Nestlé's food, Imperial Granum, Ridge's food, and some others are made very carefully from selected wheat by this process. Nestlé's food contains dried milk.

These foods are all valuable when made into gruel or porridge, but should be used very sparingly under the age of twelve months, and then only as attenuants for milk, *not as substitutes* for it.

Dr. Mary Putnam Jacobi, editor of "Domestic Hygiene of the Child," by Uffelmann (a translation), in speaking of the value of the various preparations of infants' food on the market, says: "There is not the slightest reason to prefer them to milk or its preparations, except that the latter requires more care; and for any intelligent and affectionate mother this reason is quite insufficient. . . . During the first year the baby is building up tissues and organs that are to last him throughout life; and these will work well or ill according to the degree of perfection and precision of structure which they attain at the beginning. And this depends to an immense extent upon the suitability of the food, not only to be digested, but to be absorbed, and then to be assimilated and organized.

"So mysterious are the properties of the molecules of albumen and fat, when once they have been thrown into the whirl of the living organism, that we must strive to deviate as little as possible from the exact forms given to us in nature, if only because we do not know what remote effects might result from the deviations. If nature provides the albumen of milk and a living fluid, we cannot expect the same results from any other albumen, or from long dead organic matter, as condensed milk."

The farinaceous foods have value, but they cannot replace good milk, which should be almost the sole food of the child to at least the age of ten months, and the principal nutrient to the age of two years.

When a baby is nursed, and its mother has an abundance of milk, it takes nothing else during the first ten or twelve months of life. When a baby is artificially fed, this fact should be borne in mind. The important thing is to attain as nearly as possible to the standard that nature has set.

Biedert's cream mixture and the whey mixture are valuable for young infants and those which for any reason do not thrive on milk.

Amount for Each Meal. A child is nourished, not by what it swallows, but by what it digests. Giving too much or too concentrated milk is very unwise, for the delicate system cannot manage it, and too frequently the meal becomes a source of pain rather than of strength. Each individual babe will require a little different treatment in this respect from every other.

In general, for the first six weeks from two to four tablespoons at a feeding may be given; from that age to six months, from four to eight tablespoons, gradually increasing the amount to twelve tablespoons at one year.

Dilution. Cow's milk is more easily digested when diluted with water, and we are more likely to dilute too little than too much. The amount of water used should vary with the age and strength of digestion of the child. As a rule the new-born infant should have two parts water to one of milk; at four months equal parts of milk and water; at ten months one part water and two parts milk. When digestion is particularly feeble, it may be necessary to dilute milk with six or eight times its bulk of water.

Manner of Giving. It is best to give milk from a bottle so constructed that suction is necessary, for it induces the flow of the digestive juices. Use the plain rubber nipple; those with tube attachments which extend into the bottle are to be avoided, on account of the difficulty of making them perfectly clean inside. Cultures from these tubes always give large numbers of bacteria, as do also those made from the nipples, unless they are boiled.

The *intervals* of feeding will vary somewhat with the age of the child. Once in two or two and a half hours during the day for the first six months, and every three hours from the sixth to the twelfth month, is the general rule.

The *temperature* of the meal should be 100° Fahr.

A babe needs less variety in its food than older children, and they in turn require less than grown persons; but both must have a certain proportion of the five essential food principles.

There is an impression in the minds of many that children should not have fat. This has perhaps sprung from the fact that mother's milk has a watery, thin appearance. It seems not rich; nevertheless it has a due proportion of fat, and it is extremely important that this be maintained when cow's milk is diluted, for this cream is the best addition.

Fat is needed not only for the growth of brain and nerves, which is very rapid in children, but also for the perfect formation of other tissues.

The following table is that given by Dr. Louis Starr as a guide for feeding:

GENERAL RULES FOR FEEDING.

Age.	Intervals of Feeding.	Average Am't each Meal.	Average Am't in 24 hours.
First week	2 hours	2 tablespoons	1¼ pints
Second to sixth week	2½ hours	3–4 tablespoons	1½–2 pints
Sixth week to sixth month	3 hours	6–8 tablespoons	2½–3 pints
At six months	3 hours	12 tablespoons	4½ pints
At ten months	3 hours	16 tablespoons	5 pints

For the First Week; One Feeding

1 Tablespoon of whey.[1] $\frac{2}{3}$ Tablespoon of cream.
1 Tablespoon of water. $\frac{1}{6}$ Teaspoon of sugar.

Or Biedert's cream mixture:

1 Tablespoon of cream. 3 Tablespoons of water.
  $\frac{1}{4}$ Teaspoon of milk-sugar.

Or,

1 Tablespoon of milk. 3 Tablespoons of water.
  $\frac{1}{4}$ Teaspoon of milk-sugar.

If it is desirable to make at once a sufficient quantity of Biedert's cream mixture for several feedings, the above rule multiplied by eight will furnish enough for eight bottles, and is as follows: one cup of cream, three cups of boiling water, and one tablespoon of milk-sugar. Mix all together; put the mixture in equal portions into eight feeding-bottles, and plug each with cotton. Either sterilize it or put it immediately on ice to keep.

After the First Week, and Until the Sixth Week

Use either the cream mixture, the whey mixture, or the following:

2 Tablespoons of cow's milk.
4 Tablespoons of water.
1 Teaspoon of Mellin's food.
$\frac{1}{3}$ Teaspoon of milk-sugar.

---

[1] To prepare whey: 1 pint of milk mixed with 1 teaspoon of liquid rennet. Set in a warm place until the curd is formed; then break the curd and put it into a cloth or a wire strainer to drain.

From the Sixth Week to the Sixth Month

Water and milk in equal quantities, with a little cream and milk-sugar, and some attenuant, such as Mellin's food or barley jelly.[1]

> 2 Tablespoons of cow's milk.
> 2 Tablespoons of water.
> 1 Tablespoon of cream.[2]
> 1 Teaspoon of Mellin's food.
> $\frac{3}{8}$ Teaspoon of sugar.

The above proportion to be maintained, but the amount to be varied according to the age of the babe.

If at any time this disagrees, use instead Biedert's cream mixture or the whey mixture. When both of these fail it may be necessary to peptonize the food.

To peptonize milk:

No. 1

> 2 Tablespoons of milk.
> 2 Tablespoons of water.
> 1 Tablespoon of cream.
> 1 Small measure of peptogenic milk powder.

Put all into a clean porcelain-lined saucepan and heat it, stirring slowly until the mixture boils; this should not require more than ten minutes.

No. 2

A special preparation for sick or feeble infants, or those suffering from indigestion.

---

[1] To make barley jelly: Boil two tablespoons of pearl barley in a pint of water for two hours. Strain. It will form a tender jelly.

[2] The condensed cream of the Highland Co. may be used when other cream cannot be obtained.

2 Tablespoons of milk.
2 Tablespoons of water.
1 Tablespoon of cream.
1 Small measure of peptogenic milk powder.

Put all into a bottle, shake it well, place it in a bath or kettle of hot water of a temperature of 115° Fahr. (so hot that the hand cannot be borne in it long without discomfort), and keep it at that temperature for exactly thirty minutes; then pour it into a saucepan, and heat quickly to the boiling point. By this method a very thorough predigestion takes place. The process should be stopped before the bitter taste is developed.

From the Sixth to the Tenth Month

Increase the proportion of milk and of Mellin's food, or other attenuant used.[1]

4 Tablespoons of cow's milk.
3 Tablespoons of water.
1½ Teaspoons of cream.
1 Tablespoon of Mellin's food.
½ Teaspoon of milk-sugar.

Boil the water, then add the milk, Mellin's food, cream, and sugar, or put all together in a feeding-bottle, place in a kettle of water heated to 190° Fahr., and keep it at that temperature for one hour.[2] This amount is only a general rule, and may, of course, be varied according to the age and individual need of the child. The *proportion* of the ingredients should, however, not be changed.

[1] **Malted** milk, Nestlé's food, Ridge's food, Imperial Granum, or barley-flour, may be used as attenuants.
[2] Enough for the whole day may be made by multiplying the rule by eight, dividing the quantity into eight bottles, and sterilizing all at once. Keep in a cool place until needed.

From the Tenth to the Twelfth Month

6 Tablespoons of cow's milk.
3 Tablespoons of water.
1½ Tablespoons of cream.
1 or 2 Tablespoons of Mellin's food.
1 Teaspoon of milk-sugar.[1]

Mellin's Food with Condensed Milk. Although, as has been previously stated, condensed milk is not a proper food for children, there are times when it may be necessary to use it: for instance, in traveling, or when the daily supply of milk for any reason fails.

The usual mixture of condensed milk given to babies is one part of milk to twelve parts of water, the analysis[2] of which shows the fat and casein to be in too small proportions. If more condensed milk be added, the sugar will be increased too much; but by increasing the water, and using Mellin's food and cream, a very good mixture may be obtained. The following is recommended:

1 Teaspoon condensed milk.
1 Tablespoon of Mellin's food.
8 Tablespoons of water (1 cup).
1 Teaspoon of cream.

Boil the water, then add the condensed milk, Mellin's food, and cream in the order in which they are mentioned, stirring until all is dissolved.

---

[1] Milk-sugar may be obtained without difficulty, and always, at a pharmacy. It is better for infants than cane-sugar, because it is a little easier of digestion.

[2] Water 92.60%
Fat 1.00%
Casein .... .84%
Sugar 5.40%
Ash .... .16%

Dr. Meigs.

Nothing should be used during the first twelve months except liquid food, and that must not be of too great density.

Avoid any food which contains cellulose, or starch as such.[1] Cellulose is but imperfectly if at all digested by grown persons; and starch, not being a natural kind of nourishment for an infant, is extremely liable to ferment and cause serious digestive disturbances.

It should be remembered that, although the chief function of a babe is to eat, sleep, and grow, its stomach cannot work all the time, and, consequently, the wise plan is to feed it only at regular intervals.

The best proof that a child is doing well is increase of weight, a healthy appearance, and lack of fretfulness. Sometimes, when restless, it is only a drink of water that it needs, as children suffer much from thirst in warm weather.

From the Twelfth to the Eighteenth Month

Continue with milk, *undiluted* with water, as the principal food. Use with it Mellin's food as before, Nestlé's food, Ridge's food, Imperial Granum, oatmeal porridge *strained*, soft custard, soft-cooked eggs, cocoa[2] cooked in water, with milk added or cooked in milk, and cracker-crumbs boiled in water, with milk added.

After Eighteen Months

The same diet as for the previous six months, with the addition of scraped or pounded chicken, mutton, or beef; mashed baked potatoes with beef-juice poured

---

[1] Although Mellin's food is made from grain, the starch in it has been changed in the process of manufacture into easily assimilated dextrine and sugar.

[2] The ordinary powdered cocoa, which has been deprived of oil. Dutch brands are good.

over; toasted bread or toasted crackers rolled into crumbs, and soaked in milk or broth; junket, and plain, simple puddings, such as cream-of-rice, tapioca, and arrowroot.

A diet similar to this should be the chief food to the seventh year. It may be varied by farina, wheat-germ, and other grain mushes, dried rusk and milk, or Zwieback[1] and milk, sponge cake with cream or milk, snow-pudding, and other wholesome and delicate desserts, and cooked fruits.

Foods to be Carefully Avoided. Veal, pork in any form except bacon,[2] highly seasoned stews, curries, canned meats or dried meats in any form, baked beans, fruit cake, also all cakes or gingerbread made with so-called "cooking-butter" or with common lard, raw fruits, lobsters and crabs, new potatoes, berries, and cabbage.

---

[1] Zwieback is a slightly sweetened and dried bread, which may be bought at any grocer's. It is like dried rusk.

[2] Bacon is very easy of digestion, and is a valuable form of fat for children four or five years old. Given with bread or potatoes, it will often be eaten when butter is refused.

DISTRICT NURSING

In England and in some parts of America district nursing, or nursing among the very poor of certain sections of a city, is an established part of a nurse's work. Her duties are to go from house to house among the sick, to administer medicine and food, and to make the surroundings of her patient comfortable.

There is no way in which one may reach the hearts and sympathies of the poor so quickly as by helping them to, or showing them how to do for themselves, those things which they think they need.

Their first consideration is for the immediate necessities of life — food, clothing, and shelter. Their days are spent in a struggle with the world for these — too often an unequal struggle, in which the world conquers. A nurse, or any other person who can gain admission to their homes and sympathies, may help them in many ways as no other can. Great good may be done by teaching them economical and simple methods of preparing their food, which as a general thing is cooked both badly and wastefully.

A nurse doing district nursing, besides administering medicine and making her patient generally comfortable, will inevitably and naturally turn to the preparation of some form of nourishment for him. If she can make it acceptably with the materials and cooking utensils at hand, or is able to ask for that which is within the means of the family, or to direct the buying of it, she will add greatly to the comfort of the household.

The object of this chapter is not, however, to deal with cooking for the sick. That will be left entirely to the judgment of the nurse, who is supposed to have studied the subject as a part of her training. But it has occurred to the author that a nurse doing district nursing would often find the opportunity to help the *families* of her patients, and that often such help would need to be given in order to prevent actual suffering. Especially would this be true if it were the mother of a family who was ill, and there was no one to prepare food for the father and children, who must be fed. Usually there is a child, either boy or girl, who is old enough to learn if there is some one to teach.

The following pages have been written for the purpose of suggesting, to such nurses as are disposed to do good in this way, some easily made and economical dishes which are really both palatable and nutritious. A few directions about building a fire, washing dishes, sweeping, etc., will be given, and then some bills of fare with recipes adapted for the use of people of small means, and taken for the most part from the Lomb Prize Essay by Mary H. Abel, entitled "Practical, Sanitary, and Economic Cooking," and published by the American Public Health Association, 1890.

Permission to use these recipes has been graciously granted by Mrs. Abel, and the American Public Health Association, through Mr. Lomb.

To Make a Fire. First, clear the stove of ashes and cinders, then put in wood-shavings, or twisted newspaper; over this foundation lay small pieces of wood, crossed, so as to leave air-spaces for draft, then larger pieces of wood, and lastly two or three fire-shovels of coal. Light the kindling from the bottom of the grate, and let it burn for a while before putting on more coal; remember that it is the heat from the burning wood which ignites the coal, and if it does not burn it is because there is not wood enough to produce sufficient heat to start the union between the combustible part of the coal—carbon chiefly—and the oxygen of the air. Add coal a little at a time, thus keeping a fresh fire.

After the fire is well started regulate the dampers often, to economize as much as possible the consumption of coal. Keep them partially or wholly closed, unless a hot fire is needed for some purpose. The cinders left from an old fire should be sifted and reburned. Many dollars' worth of coal may be saved in a year by giving attention to the drafts of a stove.

To Wash Dishes. Mixing-bowls, double boilers, and all dishes which for any reason have food clinging to them, should be put to soak in cold water as soon as used. If this has not been done, attend to it before making other arrangements for washing the dishes. See then that the dish-pan or tub, dish-cloths, and sink are perfectly clean; if not, make them so with hot water and soap. Wash the dishes in hot soapy water, not hot water alone, even if they are not greasy, and rinse them in a pan of clear hot water. Take glassware, silver, and china first, then steel knives and forks, granite-ware, kettles, tins, etc. When the dishes are finished, wash thoroughly and dry, or put to dry, both the wiping-towels and the dish-cloths; unless they are white, clean, and sweet when done, boil them in clear soapy water until they become so, changing it frequently if it looks dark.

Sweeping and Dusting. Sweep slowly and carefully, holding the broom close to the floor, so that the dust shall not be thrown into the air. *Burn the dirt;* never allow it to be thrown into a box or into the coal-hod.

Dusting should be done with a damp cloth, wiping up the dust, not brushing it into the air, from which it will settle upon some other object. When you have finished, wash the duster and hang it to dry. Never use a feather duster. With it one simply brushes the dust from one place only to have it settle in another.

BILLS OF FARE

Mrs. Abel says, in her chapter headed "Bills of Fare": "The following bills of fare are made out for a family of six persons, consisting of a workingman, two women, and three children between the ages of six and fifteen.

"The amount of food, and the proportion in which the great food principles are represented, approximate to that which is demanded by standard dietaries for such a family. . . .

"To keep us in health and in working order, we ought to have a certain amount of what is best furnished by meat, eggs, milk, and other animal products, and we must also have fats, as well as what is given us in grains and vegetables." The following bills of fare are made up with this object in view:

For a family of six; average price, seventy-eight cents per day, or thirteen cents per person.

SATURDAY, MAY

Breakfast.	*Dinner.*	*Supper.*
Soda-biscuit.	Bread Soup.	Browned Flour Soup
Sugar-syrup.	Beef-neck Stew.	with Fried Bread.
Coffee.	Noodles.	Toast and Cheese.
	Cream-of-rice Pudding.	

The recipe for **Soda-biscuit** will be found on page 242.

Bread Soup. *Ingredients*, dry bread broken in small bits, water, salt, pepper, onion, and a little fat. Soak the bread in the water for a few minutes. Fry the onion, sliced, in the fat, and add it to the soup, with the salt and pepper.

Or, use milk instead of water, and toasted or fried bread. Boil slowly for five minutes to perfectly soften the bread.

Beef-neck stew, page 186.

Noodles. *Ingredients*, three eggs, three tablespoons of milk or water, one teaspoon of salt, and flour.

Make a hole in the middle of the flour, put in the other ingredients, and work to a stiff dough, then cut it into four strips. Knead each till fine grained, roll out as thin as possible, and lay the sheet aside to dry. When all are rolled, begin with the first, cut it into four equal pieces, lay the pieces together, one on top of another, and shave off very fine, as you would cabbage; pick the shavings apart with floured hands and let them dry a little.

To use. Boil the strips a few at a time in salted water, taking them out with a skimmer, and keeping them warm. Strew over them bread crumbs fried in butter, or use like macaroni.

These noodles will keep indefinitely when dried hard. Therefore, when eggs are cheap, they may be made and laid up for the winter. The water in which they are boiled is the basis of noodle soup. It needs only the addition of a little butter, a teaspoon of chopped parsley, and a few of the cooked noodles.

Cream-of-rice Pudding, page 206.

Browned Flour Soup.

2 Tablespoons of butter or fat.
½ Cup of flour.
2 Pints of water.
1 Pint of milk.
1 Teaspoon of salt.

Cook the flour brown, in the fat over a slow fire, or in an oven. Add slowly the water and other ingredients. Serve with fried bread.

Toast and Cheese. Toast some slices of white or Graham bread, arrange them in a platter, and pour over sufficient salted water to soften them. Grate over enough old cheese to cover the toast. Set it in the oven to melt, and place the slices together as sandwiches. This is the simplest form of "Welsh Rarebit."

SUNDAY, MAY

Breakfast.	*Dinner.*	*Supper.*
Milk Toast.	Beef Stew.	Noodle Soup.
Coffee.	Creamed Potatoes.	Broiled Herring.
	Dried Apple Pie.	Bread.
	Bread and Cheese.	Tea.
	Corn Coffee.	

Milk Toast, page 130. **Beef Stew**, page 186. **Creamed Potatoes**, page 166.

Dried Apple Pie. Make a crust in the following manner: One quart of flour, one teaspoon of salt, one tablespoon of butter or lard, or butter and suet, one scant pint of sweet milk, or water, with one teaspoon of soda and two of cream of tartar, or three teaspoons of baking powder.

Sift the flour, salt, cream of tartar, and soda together twice, put it into a chopping-tray, and chop in the shortening, which should be cold and hard, till all is fine and well mixed. Now add the milk a little at a time, still mixing with the chopping-knife. Turn the dough on to a molding-board, and roll it out quickly. When half an inch thick, bake in a sheet or cut it into rounds, and bake in layer cake tins.

When done, split it in two, and spread each half with dried apples, stewed with a little lemon-peel and sugar. Lay the two pieces together, and eat while warm.

Any other fruit may be used in the same way, and if a richer crust is wanted, two tablespoons of fat instead of one may be used.

Corn Coffee. Roast common field corn as brown as possible without burning. Grind coarsely, and steep like coffee. Add milk and sugar, and you will find it a delicious drink.

Noodle Soup, page 305.

MONDAY, MAY

Breakfast.	*Dinner.*	*Supper.*
Oatmeal Mush, with Milk and Sugar.	Pea Soup.	Bread Pancakes.
Bread.	Mutton Stew.	Fried Bacon.
Coffee.	Boiled Potatoes.	Tea.
	Bread.	

Oatmeal Mush, page 91.

Pea Soup. *Ingredients,* one pound of peas, one onion, two tablespoons of beef fat, salt and pepper. Additions to be made according to taste. One fourth of a pound of pork, or a ham-bone, a pinch of red pepper, or, an hour before serving, different vegetables, as carrots and turnips, chopped and fried.

Soak the peas over night in two quarts of water. In the morning pour it off, put on fresh water, and cook with the onion and fat until very soft. Then mash or press the peas through a colander or soup-strainer to remove the skins, and add enough water to make two quarts of somewhat thick soup. Season.

Mutton Stew, page 187.

Bread Pancakes. Make in the following manner: One quart of milk, three eggs, one tablespoon of butter, one teaspoon of salt. Add to this one cup of flour, and two cups of bread crumbs that have been soaked soft in milk or water and mashed smooth. The batter should be rather thick. Bake in small cakes, adding more flour if they stick.

TUESDAY, MAY

Breakfast.	Dinner.	Supper.
Oatmeal Mush and Milk.	Fried Fish, with Mint Sauce.	Fried Farina Pudding.
Buttered Toast.	Fried Potatoes.	Broiled Salt Pork.
Coffee.	Bread.	Bread. Tea.

Mint Sauce. Two tablespoons of chopped green mint, one tablespoon of sugar, one half cup of vinegar. Mix and let stand an hour or two.

Fried Farina Pudding. One pint of water, one pint of milk, one teaspoon of salt, one half pint of farina, two eggs. Mix the flour and eggs smooth with a part of the milk. Heat the remainder to boiling, and stir in the egg and flour. Continue stirring until it thickens, then cook for fifteen minutes in a double boiler. When cold, cut it in slices and fry them brown on a griddle.

SATURDAY, SEPTEMBER

Breakfast.	Dinner.	Supper.
Soda-biscuit.	Pea Soup.	Corn Mush and Molasses.
Baked Potatoes, with Drawn Butter Sauce.	Irish Stew. Bread.	Bread and Grated Cheese. Tea.
Cocoa.		

Drawn Butter Sauce. Make according to the rule for White Sauce (page 130), except use water instead of milk, and part beef fat instead of all butter.

Irish Stew (page 186).

SUNDAY, SEPTEMBER

Breakfast.	Dinner.	Supper.
Oatmeal and Milk.	Broiled Beef Liver.	Lentil Soup, with
Bread and Butter.	Boiled Potatoes	Fried Bread.
Cocoa.	and Carrots, with	Smoked Herring.
	Fried Onions.	Bread.
	Bread and Cheese.	Barley Porridge.

Boiled Potatoes, and Carrots with Fried Onions. Slice hot boiled potatoes and boiled carrots together. Season them with salt and pepper, and pour over them hot fried onions.

Lentil Soup. Made like Pea Soup, page 307.

Fried Bread. Cut bread into small cubes and fry it in hot fat until light brown.

Barley Porridge. Made with pearl barley soaked over night in water, and then cooked for two hours, or until it is soft. During the last hour add milk instead of water. Flavor with salt and butter.

MONDAY, SEPTEMBER

Breakfast.	Dinner.	Supper.
Buckwheat Cakes.	Giblet Soup.	Codfish Balls.
Fried Bacon.	Baked Potatoes, with	Cheese.
Coffee.	Drawn Butter Sauce.	Bread.
	Bread.	Tea.

Giblet Soup. Giblet soup is made from the heart, liver, and neck of chicken and other fowls, which in city markets are sold separately and very cheap. Clean them very carefully, wash in cold water, cut into small pieces, and boil for two hours with onions and herbs. Then add a little butter, thickening, salt, and pepper.

Codfish Balls *(Salt Cod).* Codfish is one of the cheap foods that seems to be thoroughly appreciated among us, and good ways of cooking it are generally understood. It must be freshened by laying it in water over night. When soaked, put it into cold water, and bring gradually to the boiling point; then set the kettle back where it will keep hot for half an hour; at the end of that time separate it into fine shreds, add an equal amount of fresh mashed potato, make into balls, and fry on a griddle.

TUESDAY, SEPTEMBER

Breakfast.	*Dinner.*	*Supper.*
Fried Bacon.	Boiled Corned Beef,	Pea Soup.
Boiled Potatoes.	with	Yeast Biscuit and
Bread.	Horse-radish Sauce.	Butter.
Coffee.	Stewed Cabbage.	Stewed Fruit.
	Bread.	
	Barley Porridge.	

Boiled Corned Beef. Boil the beef for three hours, very slowly at first, changing the water once if it is very salt.

Horse-radish Sauce. Add grated horse-radish to drawn butter sauce. Simmer a few minutes.

Barley Porridge, page 309.

SATURDAY, JANUARY

Breakfast.	*Dinner.*	*Supper.*
Fried Bacon.	Browned Flour Soup.	Baked Beans.
Corn Bread.	Stewed Mutton.	Bread.
Coffee.	Mashed Potatoes.	Apple Dumplings, with
	Bread.	Pudding Sauce. Tea.

Corn Bread. (1) Plain. One cup of sweet milk, one cup of sour or buttermilk, or both of sour milk, one teaspoon of salt, one teaspoon of soda, one tablespoon of butter or suet or lard, three cups of Indian meal, and one cup of wheat flour, or all of Indian meal. Mix, pour into a tin, and bake forty minutes.

(2) *Richer.* The same, with an egg and one half cup of sugar added.

(3) *Very nice.* No. 1, with the addition of three eggs, one half cup of sugar, and one third of a cup of butter, one cup of meal being omitted.

Browned Flour Soup, page 305.

Apple Dumplings, with Pudding Sauce. *The Dumplings.* Make a crust like that used in dried apple pie. Cut it in squares; place sliced apples in the middle, and gather up or pinch the corners. Bake or steam.

Sauce. One pint of water made into a smooth paste with a heaping tablespoon of flour. Cook ten minutes. Strain if necessary, sweeten to taste, and pour it over one tablespoon of butter, and the juice of a lemon, or other flavoring. If lemon is not used, add one tablespoon of vinegar. This can be made richer by using more butter and sugar. Stir them to a cream with the flavoring, and then add the paste.

SUNDAY, JANUARY

Breakfast.	*Dinner.*	*Supper.*
Fried Codfish.	Sheep's-head Stew, with Soda-biscuit Dumplings.	Potato and Onion Salad.
Bread and Butter.		Broiled Salt Pork.
Coffee.	Baked Potatoes.	Bread.
	Bread and Cheese. Cocoa.	Grated Corn Mush, with Pudding Sauce.

Sheep's-head Stew (see Mutton Stew, page 187).

Potato and Onion Salad. Slice some potatoes (fresh boiled and slightly warm are best). Sprinkle them with minced onion, salt, and pepper. Dress with a little melted butter and vinegar.

Pudding Sauce, the same as that for Apple Dumplings.

MONDAY, JANUARY

Breakfast.	Dinner.	Supper.
Fried Mush and Molasses.	Soup from Boiled Beef, with Macaroni.	Boiled Potatoes, with Butter Gravy.
Bread.	Boiled Beef Flank, with Mustard Sauce.	Dried Apple Roly-poly Pudding.
Coffee.	Bean Purée. Bread.	Bread. Tea.

Mustard Sauce. Make some drawn butter in the following manner:

A heaping tablespoon of butter, or beef fat, is put into a saucepan. When it boils, one heaping tablespoon of flour is added, and stirred as it cooks. To this add gradually one pint of water, one teaspoon of salt, and one fourth of a teaspoon of pepper. If you wish to unite economy and good flavor, use one half teaspoon of beef fat in making the sauce, and add one half teaspoon of butter cut in small pieces just before serving. Add a little mustard, and you have mustard sauce.

Bean Purée. Make like Pea Soup, page 307.

Dried Apple Roly-poly Pudding. Make the soda-biscuit dough which is used in dried apple pie. Roll it out into a thin sheet, and spread with stewed and flavored dried apples. Roll it into a round or loaf, and bake in a pan containing a little water.

TUESDAY, JANUARY

Breakfast.	Dinner.	Supper.
Fried Potatoes.	Browned Farina Soup, with Toast.	Bean Soup.
Bread.	Stewed Mutton, with Yeast Dumplings.	Milk Toast.
Coffee.		Tea.

Browned Farina Soup. Make like Browned Flour Soup, except use farina.

For other similar bills of fare and recipes, see the Lomb Prize Essay, entitled "Practical, Sanitary, and Economic Cooking," which is published and sold at a low price by the American Public Health Association, and may be bought at any book-store. It is most heartily recommended to nurses who do district nursing as a book which will be found useful among the poor and those possessed of moderate means.

LITERATURE

In preparing the preceding pages the following authorities have been consulted. Their works will be found useful for reference on subjects connected with the chemistry of food, bacteriology, nutrition, health, practical cooking, and allied topics.

"The Chemistry of Cookery." W. MATTIEU WILLIAMS. 1885.
"Food Materials and their Adulterations." ELLEN H. RICHARDS. 1886.
"The Chemistry of Cooking and Cleaning." ELLEN H. RICHARDS. 1882.
Various Articles on Food in "The Century Magazine." W. O. ATWATER. 1887-88.
"Elementary Manual of Chemistry." ELIOT AND STORER. Compiled by W. RIPLEY NICHOLS. 1880.
"A Manual of Practical Hygiene." EDMUND A. PARKES. Edited by FRANÇOIS DE CHAUMONT. 1887.
"A Simple Treatise on Heat." W. MATTIEU WILLIAMS. 1880.
"Food for the Invalid." J. MILNER FOTHERGILL. 1880.
"Food and Feeding." SIR HENRY THOMSON. 1880.
"The Boston Cook Book." D. A. LINCOLN. 1884.
"New England Breakfast Breads." LUCIA GRAY SWETT. 1890.
"Miss Parloa's New Cook Book." MARIA PARLOA. 1880.
"Diet for the Sick." MARY E. HENDERSON. 1885.
"Food in Health and Disease." I. BURNEY YEO.
"Delicate Feasting." THEODORE CHILD. 1890.
"The Story of the Bacteria." T. MITCHELL PRUDDEN. 1890.
"Dust and its Dangers." T. MITCHELL PRUDDEN. 1890.

"Bacteria and their Products." GERMAN SIMS WOODHEAD. 1892.

"The Methods of Bacteriological Investigation." FERDINAND HEUPPE, M. D. 1886.

"Microbes, Ferments, and Molds." E. L. TROUESSART. 1886.

"Principles of Bacteriology." ALEXANDER C. ABBOTT, M. D. 1892.

"The Human Body." H. NEWELL MARTIN. 1890.

"A Text-book of Human Physiology." AUSTIN FLINT, M. D., LL. D. 1888.

"Domestic Hygiene of the Child." JULIUS UFFELMANN, M. D. (A Translation.) Edited by MARY PUTNAM JACOBI, M. D. 1891.

"A Treatise on the Diseases of Infancy and Childhood." J. LEWIS SMITH, M. D. 1886.

Article in the "Medical News" on "Diseases of Children Incident to Summer." VICTOR C. VAUGHAN. June 9, 1888.

"Practical, Sanitary, and Economic Cooking." MARY H. ABEL. 1890. (The Lomb Prize Essay.)

"The Town Dweller." DR. FOTHERGILL.

"A Guide to Sanitary House Inspection." W. PAUL GERHARD. 1890.

"Papers of the American Public Health Association." 1892.

"Foods." EDWARD SMITH. 1883.

CHARTS

Charts of the composition of various foods may be made like the following, for use in a cooking school. They are valuable and convenient for reference.

CHEMICAL COMPOSITION OF AN EGG

Shell.
    Carbonate of lime.

Yolk.
    Nitrogenous matter...................16.00%
    Fat................................30.70%
    Salts...............................1.30%
    Water..............................52.00%

White.
    Nitrogenous matter...................20.40%
    Salts................................1.60%
    Water...............................78.00%

COMPOSITION OF COW'S MILK

Water	87.4%
Fat	4.0%
Sugar and soluble salts	5.0%
Nitrogenous matter and insoluble salts	3.6%

Dr. Miller.

COMPOSITION OF COCOA

Cocoa butter	48.00%
Nitrogenous matter, albumen, etc.	21.00%
Theobromine	4.00%
Starch and traces of sugar	11.00%
Cellulose	3.00%
Coloring matter and aromatic essences	Traces
Mineral matter	3.00%
Water	10.00%

Payen.

COMPOSITION OF BREAD

Nitrogenous matter	8.10%
Carbohydrates, starch, sugar, etc.	51.00%
Fatty matter	1.60%
Mineral matter	2.30%
Water	37.00%
Cellulose	0.00%

COMPOSITION OF POTATO

Water	75.00%
Starch	18.80%
Nitrogenous matter	2.00%
Sugar	3.00%
Fat	0.20%
Salts, principally potash	1.00%

APPARATUS

The following is a list of the necessary furniture, utensils, china, and miscellaneous articles for furnishing a cooking school.

CHINA FOR SERVING

3 Glass cream pitchers.
6 Small china cream pitchers.
6 Coffee-cups and saucers.
6 Tea-cups and saucers.
3 Cocoa-cups and saucers.
2 Bouillon-cups and saucers.
3 Egg-cups.
3 Egg-glasses.
6 Tall, slender glasses for milk-punch, egg-nog, etc.
1 Small red goblet for serving beef-juice.
6 Tumblers.
1 Spoon-holder.
3 Glass sugar bowls.
2 Soup bowls.
2 Salad bowls.
2 Finger bowls.
3 Small teapots.
1 Cocoa-pot.
1 Tête-à-tête set.
1 Oatmeal set.
1 Cracker jar.
6 Dinner plates.
6 Tea plates.
6 Individual bread plates.
6 Individual Butter plates.
6 Glass sauce dishes.
6 Bone dishes.
1 Vinegar cruet.
2 Individual salt-cellars.
2 Individual pepper-bottles.
3 Small oval platters.
3 Medium-size oval platters.
3 Silver or planished tin covers, for platters or vegetable dishes.
6 Silver knives.
6 Silver forks.
6 Silver spoons.
1 Pair of silver sugar-tongs.
1 Champagne tap.

COMMON KITCHEN CHINA

3 Large pitchers.
3 Small pitchers.
6 Half-pint cups.
6 Saucers.
12 Custard cups.
6 Individual scallop dishes.
3 Mixing bowls.
6 Quart bowls.
6 Pint bowls.
3 Large vegetable dishes.
3 Small vegetable dishes.
3 Pudding dishes.
1 Large jelly-mold.
6 Small jelly-molds.

GRANITE-WARE

2 Six-quart covered kettles.
1 Six-pint double boiler.
2 Three-pint double boilers.
1 Quart double boiler.
1 Coffee-pot.
3 Stew-pans.
6 Saucepans.
2 Omelet-pans.
2 Hand-basins.

APPARATUS

IRON AND TIN WARE

1 Tin tea-kettle.
6 Half-pint measure **cups in** thirds.
6 Half-pint measure cups in fourths.
2 Tin jelly-molds.
1 Large-mouthed **tunnel.**
3 Small tunnels.
1 Colander.
1 Taper soup-strainer.
3 **Coarse** wire strainers.
3 Fine wire strainers.
2 Tea-strainers.
1 Flour sieve.
1 Dredging box.
1 Egg-poacher.
1 Grater.
1 Whip-churn.
2 Dover egg-beaters.
1 Lemon-squeezer.
1 Meat-press.
1 Potato-masher.
2 Large wire broilers.
2 Small wire broilers.
1 Oyster-broiler.
1 Wire cake-rest.
2 Large **tin pans.**

3 Frying-pans.
2 Iron baking-pans for bread.
2 Sponge-cake pans.
1 Iron gem pan.
2 Muffin tins.
1 Chafing-dish.
3 Lacquered trays.
3 Small trays.
12 Japanned boxes **of different** sizes, for flour, etc.
6 **Tea-caddies.**
1 **Biscuit-cutter.**
4 Cutting-knives.
3 Vegetable knives.
1 Chopping-knife.
1 Meat-cleaver.
6 Forks.
1 Set of steel skewers.
1 Corkscrew.
1 Can-opener.
1 Ice-pick.
1 Sugar-scoop.
1 Basting-spoon.
6 Mixing-spoons.
12 Tablespoons.
12 Teaspoons.

WOODEN WARE

1 Coffee-mill.
1 Ice-cream freezer.
1 Salt-box.
1 Spice-box.
1 Dish-tub.
1 Large oval chopping-tray.
2 Meat-boards.
1 Bread-board.

1 **Molding-board.**
1 **Rolling-pin.**
2 Butter-spatters for butter-balls.
2 Cake-spoons.
2 Salt-spoons.
2 Vegetable brushes.
2 Scrubbing brushes.

APPARATUS

LINEN

Table-cloths.
Napkins.
Hand-towels.
Tea-towels.
Dish-cloths.

Mops.
Ice-bag.
Jelly-bags.
Cleaning-cloths.

MISCELLANEOUS

1 Chemists' thermometer.
1 Oven thermometer.
1 Arnold sterilizer.
1 Feser's lactoscope.

1 Quevenne's lactometer.
1 Hamper for soiled linen.
6 Quart Mason jars.
6 Pint Mason jars.

FURNITURE

1 Cooking stove, with appurtenances.
1 Coal-hod.
1 Coal-shovel.
1 Galvanized iron covered waste-pail.
1 Galvanized iron sink.
2 Towel-racks.

2 Tables.
1 Refrigerator.
1 China-closet.
1 Open dresser.
6 Chairs.
1 Broom.
1 Dust-pan.
1 Dust-brush.

INDEX

Absorption, 68.
Adaptation of food to particular needs, 69.
Air, 14, 15, 18, 20, 38–44, 54, 56, 64.
Albumen, 17, 25, 27, 52, 59, 61, 76, 146, 152, 168, 169, 283, 292.
Albuminoids, 17, 25, 62.
Ale, 119.
Apparatus for furnishing a cooking-school, 315.
Apple dumplings, 311.
Apple (dried) pie, 306.
Apple soup, 144.
Apples, 130; baked, 225, 226; stewed, 226.
Apple-tea, 106.
Arrowroot, 32, 34, 85.
Atmospheric pressure, 38.

Bacon, 300.
Bacteria, 23, 49, 99, 285.
Bacterial poisons in milk, 285, **286**.
Bacteriology, 5, 313.
Baking-powder, 236, 245.
Barley jelly, 296.
Barley porridge, 309.
Barley pudding, 205.
Barley water, 101, 284.
Beef, 169, 170, 310.
Beef-juice, 75.
  Bottled, 76.
  Broiled, 76.
Beefsteak, 27, 170, 171.
Beef-tapioca soup, 140.
Beef-tea, 75, 116.
  Bottled, 77.
  With hydrochloric acid, 77.
Beer, 119.
Biedert's Cream Mixture, 293, 295.
Bile, 51, 61.
Bills of fare, 304.
Birds, 175.
  Field-larks, 180.
  Grouse, 179.
  Partridge, 176.
  Pheasants, 178.
  Reed-birds, 179.
  Squabs, 176.
  Snipe, 177.
  Woodcock, 178.
Biscuits, cream-of-tartar, 242.
Biscuits, twin, 243.
Blanc-mange, 209, 210.
Boiled corned beef, 310.
Boiled potatoes and carrots, with fried onions, 309.

Bouillon, 143.
Brandy-milk, 98.
Bread, 34, 76, 232.
  Composition of, 315.
  Cream-of-tartar biscuit, 242.
  Gluten, 245.
  Graham, 241.
  Graham gems, 244.
  Milk, 239.
  Oatmeal muffins, 244.
  Rusk, 240, 241.
  Snow-cakes, 243.
  Sticks, 240.
  Water, 238.
Bread pancakes, 307.
Bread soup, 304.
Broths, 27, 75.
  Beef, 78.
  Beefsteak, 79.
  Chicken, 80.
  Clam, 82.
  Mutton, 81.
  Oyster, 82.
  Scotch, 80.
  Serving of, 275.
Browned farina soup, 312.
Browned flour soup, 305.
Butter-cream, 193.
Buttered water toast, 129.

Cake, 246.
  Care in baking, 247.
  Chocolate, 250.
  Dream, 252.
  Feather, 249.
  Invalid's sponge, 248.
  Layer, 250.
  Process of making, 247.
  Rose, 250.
  White, 251.
Cake filling and frosting, 252.
  Caramel, 252.
  Chocolate, 253.
  Cream, 253.
  White mountain, 252.
Calf's-foot jelly, 28.
Caramel, 37, 38, 115.
  To make, 197.
Carbohydrates, 18, 19, 31, 62, 63, 64, 65, 58, 71.
Carbon, 12, 13, 14, 16, 17, 18, 29, 36, 37, 171.
Carbonic acid, 10, 11, 14, 15, 21, 40, 42, 54, 107, 234, 235.
Carmine for coloring, 210.
Carrageen, 209.
Cellulose, 299.

INDEX

Charts, 314.
Chemical changes, 10, 11, 15.
Chemistry of foods, 313.
Chicken, broiled, 174.
Chicken jelly, 126.
Chicken panada, 141.
Chicken soup, 135.
Chicken-tapioca soup, 139.
China for serving, 316.
Chocolate, 108, 110, 200.
   Serving of, 269.
   To make, 109.
Clam broth, 82.
Cocoa, 108, 299, 315.
Cocoa cordial, 119.
Cocoa-nibs, 109.
Cocoa-shells, 109.
Codfish balls, 309.
Coffee, 9, 22, 23, 114, 307.
   Composition of, 116.
   Serving of, 269, 275.
   To make, 117, 118.
Coffee jelly, 124.
Coffee-syrup, 104.
Composition of the body, 16, 17, 18, 24.
Condensed milk, 288, 298.
Consommé, 142.
Contagious diseases, care of dishes in, 271.
Convalescent's diet, 260.
Corn bread, 310.
Corn coffee, 307.
Cream, 30, 63, 104.
Cream, condensed, 296.
Cream-of-celery soup, 137.
Cream-of-rice soup, 138.
Cream of tartar, 10, 236.
Cream-of-tartar biscuit, 242.
Creams, 127, 195.
   Chocolate, 200.
   Coffee, 199.
   Egg, 198.
   Peach foam, 202.
   Rice, 202.
   Tapioca, 201.
   Velvet, 199.
Cream sauce, 149.
Cream toast, 130.
Croutons, 132, 135.
Custards, 195.
   Soft, 195, 278.
   Baked, 196.
   French, 197.
   Rennet, 197.

Dextrine, 33, 63, 128, 163, 290.
Diastase, 34, 50.
Diet, 72.
Diet lists or menus for the sick, 254.
Digestibility of foods, 9.
Digestion, 9, 49, 66, 110, 116.
Digestive fluids, 50, 51.
District nursing, 301.
Drawn butter, 194.
Drawn butter sauce, 308.

Dried apple pie, 306.
Drinks, 95.

Egg-nog, 95.
Eggs, 25, 26, 52, 152, 314.
   Composition, 152.
   Omelets, 156.
     Creamy, 157.
     Foamy, 158.
     Orange, 160.
     Spanish, 160.
     To serve, 277.
     With chicken, 159.
     With ham, No. 1, 158.
     With ham, No. 2, 159.
     With jelly, 159.
     With parsley, 160.
     With tomatoes, 159.
   Poached, 155.
   Scrambled, No. 1, 156.
   Scrambled, No. 2, 156.
   Soft-cooked, 154.
Egg toast, 131.
Elements, 12, 13, 14, 16, 17, 18, 19, 56, 57, 59.
Ether, boiling-point of, 30.
Extractives, 24, 25, 26, 28, 59.

Farina, 87, 91, 92.
Farinaceous foods, 289, 291, 292.
Fats, 17, 18, 19, 28, 29, 30, 31, 58, 60–65, 68, 71, 169, 292, 294.
Feeding of children, 280.
   Analysis of Mellin's food prepared for use, 291.
   Care of feeding-bottles, 287.
   Condensed milk, 288.
   Farinaceous foods, 289.
   Food.
     Amount at each meal, 293.
     Dilution, 293.
     First week, 295.
     From the first to the sixth week, 295.
     From the sixth week to the sixth month, 296.
     From the sixth month to the tenth, 297.
     From the tenth to the twelfth month, 298.
     From the twelfth to the eighteenth month, 299.
   Food after eighteen months, 299.
   Foods to be carefully avoided, 300.
Field-larks, 180.
Fire, 14, 302.
Fish, 5, 191.
   Boiled, 194.
   Broiled, 193.
   Creamed, 193.
   To prepare, 191.
   When in season, 192.
Flavors, 9, 59, 79.
Flaxseed tea, 105.
Food, 9, 14, 18, 25, 49, 53.

INDEX

French toast, 131.
Fried bread, 309.
Fried farina pudding, 308.
Fruits, 224, 71, 208, 225, 229.
  Apple compote, 226.
  Apple jelly, 230.
  Apples, baked, 225, **226**.
  Apples, stewed, 226.
  Cranberry jelly and sauce, 227.
  Grape jelly and sauce, 228.
  Prunes, stewed, 227.
  Serving of, 276.
Fuel and kindlings, **16**.

Gastric juice, 50.
Gelatin, 28, 53, 59, 76, 120, **122**, **168**, **169**.
Gelatine, 120, 121, 222.
Gelatinoids, 17, 25, 28.
General rules for the **feeding of children**, 294.
Giblet soup, 309.
Glucose, 35, 37, 52, **63**.
Graham bread, 241.
Graham gems, 244.
Granite-ware, 316.
Grape jelly, 228.
Grape juice, 105.
Grouse, 179, 180.
Gruels, 83.
  Arrowroot, **84**.
  Barley, **84**.
  Cracker, **87**.
  Farina, **87**.
  Flour, **86**.
  Imperial Granum, **88**.
  Indian meal, **89**.
  Oatmeal, **85**, **86**.
  Racahout des Arabes, **88**.
  Serving of, 83, 275.
Glycerin, 30.
Glycogen, 63, 64, 65.

Hamburg steak, No. 1 (scraped beef), 172.
Hamburg steak, No. 2, 173.
Heat, 2, 10, 13, 14, 15, 20, 56, 54, 61, 169, 218.
Hemoglobin, 17, 59.
Horse-radish sauce, 310.
Human milk, 281.
Hydrochloric acid, 10, 11, 28, 52, 77, 78.
Hydrogen, 12, 13, 16, 18, 19, 24, 29.

Ice-cream, 217.
  Frozen custard, 221.
  Philadelphia, 220.
  Royal, 220.
  With an improvised freezer, 221.
Ice-cream freezers, 217.
Ices, 217.
  Apricot, 224.
Ideal diet, 68.
Imperial Granum, 291, 297.
Inorganic matter of the body and of food, 18, 65, 66.

Jellies, 120.
  From fruits:
    Apple, 230.
    Cranberry, **227**.
    Grape, 228.
    Serving of, **276**.
    To preserve, **230**.
  From gelatine, 120.
    Chicken, 126.
    Coffee, 124.
    French, 125.
    Lemon, 123.
    Orange, 123.
    Puncheon, 126.
    Wine, No. 1, **122**.
    Wine, No. 2, **122**.
    Restorative, **125**.
Junket, 198, 278.

Kitchen china, 316.
Kumiss, 106, 107.

Lactometer, **46**.
Lactoscope, **46**.
Lactose, **18**, **37**.
Lamb chops, 184.
Lead, 12.
Lemonade, 97, 275.
Lemon jelly, 123.
Lentil soup, 309.
Lettuce salad, 213.
Light diet, 256.
Lime-water (experiment with), 21.
Linen, 318.
Liquid diet, 254.
Literature, 313.
Liver, 63.
Lobsters, 300.
Lomb prize essay, 302.

Malted milk, 290, 291.
Meats, 5, 168.
Mellin's food, 283, 284, 290, 297, 298, 299.
Menus for the sick, 254.
Micro-organisms, 1, 2, 22, 23, 40, 46, 47, 49, 98, 230, 281, 284, 285.
Milk, 30, 44–49, 57, 273.
  Composition of cow's, 45, 281, 315.
  Condensed, 298.
  Malted, 290.
  Pasteurized, 288.
  Preserved, 289.
  Serving of, 275.
  Sterilization of, **47**, **48**, **49**, 99, 100, 281, 284, 287.
  Supplies, **49**, 281, 282.
Milk and seltzer, 100.
Milk and soda-water, 101.
Milk lemonade, 97.
Milk-punch, 95, 275.
Milk toast, 130.
Milk-sugar, 298.
Mineral matter in milk, 283.
Mineral salts, 18, 57, 65, 66, 71, 111, 162, 175, 226.

INDEX

Mint sauce, 308.
Mock-bisque soup, 135.
Mulled wine, 118.
Mush and porridge, 90.
  Cracked wheat, 93.
  Farina, 92.
  Granula, 93.
  Hominy, 94.
  Imperial Granum, 93.
  Indian meal, 94.
  Oatmeal, 91.
  Wheat germ, 92.
Mustard sauce, 312.
Mutton, 181, 182.

Nestlé's food, 291, 297.
Nitrogen, 12, 13, 14, 16, 17, 24, 42, 59.
Nitrogenous compounds, 53, 58, 62.
Noodles, 305.
Noodle soup, 305.
Nutrition, 53, 57, 313.
  Absorption, 68.
  Adaptation of foods to particular needs, 69.
  Definition, 54.
  Ideal diet, 68.
  Imperfect, 70.
  Inorganic matters and vegetable acids, 65.
  Summary of the digestibility of foods, 68.
  Value of protein, fats, carbohydrates, and extractives, 58–65.
  Ways in which food supplies the wants of the body, 56.

Oatmeal, 80, 85, 86, 90, 91.
Oatmeal muffins, 244.
Oil, 10, 30.
  Cod-liver, 63.
  Fixed and volatile, 28.
  Olive, 30, 31, 211.
Omelets, 156.
Orange jelly, 123.
Oxygen, 12, 13, 14, 15, 16, 17, 18, 29, 40, 42, 59, 64.
Oysters, 145.
  Broiled, 149.
  Broth, 150.
  Chafing-dish, 151.
  Composition, 145.
  Creamed, 148.
  Fancy roast, 150.
  Pan-broiled, 150.
  Raw, 147.
  Roasted in the shell, 147.
  Serving, 277.
  Soup, 134.
  Stew, 148.
  Tea No. 1, 82.
  Tea No. 2, 82.

Panada, 79, 141.
Pancreatic juice, 51, 61, 290.
Paraffin, 230.
Partridges, 176.
Pasteurized milk, 288.
Peach foam, 202.
Peas, 190.
Pea soup, 307.
Peptogenic milk powder, 284.
Peptonized milk, 296.
Pheasants, 178.
Phosphated gelatine, 121.
Physical changes, 10, 11, 12.
Pigeons, 180.
Pink blanc-mange, 210.
Pink sugar, 209.
Poisons in milk (bacterial), 22, 285, 286.
Porridge, 90, 91.
Porter, 119.
Potato and onion salad, 311.
Potatoes, 32, 34, 70, 161.
  Baked, 165.
  Boiled, 163.
  Composition, 161.
  Creamed, 166.
  Duchess, 166.
  Mashed, 164.
  Roasted, 165.
Potato soup, 136.
Preserved milk, 289.
Protein, 17, 18, 19, 24, 25, 52, 53, 56, 58, 59, 60, 62, 64, 68, 71.
Puddings, 195.
  Baked custards, 196.
  Barley, 205.
  Chocolate cream, 200.
  Coffee cream, 199.
  Corn-starch, 204.
  Cream-of-rice, 206.
  Egg cream, 198.
  French custard, 197.
  Fruit tapioca, 207.
  Irish moss blanc-mange, 209.
  Orange baskets, 208.
  Orange layers, 208.
  Orange omelet, 160.
  Peach foam, 202.
  Pink blanc-mange, 210.
  Princess, 204.
  Rennet custard, 197.
  Rice cream, 202.
  Slip, 197.
  Soft custard, 195.
  Snow pudding, 203.
  Tapioca cream, 201.
  Tapioca jelly, 207.
  Velvet cream, 199.
Puncheon jelly, 126.

Racahout des Arabes, 88, 89.
Reed-birds, 179.
Rennet, 198.
Restorative jelly, 125.
Rice, 76, 79, 81.
Rice-water, 102.
Ridge's food, 291, 297.
Roly-poly pudding, 312.
Rules for the feeding of children, 294.

INDEX

Salads, 10, 71, 211.
  Celery, 216.
  Chicken, 214.
  Lettuce, 213.
  Potato, 215.
    " with olives, 216.
Salad Dressing, 211.
  French, 212.
  Mayonnaise, 212.
Saliva, 50, 290, 51.
Salt (sodium chlorid), **11, 18, 66**.
Scotch broth, 80.
Scraped beef, 172.
Serving, 267.
Sherbets, 217, **277**.
  Lemon, 222.
  Orange, 223.
Sherry and egg, 98.
Sippets, 132.
Snipe, 177.
Soda-water, 101.
Sodium chlorid, 11, 18.
Soups, 4, 27, 134.
  Apple, 144.
  Beef-tapioca, 140.
  Bouillon, 143.
  Bread, 304.
  Browned farina, 312.
    " **flour, 305.**
  Chicken, 135.
  Chicken panada, 141.
  Chicken-tapioca, 139.
  Consommé, 142.
  Cream-of-celery, 137.
  Cream-of-rice, 138.
  Giblet, 309.
  Lentil, 309.
  Mock-bisque, 135.
  Noodle, 305.
  Oyster, 134.
  Pea, 307.
  Potato, 136.
  Queen Victoria's favorite, 139.
Spores, 23, 24, **48**, 99.
Squabs, 176.
Starch, 31, 33, 34, 35, 62, **63**, 65, 68, 51, 18, 58, 83, 85, 128, 161.
  Digestion of, 51, 52, 84, **290**.
  Composition, 32, 58.
  Tests for, 32.
Steak (beef), 27, 70, 171.
  A la Maitre d'Hôtel, 173.
  Hamburg. No. 1 (scraped **beef**), 172.
    " " 2, 173.
  Tenderloin, 173.
Steam, 12, 20, 29.
Sterilization,
  of Milk, 47, 48, 98, 99, 100, 237, 284.
  of Vessels for holding milk, 281.
  of **Water**, 19, 23, 24.
Stews, 185.
  Chicken, 185.
  Beef, 186.
  Mutton, 187.
Strawberries, 102, 103, 105, 121, 224.

Sucrose, 36, 52.
Sugar, 18, 32, 35, **36**, 37, **38, 52, 58, 63,** 65, 68, 283.
Sweeping and dusting, 303.
Sweetbreads, 188.
  Creamed, 189.
  Fricasseed, 189.
  With peas, **190**.
Syrups, Apple, **103**.
  Apricot, 103.
  Chocolate, 104.
  Coffee, 104.
  Currant, **103**.
  Orange, 103.
  Peach, 103.
  Raspberry, 103.
  Strawberry, 102.
  Vanilla, 104.

Tapioca, 34, 76, 79, **81**, 201, 207.
Tea, 22, 110, 269.
  Composition, 111.
  Kinds, 112, 113.
  Serving of, 275.
  To prepare, 113, 114.
  Value as food, 110, 23.
Tenderloin (steak), 173.
Thermometers (oven), 239.
Toast, 128.
  Cream, 130.
  Croutons, 132.
  French, 131.
  Milk, 130.
  Sippets, 132.
  Vermicelli, 133.
  Water (buttered), 129.
Toast and cheese, 306.
Tomatoes, 135.

Vanilla syrup, 104.
Veal broth, 284.
Venison, 70, 180.
Ventilation, 42.
Volatile oils, 28.

Washing of dishes, 303.
Waste, 19, 67.
Waste-pails, 5.
Water, 11, 12, 17, 18, 19, 20, 21, 22, 23, 54, 65, 218.
Water-ice, 217, 224.
Wheat-flour, 232.
Whey, 295.
  Wine, 96.
  With rennet, 96.
White-sauce, 130.
Wine jelly. No. 1, 122.
Wine jelly. No. 2, 122.
Wine, mulled, 118.
Wine whey, 96.
Woodcock, 178.
Wooden ware, 317.

Yeast, **232, 233.**
  Liquid, 237.

Zwieback, 300.

www.ingramcontent.com/pod-product-compliance
Lightning Source LLC
Chambersburg PA
CBHW021213240426
43667CB00038B/553